Joseph Glover Baldwin

Party Leaders

sketches of Thomas Jefferson, Alex'r Hamilton, Andrew Jackson, Henry Clay and

John Randolph of Roanoke

Joseph Glover Baldwin

Party Leaders

sketches of Thomas Jefferson, Alex'r Hamilton, Andrew Jackson, Henry Clay and John Randolph of Roanoke

ISBN/EAN: 9783744677981

Printed in Europe, USA, Canada, Australia, Japan

Cover: Foto ©Thomas Meinert / pixelio.de

More available books at **www.hansebooks.com**

SKETCHES

OF

THOMAS JEFFERSON, ALEX'R HAMILTON,
ANDREW JACKSON, HENRY CLAY,
JOHN RANDOLPH, OF ROANOKE,

INCLUDING

NOTICES OF MANY OTHER DISTINGUISHED AMERICAN STATESMEN

BY

JO. G. BALDWIN,

AUTHOR OF "THE FLUSH TIMES OF ALABAMA AND MISSISSIPPI."

NEW YORK:
D. APPLETON AND COMPANY,
443 & 445 BROADWAY.
LONDON: 16 LITTLE BRITAIN.
1868.

Entered according to act of Congress, in the year 1854, by
CORNELIUS C. BALDWIN,
in the clerk's office of the District Court of the United States for the Western District of Virginia.

TO THE MEMORY OF THE LATE

BRISCOE G. BALDWIN,

Recently one of the Justices of the Court of Appeals of Virginia.

In grateful acknowledgment of the obligations conferred upon the author in his youth, and as a feeble expression of veneration for the honored dead, this book, with reverential affection, is dedicated.

PREFACE.

THE design of this work is to give some account of the prominent events, and of some of the eminent personages, connected with the political history of the United States. It was obviously impossible, within the compass of a small volume, to compress an elaborate review of the lives of all the men who have figured, and of all the measures that have been agitated, in the course of the eventful period, extending through three quarters of a century, comprehended within this work. The *leading* events of this public and private history, therefore, are all that have been attempted.

The author has sought to perform his task with

candor, both in the narrative and criticism, and especially in entire freedom from all partisan bias. How far he has succeeded, it is for others to judge. The work makes no pretension to research. The events are matters of familiar history. All that the writer has attempted has been a concise narrative of the facts, grouping them together in a compact and perspicuous shape, with such reflections as seemed to him to be just and appropriate. If he has succeeded in this, and in giving to his narrative a fresh and attractive form, his object has been accomplished.

If it be objected that the work is wanting in the sober gravity and subdued tone, by some supposed to be the only legitimate style of history, he begs to remind the critic that he sought to blend interest with instruction, and, especially, to make his pages attractive to young men. To secure this end, he has labored to unite biography with political history; and, by placing rival leaders in antagonism, to make events and principles stand out in bold relief, and to give a more striking expression to the characters he has ventured to sketch.

An ardent admirer of some of the great personages of whom he has written, and disposed to look with a charitable, rather than a censorious, eye upon the conduct of men, he may have been insensibly seduced into extravagant appreciation of some of the illustrious characters treated of. If so—though historic error should of course in all cases be avoided—he deems it better to err upon the side of unmerited praise than of unjust depreciation; especially where the memories of men are concerned, whom the general voice concurs in pronouncing public benefactors.

It was the design of the author to have embraced in his work two other eminent party leaders, Daniel Webster and John C. Calhoun. But—besides that their eulogies and their writings have been so recently published, and the further fact that it would not be possible to include even a meagre account of men so eminent, and whose lives were so fertile of political incident, within the compass of this volume—the short time at the disposal of the author forbade the execution of this design. Should the public favor be accorded to this work, the original scheme may, in some other form than the present, be carried out, at some future time.

Only one of these papers—Jackson and Clay—in a somewhat ruder form, has been heretofore published. The favor, kindly extended to that paper, by gentlemen of high position and distinction, has suggested the idea of this larger design, and this more ambitious mode of publication.

LIVINGSTON, ALA., July, 1854.

CONTENTS

THOMAS JEFFERSON AND ALEXANDER HAMILTON.

CHAPTER I.
The American Revolution—Its General Character—Its Leaders, . . . 17

CHAPTER II.
Thomas Jefferson—His Birth—His Education—Studies Law—Hears Patrick Henry—Henry's Eloquence—Its Influence on Jefferson—Elected to the Legislature of Virginia—Sent to the Continental Congress—Writes the Declaration of Independence, ... 24

CHAPTER III.
Alexander Hamilton—His Birth and Education—Sent to Columbia College, New York—His First Public Speech, in 1774—A Distinguished Writer and Orator at Seventeen—Elected Captain of Artillery—Appointed Aid to Washington at Twenty—His Military Services—Washington's Estimate of them—Advocates a National Government in 1781—A Lawyer—A Leader in the Continental Congress—Writes "Publius"—The Constitution Adopted, ... 29

CHAPTER IV.
Jefferson in the Legislature of Virginia—In 1779, Governor of Virginia—In 1783 in Congress—Minister to France in 1785—In 1789, Returns Home—Washington Organizes his Cabinet—Jefferson, Secretary of State—Hamilton, Secretary of the Treasury—Their Official Conduct—Their Personal Relations—Their Talents and Characters—Their Jealousies and Collisions—Hamilton's Financial System, 85

CHAPTER V.

The French Revolution—Jefferson's and Hamilton's opposite feelings towards France—The French difficulty—Peace with France, ... 44

CHAPTER VI.

Jefferson and Hamilton retire from the Cabinet—Their Cabinet Controversies—Jefferson's Anomalous Position in the Cabinet—The Head of the Opposition—Sustains Freneau's Abusive Paper—Opposition to Washington's Administration Considered—Success of Washington's Administration—Jefferson Returns Home—Denounces the Administration—John Adams elected President—Jefferson Vice-President—Hamilton defends the Administration—Jefferson's Opinion of Hamilton as a Writer—The Federal Party—John Adams—His Conduct towards France—The Alien and Sedition Laws—Jefferson elected President, 49

CHAPTER VII.

Jefferson as a Party Tactician—As President—His Inaugural Address—His Conciliatory Policy—Acquisition of Louisiana—Strict Construction—The Embargo and Non-Intercourse Acts—Our Relations with England—Decline of the Federal party—Jefferson's Policy, ... 61

CHAPTER VIII.

Hamilton as a Lawyer—His Death—Personal Traits, &c., ... 69

CHAPTER IX.

The Republican and Federal Parties—Characteristics of each—Jefferson's Democracy—Hamilton's Conservatism—Errors of both, ... 71

CHAPTER X.

Jefferson as a Statesman—Individual Freedom—State-Rights—The "General Welfare" Clause—Consolidation—Personal Freedom—Liberty—Free Popular Government—State-Rights Doctrines—Their Influence, ... 79

CHAPTER XI.

Jefferson's Political Speculations—Their Influence—His Death—His Character—His Letters—His Published Correspondence—His Ana—His Influence on the State and National Governments, ... 88

CHAPTER XII.

Jefferson as a Popular Leader—His Inconsistencies—His Record of Private Conversations—Professor Tucker's Life of Jefferson—His Conduct in Burr's Trial—

CONTENTS. 13

In the Impeachment of Judge Chase—His Sensibility to Slander—His Opinion of
Newspapers, ... 105

CHAPTER XIII.

Hamilton—His Position, Influence, and Character, ... 120

CHAPTER XIV.

Hamilton and Jefferson Contrasted—Their True Greatness—Conclusion, . 129

JOHN RANDOLPH OF ROANOKE.

CHAPTER I.

Introduction—Garland's Life of Randolph—John Randolph—Public Opinion of him
—His Birth, Family, Education, and Politics, ... 135

CHAPTER II.

The French Revolution—Randolph, in early Youth, a Jacobin—Burke's Pamphlet—
Its Influence on Randolph—Points of Resemblance between Burke and Randolph
—Randolph's Early Character—Death of his brother Richard and of other Relatives
—His Physical Organization, ... 143

CHAPTER III.

Virginia at the date of the Federal Constitution—Contrast between the New-Englander and the Virginian, ... 148

CHAPTER IV.

The first Constitution of Virginia—Randolph opposed to equal Descents and Distribu-
tions—Virginia cherishes her Talent—Her State pride and jealousy of external
power—Opposition to the Federal Constitution—Barely adopted by Virginia—
Randolph subsequently against it—Strict Construction—Washington's Adminis-
tration—Adams's—Alien and Sedition Laws—Callender's Trial—Opposition to
Adams's Administration—Resolutions of 1798—Report of 1799—Madison—His
Character—Patrick Henry joins the Federal Party—His Character—His and
Randolph's Speeches at Charlotte Court-House—Henry's Eloquence—His
Death, ... 156

CHAPTER V.

Randolph in Congress—His Political Creed—State-Rights—Opposes Adams's Administration—Election of Jefferson—Randolph and Hamilton—Excise Abolished—Policy of this—Acquisition of Louisiana—Impeachment of Judge Chase—Randolph as a Party Leader—His Unhappiness—Disappointed Love—His Friendships—Death of his Friends, Thompson and Bryan, . . . 169

CHAPTER VI.

Jefferson's Second Term—Our Foreign Relations—State of Europe—President's Conduct—Randolph Opposes the Administration—Denounced by his Party—Returns Home—Illness and Unhappiness, ... 189

CHAPTER VII.

Difficulties with England—Monroe's Treaty—The Affair of the Chesapeake—The Embargo—Randolph opposes it—Jefferson against a Navy—Gun-Boats—Non-Importation Act—Madison's Election—Randolph prefers Monroe—War Measures—War—Randolph opposes it—Clay and Calhoun in Congress, . . 197

CHAPTER VIII.

Clay—Calhoun—Contrast between Clay and Randolph, . . . 205

CHAPTER IX.

Randolph's Speeches against the War—His Moral Heroism—Calhoun's—Randolph's Feelings towards England—Excitement against Randolph—Defeated for Congress by Eppes—Goes into Retirement, ... 217

CHAPTER X.

Randolph's Religious Sentiments and Conduct—Death of his Nephew, Tudor Randolph—Extracts of Randolph's Letters, ... 222

CHAPTER XI.

Randolph for Vigorous Prosecution of the War—His Letter to the New England States—Re-elected to Congress—Opposes the U. S. Bank and the Tariff—His Illness and Despondency—Monroe's Administration—Randolph Opposes it—The Missouri Question—His Letters to Dr. Dudley—His Will—Denounces the Slavery Agitation—Opposes the Bankrupt and Apportionment Bills—Visits Europe—His Impressions of England—Opposes the Greek and South American Resolutions—Opposes Internal Improvements—Opinion of Chief Justice Marshall—Opposes the Tariff of 1824—Visits England and France, ... 231

CHAPTER XII.

Presidential Election of 1824—Election of Adams by the House—Randolph opposes the Administration—Elected to U. S. Senate—Proceedings in the Senate in relation to the Panama Mission—President's Message in reply—Randolph's Speech on the Message—His Expression "The Puritan and the Blackleg"—Duel with Clay—Third visit to Europe—Defeated for the Senate by Tyler—Elected to the House—Opposes the Administration throughout—Advocates Jackson's Election—Retires from Congress—Elected to the Virginia Convention to amend the State Constitution—Opposes all Innovations—Mission to Russia—Returns Home—Nullification—The Proclamation and Force Bill—Randolph denounces Jackson—Sustains South Carolina, ... 248

CHAPTER XIII.

Randolph as a Statesman—The Leader of the State-Rights Party—Contrast between his Policy and Clay's—His Consistent and Heroic Devotion to his Principles, ... 258

CHAPTER XIV.

Randolph's Character and Death, ... 266

ANDREW JACKSON AND HENRY CLAY.

CHAPTER I.

Party Strife from 1835 to '45—Party Contests in America—Jackson and Clay—Points of Resemblance—A New Country—Jackson—His Character, Public and Private—As a General—As a Party Leader—Adams's Election—Clay's Blunders, ... 277

CHAPTER II.

Clay's Party Tactics—Adams's Administration—Jackson's and Clay's Mutual Hatred—Charge against Clay—Jackson as President—Clay in the Senate—The War of the Giants—The "Spoils" Doctrine—The Proclamation and Force Bill—John Randolph—His Character—Jackson's Influence, . . : 304

CHAPTER III.

Removal of the Deposits—Jackson's Critical Position—His Iron Nerve—Removal of Duane—The Whig Party—Union of the Purse and the Sword—Difference between the English and American Governments—Jackson's Charges against th

United States Bank—His Issue before the People—The Conduct of the Bank—Biddle—His Blunders—Commercial Distress—Jackson's Tact—His Appeal to the Farmers—Effect of the Deposits on the State Banks—Increase of Banks and Paper Money—Error of the Democratic Party—Jackson's Triumph—The Monetary and Speculative Excesses of 1835-36—The Specie Circular—Its Effects, 327

CHAPTER IV.

Jackson's Second Term—Van Buren Elected President—Commercial Distress—Party Excitement—Harrison's Election and Death—Tyler's Administration—Clay's Defeat—Jackson's Death—His Achievements and Character, . 840

CHAPTER V.

Clay in the Senate—His Patriotic Course—Compromise of 1850—Analysis of Clay's Character—His rank as a Statesman—Compared with Calhoun and Webster—His Death, ... 853

PARTY LEADERS.

THOMAS JEFFERSON AND ALEXANDER HAMILTON.

CHAPTER I.

The American Revolution—Its General Character—Its Leaders.

THE AMERICAN REVOLUTION is not only one of the most important, but one of the most interesting events in the history of the world. A young people oppressed and persecuted, rising to throw off a foreign yoke, and preferring all extremes of danger and disaster, of hardship and of privation, to submission to personal and political degradation, are necessarily objects of peculiar sympathy and regard. But the Colonies of Great Britain brought to *their* struggle an uncommon degree of this interest and consideration The movement of the Colonists was the furthest possible from a sudden outburst of popular passion. It had nothing of the temper, or purposes, or unrestrained impulses, or wild excesses of a mob. It preserved throughout the war the order, the system, the conservatism of loyalty to law and organized civic institutions. It proposed, it is true, an overthrow of government; but it set up another and better government, before it started to put down the old. It proposed armed and violent resistance to English rule; but it resisted in the name and by the authority of public law regularly enacted. It was not a paroxysm of popular rage, roused by sudden provocation. Neither was it undertaken without due preparation of the public mind, nor, as far as could be, of material resources, nor in ignorance of the advantages rationally to be expected from success, and of the dangers and evils which would certainly accrue from failure. The point of violent resistance was reached as a logical conclusion from foregone premises and by slow stages. It was attained only after exhausting all means of peaceable redress. It was only reached after the most elaborate discussion and the most deliberate consideration. The questions involved, were all public questions. Private griefs and personal considerations were, in a singular degree, wanting in the canvass of motives and reasons for opposition to the crown.

The whole history of the struggle was heroic. Whatever elements make up true glory, national and personal, were all found in that long travail for Independence. Fortunately, a pure, elevated and singularly brave generation of men led the movement; and every quality that can make or develope heroism was stimulated and forced into exercise. The affairs of a government, now just organizing and calling for the most varied skill of the politician to meet crises, and unexpected exigencies and new relations, required statesmanlike abilities, both legislative and executive; while, in the field, every martial quality was of course demanded and developed. Success, too, was not a sudden thing. It was not a mere brilliant exploit, turning the heads of the victors. It was long in doubt. Nay, for many long campaigns it seemed improbable, at times almost hopeless. Nor were there wanting difficulties of all sorts, in the cabinet and in the field, and even in the camp, to darken the prospects and to chill the hearts of the patriots. Great and unexpected reverses; sad defections, the weak vessels, once trusted brothers, falling off; miserable rivalries, even in the face of danger; bickerings, envy, insubordination in camp; disease, want of munitions of war, and of food, clothing, and shelter; the hope long and still deferred; the flag almost fainting in the breeze; the country, deserted in all its busy avocations, under a thick cloud of gloomy and of dreary silence; the forays of domestic enemies; the dwellings of the patriots blazing at midnight; the path ambushed by day; the dark deeds, too horrible for description, of the savages on the frontiers; the church closed or become the rendezvous of revelling soldiers; the schoolhouse on the hill deserted and the windows broken in; the sudden incursion of hostile cavalry into peaceable neighborhoods, scattering the women and children from the houses the marauders pillaged; the plough stopped in the furrow, and the dilapidated farm overgrown with briers; the towns and villages depopulated and in ruins; and the streets of cities deserted, or only exhibiting, here and there, under some creaking sign, a little knot of busy idlers discussing the last news from headquarters. This condition of their country, so bleak and desolate, was trying enough to the fortitude and constancy of the patriots. It is the highest of all human praise to say, that their constancy and fortitude were equal to such a trial. Indeed, we think these masculine virtues, indicating, or making the strength and greatness of the soul, more truly glorious than the noisy and brilliant courage and daring, which charge over batteries, or lead forlorn hopes up bastions. It may well be doubted whether the records of ancient or modern times give us, even in the history of Bruce or Frederick, any authentic example of a constancy more noble and triumphant, than that exhibited by Washington and his compatriots during the protracted war of the Revolution.

But the popular element of interest to a struggle, its triumph, was to succeed all this privation and trial. It came, at last, like gleams of grateful sunshine after a long and disastrous storm. And such a triumph! A triumph, in which the personal renown of the victors fades, in the splendor of a benefaction to their country and to their race, shining down, like a sun, on countless generations of mankind.

And scarcely less interesting, and not less instructive,

was that period of our public history, in which, after peace had come again, were laid the foundations of empire, and was reared up, on the ruins of old systems, that structure of civil government, which, by the blessing of God, secured, and which alone, probably, could have secured, the liberties and happiness, without which the preceding struggle had been a curse.

It was a happy characteristic of the times adverted to, that the country was under the direction of its virtue and its talent, and that of these so much existed. The Revolutionary era was emphatically the intellectual and patriotic period of the confederacy; not intellectual, perhaps, so far as the masses were concerned, but pre-eminent for the virtue and intellect of the men who were called to the higher posts of the public service.

We go back to those early times and revive our patriotism at the fountain-heads of the public liberty. We feel better nerved to the performance of our duties, by our intimacy with those who accomplished the great deeds of the Revolution. We find among them, and especially in the chief of them, what is so important to a people, an *ideal of patriotism and excellence*. Not a lesson, merely, nor a teacher, but a warm and living example, an impersonation of every moral, political, social and heroic virtue. The very existence of such a man, the mere fact that he lived, is a treasure of inestimable value to our people. It may keep them from falling, or, if, unhappily, they *should* fall, it furnishes the means of their recovery.

It is almost an amiable weakness that we are prone to look back upon the men of those times with superstitious reverence. We exempt them, in our partial veneration, from the frailties and imperfections of humanity. We endow them with fabulous powers. We endue them with a superhuman virtue. We forget that they were but men, and, too frequently, men disfigured by petty weaknesses, and a few of them stained by crime. The same passions that riot now in the vulgar breast, in some degree inflamed theirs. The same bitter rivalries, the same cabals, cliques, and partisan schemes and selfish intrigues, that now degrade ambition into a huckstering squabble for office, were then known. The same railing animosities and deadly feuds; the same ungenerous decrial and uncharitable imputations; the same tergiversations and lust of place and money, that now degrade politics into the dirtiest of trades, *then* had sway, though, doubtless, in far fewer instances than in this age of their full-blown development.

And yet, who can go back to the Revolutionary era, and fail to see, in the forms of the men who made that age illustrious, types of a noble and chivalrous manhood, such as he looks for in vain in all past history? What familiar figures and faces rise up to the memory, as if exhumed from the buried past, in all the fire and perfectness of their midday prime! The able and comprehensive Greene, most like his commander; the rough and dashing Morgan, the Lannes of the war; the brilliant and enterprising Harry Lee; the adventurous and brave Col. Washington; the calm but enthusiastic Lafayette, lifting eyes of reverent admiration to his chief; the bold and frank Henry Knox, loved of Washington; the accomplished and knightly Charles Cotesworth Pinkney; the hot and rash " Mad Anthony " Wayne, dashing like a tempest on the enemy; the elegant and courtly Edmund Randolph; the philosophic Franklin, his quiet face beaming with benignity and thought; the Adamses, the Otises, the Quincys, glowing with zeal and eloquence; Jefferson and Hamilton; and he—Virginia's greatest orator, now, at the organization of the new government, full of years as he was full of honors; near the close of a life now rewarded by the opening glories, which his prophetic eloquence had unveiled to his country: while the CENTRAL FIGURE of this august group towers above them all, not less in the regal majesty of his form, than in the sublime purity of his character, and in the sound judgment and wise moderation of his ripe statesmanship.

In this group were *two* names, not the oldest, nor, at the close of the Revolution, the most distinguished, of the bright array we have glanced at, but who were destined to impress upon their country a more lasting and important influence than any other men, with one or two exceptions, who have, to this day, appeared on the stage of action. These were the characters whose names head this paper.

CHAPTER II.

Thomas Jefferson—His Birth—His Education—Studies Law—Hears Patrick Henry—Henry's Eloquence—Its Influence on Jefferson—Elected to the Legislature of Virginia—Sent to the Continental Congress—Writes the Declaration of Independence.

THOMAS JEFFERSON was born on the 2d day of April, 1743, (O. S.,) at Shadwell, in the county of Albemarle, in the State of Virginia. If, as some suppose, the characters of men are modified by the physical scenery around them as they grow up to manhood, Jefferson was fortunate in the home of his youth; for it is difficult to conceive of a landscape more beautiful and romantic than that which greeted his youthful vision. A lovely valley, smiling at the feet of the high lands swelling above it; luxuriant plains, shadowed by the mountains towering, peak after peak, all around; the river dashing between the hills and bursting, with exulting song, into the glittering sunshine; the Blue Ridge with its soft haze marking the horizon with a long indented line of azure, until the eye loses its form far away in the dim distance; picturesque farmsteads crowning the hills, and green meadows nestling in their laps, make up a scene of almost unequalled beauty and grandeur. Such a home was fit to inspire a spirit of Liberty, and to nurse and nurture into strength and maturity her favorite champion.

In his seventeenth year, Jefferson was sent to William and Mary College, at that time, and for many years subsequently, the most approved institution of letters in the State; in whose venerable halls so many of the most eminent sons of that honored commonwealth were furnished forth with the first preparation for the distinguished parts they played in later life.

It was in his twenty-third year, while a student of law at Williamsburg, under the pure and learned Wythe, that Jefferson heard Patrick Henry, in the House of Burgesses, declaiming against the Stamp Act. For a young man to hear Henry and to adopt his cause, were the same thing; for the great orator spoke under the double inspiration of Eloquence and Liberty. Henry was in the prime of his powers, and this speech was one of the greatest of his life. The scene then enacted was worthy of the historic pencil; the orator, kindling with the fire of Ezekiel, and pouring forth from his impassioned soul, aflame with liberty, the thoughts so long imprisoned and burning for utterance in the solitude of the forest; quelling opposition; cowing the bold by greater boldness; inspiriting the timid; and pleading the cause of his countrymen with a rapt enthusiasm akin to inspiration; his voice swelling out its thunder tones, his form dilated, and his countenance transfigured.

And then, the young auditor in the lobby, strangely thrilling and carried away captive by the new influence throbbing in his heart and firing his brain; that stranger, a rude unfashioned youth then, but predestinated to be, and receiving then the impulse which was to make him, one of the most effective of all the champions of freedom in the world. It is barely too extravagant a figure to say, that the neophyte votary was thus baptized to Liberty in the fire and the flood of Henry's eloquence.

We pass rapidly over other passages in the life of Jefferson; his election, in 1769, by the people of his county to a seat in the Legislature, which he held to the time of the Revolution, and signalized by his unsuccessful proposition for the emancipation of the slaves of the State; his appointment, as member of the Correspondence Committee, established by the colonial legislature; his address to the king, in 1774, so commended by Burke, vindicating the claims of the colonies; and his election, in 1775, as one of the delegates of Virginia to the Continental Congress.

And now discontent had grown into agitation, and agitation had passed to the verge of Revolution. The colonies were ripe for open revolt; indeed, the field had been taken in Massachusetts, and the first blood of the war shed. Mighty events were on the wing. The country stood still and silent, as men stand on the eve of a great explosion. The crisis had come when the work of a moment controls the events of centuries, and tells the destiny of millions. The crisis was boldly met, and the venture boldly taken. It fell to the task of Jefferson to announce the decision to the world, and to appeal to that world in vindication of its justice. No hope was left of conciliation, and no chance of retreat; and **The Declaration** rang out its burning words of defiance and resolute resistance. The country answered back with shouts and huzzas.

CHAPTER III.

Alexander Hamilton—His Birth and Education—Sent to Columbia College, New York—His First Public Speech, in 1774—A Distinguished Writer and Orator at Seventeen—Elected Captain of Artillery—Appointed Aid to Washington at Twenty—His Military Services—Washington's Estimate of them—Advocates a National Government in 1781—A Lawyer—A Leader in the Continental Congress —Writes "Publius"—The Constitution Adopted.

A YOUNG man, just entering his nineteenth year, a student in one of the colleges of New York, heard the summons to arms, for which he had long been impatiently waiting, and repaired at once to the standard of his country. He was born in the little isle of Nevis, one of the leeward West India group, in the year 1757. From early youth, he had given promise of great eminence. He had published, in his fifteenth year, an account of the desolation, by a hurricane, of some of the West India islands; and the paper containing it falling into the hands of some gentlemen of St. Croix, they were so struck with its ability and eloquence, that they sought out the author. They found him, a clerk in the counting-room of one Nicholas Cruger. Thinking that such talents should not be unimproved, with the noblest and wisest generosity they proffered to send him, and prevailed upon him to go, to the city of New York, to be educated. He was, accordingly, entered a student of Columbia College. He rose rapidly from class to class, mastering whatever branch of study he essayed, without difficulty. He joined the Debating Society of the college, and, from the start, as by a natural gift of oratory, he bore the palm of eloquence from all his young associates.

At the age of seventeen, he wrote for the press essays upon the political topics then agitating the country, which were distinguished by graces of style and maturity of thought; no mere sophomore affairs, with gleams of genius here and there shining through the pruriency and flashy wordiness of boyish composition, but strong-sensed, well-reasoned articles, in which the fancy and the imagination only set off, illustrated and intensified the close and vigorous argument.

On the sixth of July, 1774, the people of New York met in the open fields. A vast concourse of men, under the excitement of the events that were driving forward the Revolution, met to hear discussed the great questions of the day. New interest had been imparted to the proceedings, by one of those acts of individual oppression (the imprisonment of McDougal), which, more than abstract principles, exert a deep and active influence on the public mind. The meeting, after a protracted and interesting session, lasting until nearly sunset, was about to disperse, when a youth, pale, of slight, but manly form, high and broad forehead, and eagle eyes, rose to address the people. Curiosity, as much as interest in the subject, turned all eyes upon the youthful speaker. But curiosity soon gave place to other sentiments and emotions; for the orator, after the first blush of embarrassment had faded from his cheek, launched out boldly into his argument; and eloquent appeal and strong reasonings, burning invective and prophetic augury came up as he called them. The duty of resistance, and the majesty and sacredness of the popular cause, were so enforced and vindicated, that, when the speaker closed a strain of eloquence which enchained attention in breathless silence, he was greeted with long shouts of approval and applause.

He sat down, at seventeen years, a distinguished man. We say a *distinguished man*, because in self-appreciation, in knowledge, in intellect, in matured force and steadiness of character, in every thing, save a complete physical development, he *was* a man, fashioned, furnished and prepared, for a full discharge, even in difficult and trying times, of all the duties which devolve on men.

A company of artillery was raised, and now, at nineteen years of age, Hamilton was chosen to command it. A year passed, and the commander-in-chief, in his retreat through the Jerseys, was struck by the courage and skill of the young captain in his passage of the Raritan. He sent for him and invited him to his tent. The interview resulted in his becoming " the principal and most confidential aid" of Washington, with the rank of lieutenant-colonel. And, sharing the tent, the counsels, and the confidence of his chief, the youth remained with him during the long war; assisted in planning the campaigns North and South; was with him in victory and in defeat; was by his side at Brandywine and Germantown; was near him when the flag trailed in the retreat from New York; when it flew in triumph at Trenton; when it drooped over the snows of Valley Forge; when it rose again over the hot field of Monmouth; then following the track of Cornwallis through the South, and closing the lines around him, until, encircled at Yorktown, without hope of escape by land or sea, the aid led " with conspicuous gallantry," the last charge upon the British redoubts—the crowning service of the war—and saw seven thousand troops march out as prisoners, and stack their arms before him.

And, soon afterwards, the war ended, after a series of campaigns, of which it may be said, that the very reverses were prominent accessories of its true glory.

How much the services of Hamilton were of benefit to the commander, cannot be rightly comprehended except by the testimony of the chief; since the aid, having no independent command or office, is sunk in the General. But we may readily conceive that Washington, whose genius was even more eminently appreciative than suggestive, derived no small assistance from the fertile resources, the bold conceptions, and the quick eye of his gifted aid. And this tribute to Hamilton's merits is enforced by the appointment Washington made him, fourteen years afterwards, to the office of Senior Major-General, over older officers, to serve in the French war. In September, 1778, Washington wrote to President Adams: " I have no hesitation in saying that, if the public is to be deprived of the services of Col. Hamilton in the military line, the post he was destined to fill will not be easily supplied."

In 1779, Hamilton proposed a mode of extricating the country from its embarrassments, by suggestions which prepared the way for the United States Bank. In 1780, he proposed, in his celebrated letter to Duane, the establishment of a constitution for a national government; and is thus entitled to the high merit of being among the first to see, and the ablest to vindicate, the wisdom of that measure.

Retiring, in 1781, from the active duties of his office of aid to Washington, and relinquishing its emoluments, though he retained the commission, to be in readiness for future service, he commenced the study of the law. He came to the bar in 1782, and rapidly took position. In the same year he was elected to the Continental Congress, and rose at once to a first place in that body. The reports he drew, as chairman of the most important committees, amply vindicate his claim to this consideration. He resumed the practice in the spring, and won for himself such distinction, at a bar as eminent as any in the world, that Chancellor Kent, in discussing some intricate question of law, goes out of his way to acknowledge the light he had received on the question from an argument of Alexander Hamilton, which he was once so fortunate as to hear. In 1786, a member of the New York Assembly; in 1787, a delegate to the Convention which framed the Federal Constitution, of which body he was one of the ablest members;—is it too much to say the very ablest? An eminent French minister says of him in this connection: " There is not an element of order, strength, or durability in the Constitution, which he did not powerfully contribute to introduce into the scheme, and cause to be adopted."

The essays published by him and Jay and Madison, about this time, under the signature of *Publius*, subsequently collected in " *The Federalist*," constitute a political text-book for the American student, and, perhaps, have not been exceeded in ability, by any similar papers ever written. Three fourths of these papers are from the pen of Hamilton; and we think it must be conceded that the proportion of ability in these rare contributions is as great in his favor as the number. When we reflect that these papers were written in haste, and at arbitrary intervals, amidst the distractions and cares of political and professional engagements; and by a man who had not yet attained his thirtieth year they must be regarded as curiosities of political literature.

This task despatched, Hamilton was called into the Convention of New York, met to decide upon the ratification of the new Constitution; and there, against various and powerful opposition, he fought the great work, inch by inch, through that assembly, as Madison and Marshall had done, under the fire of a scarcely more formidable antagonism, through the Convention of Virginia.

We had, at length, a government worthy of our people That shackling thing patched up by the old Articles of Confederation, and which needed the iron pressure of a foreign war to hold its rickety staves together, was superseded by a national government, with an established constitution, and ample powers to enforce its own laws, and to carry into effect its wisely-limited but all-important objects. The next thing was to put it in motion. It started under a cloud. It was a sort of compromise, with which no one was entirely pleased. Some bitterly opposed it. Some were neutral, not seeing their way clearly to oppose or support it. The majority not much more than tolerated it, or took it as the best they could do under the circumstances. It was too strong for some; too weak for others. It had awful *squints*. It squinted towards Monarchy; it squinted towards Aristocracy; and it squinted towards Anarchy. Many weather-wise politicians shook their heads ominously and muttered fears and distrust. Almost every man could have made a better government. The politicians, who had a sharp eye to the future (for that sort of people are not of recent growth), stood aloof, prepared to take advantage of any result that might turn up, after the new experiment had been tried.

CHAPTER IV.

Jefferson in the Legislature of Virginia—In 1779, Governor of Virginia—In 1783 in Congress—Minister to France in 1785—In 1789, Returns Home—Washington Organizes his Cabinet—Jefferson, Secretary of State—Hamilton, Secretary of the Treasury—Their Official Conduct—Their Personal Relations—Their Talents and Characters—Their Jealousies and Collisions—Hamilton's Financial System.

WE left Jefferson reading the Declaration of Independence. From that time to the inauguration of the new constitution, his life was a busy one. Returning from Congress, we find him in the Legislature of Virginia, engaged in the laborious drudgery of revising her laws; proposing and pushing through new ones of great importance, and marking large strides of progress: the Law prohibiting the importation of slaves; the statute for Religious freedom; the laws abolishing primogeniture and regulating descents; and, what to the shame of the noble old mother of States and statemen, has never yet been effectually carried out, a law creating an efficient system of general education. In 1779, elected Governor for two years. In 1781, writing his Notes on Virginia. In 1783, in Congress again, and, as chairman of the committee, reporting in favor of the Treaty of Peace with Great Britain. In 1784, busy with the mint and coinage questions, and the author of the present system of decimal coins. Appointed in 1784, a Minister Plenipotentiary to negotiate treaties with foreign nations, he assisted in the treaties with Prussia and Morocco, and, in the next year, succeeded Franklin as Minister to France, and continued as such until 1789, when he returned home.

Washington was called, by the almost unanimous voice of the country, to the helm of affairs. He would gladly have declined the service. Besides that he was one of the very few men to whom the exercise of power brought no pleasure, and to whose thorough-grained conscientiousness office was a responsible trust, over which a solemn sense of duty sat, controlling himself, as it controlled all things else; besides this, repose was grateful to him after the long and wearing duties which had brought premature old age upon his limbs. Moreover, he was in the evening of life, and that life had been a season of almost uninterrupted public labor away from home. He had won fame enough to satisfy any man's ambition, and he was naturally less ambitious than most men. His renown, filling his own country and overflowing its bounds, had spread all over the world. He had harvested and garnered in his glory. The future was safe from all hands but his own. He had already made a name, the first probably on the roll of fame; a name, which must descend, as the best type of a noble manhood, down the line of humanity, even to its last generation. He was one of the few founders of empire, who would have been gratefully remembered, long after the country he established had gone down. He was above all opposition, all rivalry, all enmity:—these could grovel *now* only far below the heights on which he stood. The cabals and intrigues, which had dogged him in the camp, had slunk away in affright at the loud acclaim of his country and the world. That world, for once, was unanimous in a patriot's praise; and even kings and courtiers vied in eulogies to the American hero. While yet alive, he was canonized as the first patriot, philanthropist, and hero of all the world. He might well be chary of such a fame. It was natural, that, at his age, when miscarriage could not be repaired, he should feel indisposed to commit his renown to a new test, to the result of an experiment, about which speculation was various; to embark in duties untried before, when it was impossible to make new friends and unlikely to retain all the old ones; and to raise up party and opposition, when he so much desired repose. But duty prevailed, as with him it had ever done. And another chapter was to be written in his country's history, as honorable to it and to him as any in the past.

Washington proceeded to organize his administration by appointing Jefferson to the State Department, Hamilton to the Treasury, Knox to the War Department, and Edmund Randolph as Attorney General. It is difficult to decide, in the then disturbed and disordered state of affairs, foreign and domestic, when a policy was to be fixed, internal and international, which of these offices was of the first importance or required the higher order of abilities. We incline to think that the treasury, though not the first in dignity, was the first in difficulty; mainly because the principal matters of foreign relations were dependent for solution on general grounds and considerations, and were of such patent interest as invited the examination and co-operation of the whole administration; while the affairs of the treasury, depending upon knowledge of political economy and of finance, and consisting of an infinite number of particulars, must necessarily have been left, in a great measure, to the head of that department.

To Jefferson must be awarded the high praise which his celebrated report on the state of our foreign relations has ever commanded. It is one of the ablest state-papers ever issued from any department of the government; indeed, his whole correspondence in his department, while it elicited the warm approbation of Washington, throws an enduring lustre on his pen.

Hamilton's busy invention was at work on the finances. He found the public credit at its lowest ebb; the country impoverished; every interest languishing; the sources of revenue choked up. His funding system, making provision for the payment of the public debt; the system of internal taxes and excise; the assumption of the debts of the States incurred during the Revolution; laying a tariff of duties on foreign importations; these, some of them bold and sharp measures of relief, and bitterly opposed at the time, were proposed and carried through with a nerve and vigor worthy of all praise. The Whiskey Boys of Pennsylvania rose against the excise; and Washington issued his proclamation, and proceeded to collect an army to put down the insurrection; but the insurgents disbanded.

The policy of the Secretary of the Treasury found but little favor with the Secretary of State. They got along badly, we suspect, from the first. They both held the most prominent positions before the country. They were both very ambitious. They were both fond of having their own way. Neither had been accustomed to a rival, and could little brook one. There was but little agreement in political character; indeed, their political opinions, as to radical principles, were nearly antipodal; and there was but little congeniality of personal disposition. They were equally jealous of the favor of Washington; for it was every thing at that time. Each was conscious that himself and the other were making history; and we cannot doubt that each was looking, as none had better right or reason to look, to the highest office in the future; for it was not *then* discovered that great talents and great services were impediments to the first office in the nation.

Hamilton was, by fourteen or fifteen years, the younger; but this disparity was counterbalanced by the singular precocity of his genius, and his early, active, and continuous employment in various business, military, political, and professional, of the greatest moment. Every thing contributed to stimulate, mature and strengthen his judgment; for at periods teeming with such events and developments, days are not counted by the dial. A man who had lived through ten or fifteen years of such times, had the experience of a long life running in smooth and common channels. Jefferson had reached that age, when the energies, full yet of vitality and vigor, seem most vehemently directed to the attainment of the hopes and projects of life.

Hamilton, we suspect, had more force and demonstration of character. If he had not more character, it was more prominent. He had more intensity and directness of purpose. He met men and difficulties more boldly. Jefferson, if he did not shrink from controversy, was not fond of it. Hamilton liked it. The sharp collisions of intellect had for him an agreeable excitement. Jefferson had more wariness and caution. He was more adroit, but he was more circuitous. He was an able writer, and one of the best conversationists of his age, with every faculty, it would seem, for public speaking. We do not regard the want of volume of voice, alluded to by Mr. Wirt, as, by any means, an insuperable obstacle; greater defects having been overcome by orators not half so well furnished forth by nature. Yet, notwithstanding these advantages, though he often called his friends out to combat for his principles or party, he seldom or never took the field of controversy himself. There was little of the knight or the gladiator in him.

In the cabinet of Washington the illustrious rivals met *vis à vis*. We have Jefferson's word for it, that "Hamilton and myself were daily pitted in the cabinet like two cocks.' They seldom agreed. Each had adherents in and out of the council-hall. Randolph usually sided with Jefferson; Knox with Hamilton. Their deliberations generally resulted in a dead lock; the discussions ending where they began. The presiding Will, the slow-pondering, massive, patient, prudent, almost unerring judgment of the august chief turning the scale. That judgment, it must be confessed, usually sided, with conciliating modifications, when possible, with Hamilton.

The influence of Hamilton seems to have been felt by Jefferson with no little poignancy. In a letter to the President, 9th September, 1792, after complaining that he "was once made a tool of by the Secretary of the Treasury for forwarding his schemes, not then sufficiently understood by him" (alluding to one of the financial measures of Hamilton) he refers to the interferences of that gentleman in his (Jefferson's) own department. "My system," he says, "was to give some satisfactory distinctions to the former (France) of little cost to us in return for the solid advantages yielded us by them; and to have met the English with some restrictions, which might induce them to abate their severities against our commerce. Yet," he adds, "the Secretary of the Treasury, by his cabals with members of the legislature, and by high-toned declamation on other occasions, has forced down his own system, which is exactly the reverse."

"These views, thus made to prevail, their execution fell, of course, to me; and I can safely appeal to you, who have seen all my letters and proceedings, whether I have not carried them into execution as sincerely as if they had been my own, *though I ever considered them as inconsistent with the honor and interest of our country.*" The words italicised by us certainly show great frankness of acknowledgment.

The objections then urged to the financial system of Hamilton are now, with most of the other matters of opposition to the first administration, generally considered unsound. Most of them seem to us at this day as almost factious; some of them nearly puerile. The objections that the funding system led to speculation; that the scrip of the government had sunk below par, and that some of it was bought up for a trifle, and, therefore, ought not to be paid up in full, surely were answered by the words of the bond. The government, after having pledged its faith to pay *these debts*, was bound to pay them in full according to its contract. It was nothing to *it* what was the contract between assignor and assignee; while the policy, at that time, of meeting promptly its obligations, was even more clear than its justice. Nor was the objection to assuming the debts of the several States, incurred in the common war and for the common benefit, better grounded; the objection, namely, that some of them were not judiciously contracted, and to a want of precision as to the amount and direction of the appropriation. The general charge, true or not, that the money to be disbursed and the offices connected with the system, would or might be made the means of buying up partisans and corrupting the legislature, would have applied, probably, to *any* system; and is, at best, more an objection to *money* in the hands of government, than to the particular project which proposed to dispense it.

It is certain that the effect of the system was to raise the credit and character of the government; while the enormous evils predicted from it did not ensue.

CHAPTER V.

The French Revolution—Jefferson's and Hamilton's opposite feelings towards France—The French difficulty—Peace with France.

THE French difficulty began to grow apace. The country was thrown into a violent excitement. The popular sympathies, even to enthusiasm, sided with France. It was natural they should. We had been allies. Our flags had flown side by side, in the decisive battles of the war. Our soldiers had fought, shoulder to shoulder, in the late campaigns. La Fayette—so popular as a hero—was, for a time, at the head of, or prominent in, the movement there. It was the rising of the *people* against tyrants. The movement was an assertion of the principles *we* had fought for, and, as was claimed, but the following of *our* example and teachings. And, then, *our* great men, our Franklins, Washingtons, and Jeffersons, and, indeed, our whole country, were objects of the most honeyed commendation and flattery.

Great Britain and France were pitted against each other in exterminating warfare. The battle for national existence and the mastery of the world, was to be fought out, and that great European struggle, the like of which time, in all its flight of centuries, had never seen before, was just beginning to convulse the world. Never was there a greater national delusion than prevailed here, in the first stages of the French Revolution. Jefferson partook of it to intoxication. He was in France during the first unfolding of that great movement. While there, he was treated with marked kindness; had received many tokens of favor; had made many friendships; was intimate with Condorcet and D'Alembert; was toasted by the savans, and was welcomed by the philosophers; was courted by the intellect and wit, the beauty and polished graces, of the gay metropolis, then as ever abounding in the most luxurious and fascinating society of the world. He was Epicurean in his tastes, and French in his mental organization. He liked the freedom and grace of Parisian manners, and the new French ideas on religion, government, and philosophy. He saw before him the vision and dream of his youth—the equality and brotherhood of man, and his political and moral regeneration, rising over old systems, like a morning star in the firmament. He came away before the first acts of the Revolution had been succeeded by its bloodier scenes. He came away with impressions in favor of France and her movement, too deep to be obliterated; and he found prevailing at home the sentiments he brought with him.

With Hamilton it was different. He was English in his structure of mind, and in his philosophy of government. He had no French notions, tastes, or habitudes. He had more of reverence than love of novelty. He had opposed the British Government, not because he disliked *it*, but because of his love of British liberties and institutions, which the king had denied *to us*. He was any thing but a democrat. He had no great confidence in the masses. He saw in this sudden movement no hope of good. Jefferson, following him with his pen, records in his Anas, as something very heretical, that Hamilton said: "The republic of France would not last three months." Like Burke, he was not deceived by words of philanthropy covering dark deeds of crime. Murder appeared to him no better, when tricked out in philosophic robes, than in the old garb of vulgar assassination. The tyranny of an upstart mob was as hateful to him as the tyranny of a king. He did not believe in a sudden wrench, from an ignorant and besotted servility, to the self-respect and self-control necessary to a virtuous liberty. Progression and adaptation for higher enjoyments and uses following the processes of nature, are things of growth and development, and not a miraculous conversion. He did not mistake the yell of slaves, drunk with blood and license, for the shout of freedom: And when the long procession of hurdles moved down the streets of Paris to the guillotine, or returned with the ghastly heads of delicate females fixed on pikes, he did not suppose *that* to be a procession of freemen. Nor did Jefferson and *his* party. They thought these horrid outrages only the first excesses of exasperation, which, if not marking all revolutions, at least in this instance, were only the natural results of the passions despotism had planted or aroused; and that, after reason had time to resume her sway, the order, moderation and security of good government would succeed.

We think Hamilton, at this time or afterwards, if not disposed to an alliance with England, at least wished to favor her by discriminations. We think it as evident that Jefferson was disposed in the same way towards France. The sober, better judgment of Washington was for neither. With a wisdom we can find no language sufficiently expressive to extol, he determined to keep aloof from both; to have *no* entangling alliances; "not to quit our own to stand on foreign ground." He was for a judicial impartiality between the belligerents. This did not suit the temper of France, and of French partisans and sympathizers here and elsewhere. The French took to fitting out ships in our ports, and to sallying out from them for prizes, and bringing them in. Washington put his peremptory veto on this high-handed proceeding.

Mistaking the temper of the American people, and misled by the clamor of French partisans here, the French Envoy, took ground against the government, and proposed an issue before the people between himself and the administration. The insult was rebuked. The French government took up the quarrel. Public feeling was aroused. In the midst of this excitement, Jay's treaty was made and ratified. Then came such wanton outrages and insults to our ministers and country, by the upstart rulers of France, that American blood boils to this day when we recall them.

Before the acme of this excitement, Jefferson and Hamilton were out of the cabinet. Indeed, Washington, before the last of these acts, had given up the presidency, and John Adams had succeeded to it. Washington was up for war. So was Hamilton. Indeed the old military and heroic spirit, and that of the country generally, was thoroughly roused.

War measures were taken by Congress; a large army provided for; Washington put at its head, and Hamilton made the second in command; when, without consulting his cabinet, and to the astonishment of Washington and Hamilton, the President, in one of those freaks of wilfulness and eccentricity to which he was subject, sent a commission to France; and the rulers there, whose policy was to bully and not to fight, gladly availed themselves of the opportunity to make peace.

CHAPTER VI.

Jefferson and Hamilton retire from the Cabinet—Their Cabinet Controversies—Jefferson's Anomalous Position in the Cabinet—The Head of the Opposition—Sustains Freneau's Abusive Paper—Opposition to Washington's Administration Considered—Success of Washington's Administration—Jefferson Returns Home—Denounces the Administration—John Adams elected President—Jefferson Vice-President—Hamilton defends the Administration—Jefferson's Opinion of Hamilton as a Writer—The Federal Party—John Adams—His Conduct towards France—The Alien and Sedition Laws—Jefferson elected President.

In December, 1793, Jefferson resigned his office of Secretary of State. Hamilton remained as Secretary of the Treasury, until January, 1795, when he retired.

For some time before the resignation of Jefferson, the relations between him and Hamilton had grown very bitter; producing such dissensions in the administration, that Washington interposed to reconcile them and restore harmony; but this was impossible. Each of course threw the blame on the other, and crimination and recrimination followed.

Jefferson's position in the cabinet was anomalous. He disapproved of almost all the measures that marked the line of policy, and made up the political character, of the administration of which he was a part. That administration was violently attacked in Congress; and a party, formidable for its talents and the influence of its members, formed there, the basis of whose organization was this opposition; and the leaders of this party were not only representing Jefferson's principles and views, but were his political and personal friends. Nay more. He ever afterwards referred to this party as his own, and claimed a participation in the merit he ascribed to their proceedings.

The clerk in his own office, the poet Freneau, was editor of the newspaper which was the organ of the opposition; and Freneau, not contenting himself with abusing the measures and Federal ministers of the President, ventured to assail the President himself in terms of violent vituperation. It is refreshing to recur to the toleration shown at that day to the office-holder, and to witness the independence of a cabinet minister. We extract from Jefferson's Anas: "He (Washington) said he despised their attacks on him personally &c. He was evidently sore and warm, and I took his intention to be that I should interpose, in some way, with Freneau, perhaps withdraw his appointment &c. But I will not do it. His paper has saved our constitution * * checked the career of the monocrats; and the President, not sensible of their designs, cannot, with his usual good sense and *sang froid*, look on the efforts and effects of this *free* press," &c. We wonder how the distinguished patriot of the Hermitage would, with "*his* usual good sense and *sang froid*," have met the Secretary, whose little French clerk had been kept in office, after it was known that his main business was to libel the President and decry his measures; and, especially, if the little Frenchman had, like Freneau, the "*sang froid*" to send three copies of his "*free* paper" to the President, for distribution every week!

It is impossible, we think, to look back upon the administration of Washington, and not disapprove of the temper, if not of the fact of opposition to it. Consider that the government was an experiment; that successful administration was almost as essential as the constitution itself; that every thing was at sea and in chaos; that there were no precedents or lights in the past to regulate the working of this new and anomalous machinery; that almost *any* government was better than the anarchy and confusion which must have resulted from throwing off or checking the present government; that there were difficulties and trials of all sorts, external and internal; that most of these measures were really unobjectionable, some of them absolutely necessary, and none of them incorrigibly evil; that all views were represented, and all parties heard; and the final judgment pronounced by the functionary chosen by all, and against whose wisdom and disinterested patriotism no suggestion could be made by any reasonable or sober-minded man;—when these things are considered, we are amazed at the almost ferocious opposition with which every measure proposed was assailed, on grounds and pretexts, too, for the most part unreasonable and untenable, sometimes even puerile and factious. But against all this opposition the administration triumphed; and, we think, considering the obstacles arrayed against him, domestic and foreign, intrinsic and factitious, the great chief exhibited a genius for statesmanship, in no degree inferior to that which he displayed in the field. Indeed Washington, the Statesman, was even a greater man, we think, than Washington, the General.

We pass over the measures of administrative policy in the cabinet of Washington, after Jefferson's withdrawal. They were, in the main, some important measures excepted, the carrying out and fulfilment of the policy which had previously been stamped on the administration. Jefferson returned to Monticello, and seemed now, to all appearance, busy with his " peas and clover," and enjoying those calm rural delights of which he makes so much mention in his letters. He opposed the remaining course, as he had opposed the preceding acts of Washington's administration; and now in more open and unrestrained condemnation. He did not scruple now, in his letters, to charge Washington with being under the influence of Hamilton and the monocrats, and to inveigh against the administration, as monarchical in its tendencies and English in its affinities.

The genius of Jefferson could not be idle. His pen and tongue were busy in public affairs. He was the monk of letters, and Monticello the monastery from whence poured those effective missives, which no man of his time knew so well as himself how to employ. He was put in nomination at the succeeding election, and came near being elected; but the revulsion of the French enthusiasm and its re-action upon the Republicans prevented his success. On the count of the votes, it was discovered that John Adams had received the largest number, and that Jefferson was next on the list. He was, therefore, chosen Vice-President. He repaired to his post, which was little better than a sinecure, but he made it a tower of observation.

Nor had Hamilton been idle. His powerful pen was as active, in defence of the administration, in the public prints, as his brain had been busy in maturing its measures in the cabinet. The essays of Camillus and Curtius are equal to the best writings of "The Federalist." Jefferson, writing to Madison, in September, 1795, speaks of him thus: "Hamilton is really a Colossus to the Anti-Republican party. Without numbers, he is a host within himself. They have got themselves into a defile where they might be finished; but too much security on the Republican part will give time to his talents and indefatigableness to extricate them. We have had only middling performances to oppose to him. In truth, when he comes forward there is nobody but yourself who can meet him." And the letter concludes: "For God's sake take up your pen, and give a fundamental reply to Curtius and Camillus."

Up to this time the Federalists had prevailed on all important issues: the financial policy; the international questions; the British Treaty; the neutrality policy; the question of the powers of the Executive as to removals from office; the power of the Legislature to defeat a treaty by withholding appropriations to carry it into effect; the first exertion of physical force to suppress opposition to the laws, and the people, by electing Mr. Adams, who approved all these measures, over his opponent, seem to have avouched this policy. Republican stock was at a discount. Indeed, Jefferson seems to have thought the prospect rather gloomy, for, in a letter to Mr. Madison, January 1, 1797, he suggests whether it " would not be better for the public good to come to a good understanding with Adams as to his future elections," he being " the only sure barrier against Hamilton's getting in."

The weight of talents was, we think, with the Federalists. Washington, Hamilton, Marshall, Henry, Ames, the Lees, the Adamses, Otis, Pickering, Livingston, the Pinkneys, and Luther Martin, are but a few of the names that shone in the bright galaxy which revolved around or composed the first administrations; while the old military corps, in its higher and lower grades of service, generally were on the same side.

The insolence of France and its rejection of our ministers; its assaults upon our commerce; the measures taken by the new administration to avenge these indignities, and to protect our rights, swelled the popularity of the Executive, and damped the spirits and ardor of opposition.

That the party in power, for a long while at least, might have maintained its supremacy, is almost certain, had it not been for causes originating with itself. But the prudent course was not pursued. Mr. Adams was in many respects the most improper selection that could have been made for President.

It is true, he had a strong record of services, and great claims upon the gratitude of his country. He belonged to an influential family; he came from, at that time more than now, an influential section; which had contributed largely to the glory and success of the Revolution, and had stood the first and fiercest onset of tyranny. He was a man of positive character, of pure reputation, of great courage and boldness, of impassioned eloquence, and of active and untiring energies. His patriotism, honesty and magnanimity, were known to the country. He was one of the very earliest champions of freedom; had moved the appointment of Washington to the command of the army; had seconded the Declaration and was its most eloquent advocate. It was he, more than any other man, who, by his zeal, eloquence, and boldness in the Congress, kept up the hopes of the patriots, and pushed through the measures that, in the dark hours of the struggle, were needed to sustain it and give it success; and to the negotiations, so important to the achievement and security of the final victory, he had largely contributed. Indeed, his life was a sort of embodiment of the political history of the Revolution. But he had some great faults of temper and character. He was bold, but his boldness ran into rashness. He was frank, but his frankness ran into indiscretion. His confidence made him the dupe of the most transparent designs, and his suspicions alienated him from the most trustworthy. He was full of learning, and he was full of crotchets. His judgment was far from sound; yet he had such conceit of his wisdom as made him think himself nearly infallible. His vanity was enormous, irritable and itching, and was the door through which artful men easily came into his confidence. He thought himself equal to Washington, and complained that he did not get an equal number of votes, with an equal chance for the presidency. He was really, at bottom, a kind, generous, noble-hearted man; but his manners were so far from conciliating, that they conveyed a very different impression. He was incapable of concealment. He could be read as easily as his messages. Whatever he thought he spoke, and was perpetually giving offence and handles to his enemies, and getting himself into hot water with his friends. On some subjects, he was little better than a monomaniac. Among these, was his jealousy of Hamilton. He looked on Hamilton with unconquerable aversion. He seemed to regard him as his evil genius. Hamilton haunted him like a demon; he sat on him like a nightmare, disturbing his peace and marring all his enjoyments. He thought Hamilton was in a perpetual scheme and intrigue against him. In whatever irritated him, he could see the hand of Hamilton. In every squib fired at him in the papers; in every lying rumor that was bruited about the political circles, he saw the agency of the never-resting and diabolical Hamilton. He denounced Hamilton, every where and on all occasions, with as little decency as reason. He became furious when his name was mentioned. His denunciations, after a while, grew too public and notorious to be disregarded. Hamilton wrote to him, desiring an explanation. He refused to return any answer. Hamilton wrote again, denouncing him, in unequivocal terms, as a liar and a slanderer.

Unfortunately, Mr. Adams was constitutionally obstinate; more unfortunately, he was fickle and vacillating. The country was hot for war. France was not foolish enough to go to such a length. She was in no condition for it. She never intended it. She would soon have sued for peace. In one of his self-willed whims, without mentioning the subject to his cabinet, Mr. Adams, as we before remarked, in the teeth of the insults and contumelies of the French Directory, sent off envoys to France to seek a settlement of the difficulty. France clutched at the chance; and, thus, the war fever ended by a revulsion against the administration on account of its humiliating conduct. Washington, when he heard of the proposition, declared himself "horror struck." Hamilton exclaimed against it. The public spirit of the nation was disgusted and humbled. Whether the fact, that Hamilton was second, and, in case of Washington's death, would be the first in the army (an appointment wrung from Adams, with much groaning of spirit, by Washington's peremptory persistence) whether this circumstance had any thing to do with this unfortunate mission is not known; but it is pretty certain that the success of the war movement, by bringing France to terms, would have given such a head of popularity to the Federal administration, as would have made future opposition to it, for some years at least, futile.

The Alien and Sedition laws, too, contributed to the unpopularity and downfall of the administration. If the war had gone on, probably they would not have had much influence. All minor questions would have been swallowed up in the war. They gave, however, the Republicans an issue upon which they could safely go before the country. Having deprecated the war with France, they were not in a condition to avail themselves of the mission to much advantage. The war itself was popular. Not much capital was to be made of that. The Alien and Sedition laws involved distinctive principles, and made a platform broad enough, covering the whole question of the relations between the States and Federal Government, upon which a party might stand. Public opinion has long since agreed, that these measures were unconstitutional and improper. They had, however, their apologists and apologies in their day. They were passed in times of violent excitement; when thirty thousand foreign emissaries, it was said, were engaged in machinations against the government; and when the press exhibited a licentiousness never before known. But to make the mere suspicion of the President, however excited, the ground for sending into exile a person residing here; and to protect specially the characters of the officers of the general government by law of that government, seem to us clearly beyond the powers of the government. Why should the general government protect the reputation of its own officers, by special law, any more than their property? But more broadly: although defaming a man, public or private, is certainly an outrage, yet the freedom of newspapers to tell lies on public men, is so associated with their power to tell the truth, that, we think it impolitic to attempt, by law, to punish such lying. The law would afford but scant redress and no terror; and the public have long since ceased to believe any charge, made without proof, in a party paper. Besides, in high party times, such a law, if not impracticable of execution, would transfer the excitement of the stump and the hustings to the courts of justice.

Other causes soon came into play. Washington died. The great American heart had ceased to beat; and his powerful influence freely given to Mr. Adams's administration, without any personal preference *for him*, was now withdrawn. Before he died, he had summoned Patrick Henry to the field to combat for the administration. He came forward, struck one more blow for what he thought the right, but fell back, soon afterwards, into the grave. Hamilton, "the host within himself," was still left. He had helped to rally the party in 1799, and the Federalists had again carried the day in the congressional elections. But now *he* was alienated. He preferred C. C. Pinkney, of South Carolina, than whom a more chivalrous and magnanimous patriot never lived. The folly of Mr. Adams, in dismissing two of the members of his cabinet, under circumstances of irritation, completed his ruin. The tide now began to ebb, when, to cap the climax, Hamilton came out with his pamphlet denouncing Adams, on the eve of the election in New York. The Federalists were divided and disheartened; and Jefferson and Burr won the day. In the contest between Jefferson and Burr, before the House, Hamilton, much as he disliked Jefferson, threw his influence in his favor.

Hamilton was now in private life, and his great rival was in the highest seat of power. The object of Jefferson's personal ambition, after so many vicissitudes, had, at last, been attained. It remained to see, whether he could do what is often harder than to win power—retain it.

CHAPTER VII.

Jefferson as a Party Tactician—As President—His Inaugural Address—His Conciliatory Policy—Acquisition of Louisiana—Strict Construction—The Embargo and Non-Intercourse Acts—Our Relations with England—Decline of the Federal party—Jefferson's Policy.

WHATEVER may be the estimate of Jefferson as a statesman, there can be no doubt that he was one of the most adroit politicians who ever lived. We think, that, soon after the inauguration of the government, conceiving it could be safely administered only upon his own principles, he set to work to build up a party. The opposition to the first administration was composed almost entirely of his friends and adherents. The Anti-Federalists (so called from having opposed the Constitution) with Mr. Madison and a few others, who had favored the adoption of that instrument, constituted the germ and nucleus of his party.

By slow degrees, the little phalanx always kept together and always in opposition, grew into the army which, in 1801, bore Jefferson triumphantly into power. Nothing was omitted, in all that time, which could add recruits or bring strength to his ranks.

Jefferson entered upon his office, and delivered his Inaugural address. That paper stands unapproached as a masterpiece of composition of its kind and for its purposes. We think it, as a composition, in every respect, superior to the Declaration of Independence. It is difficult to see in what particular it could be improved. It set forth, as far as it went, with the distinctness and beauty of a picture, an almost perfect ideal of government under our Constitution—its powers, its means, and its ends. It preached, in eloquent strains, the beauties of moderation, of brotherly love, of a return to the kindness and confidence of old relations and friendships. It hinted at amnesty for old offences and differences, and invited, by its exhortations, new recruits.

That these fraternizing passages were the dictates of policy, Jefferson did not scruple to avow to his friends. He wished to alienate from the Federal leaders as many of their adherents as possible; and so well did he succeed, that he crushed, more effectually by conciliation, than he could have done by power, what might still have been a formidable and troublesome organization.

The remaining course of the administration was prosperous. Circumstances favored the Republicans. The old "Heroic-racy," as Jefferson called them, who had constituted the flower of the Federal party, had died or worn out. A new generation of voters, with fresher principles and newer ideas, had succeeded. Victory, too, when it comes clothed in moderation, and invites conciliation, is an advocate of moving eloquence. The old Federal spirit was broken. Its ranks were thinned by desertion. Its leaders were alienated and hostile. Besides, it was the good fortune of the Republicans to come in on abstract and general maxims, and on minor matters of objection and discontent, rather than upon any great permanent measures of opposition. The Alien and Sedition laws are not exceptions; for they were passed to last only for a limited period, and were suffered to continue, in almost nominal existence, until they expired by their own limitation. Some removals—not many—were made; and these, in those primitive times, produced a considerable outcry; but they were defended with such plausibility, that the party who had employed the last hours of their rule in providing for *their* friends, could not very reasonably complain of the new administration for providing for a small proportion of its own.

So successful was the new administration in its policy of conciliation, that even Mr. Adams yielded his support to it; and, indeed, continued, we believe, ever afterwards a supporter of the party; having been placed at the head of the Republican ticket of electors, in 1818, by the Republican party of Massachusetts.

A review of the measures of the first Republican administration would be impossible in the space left us in this paper. Upon the whole, we think, candor constrains a commendation of its general features. It left the country better than it found it. The cession of Louisiana doubled the area of the Republic, and added indefinitely to its strength and wealth. The credit due to Jefferson for this acquisition, is less, probably, than Mr. Monroe and Mr. Livingston deserve. The design originally was only to purchase the island of New Orleans and Florida. Bonaparte was first consul. He saw the instability of his hold upon Louisiana. With Great Britain mistress of the seas, he knew that his title was only an instantaneous seizin. He saw the great value of the territory to his rival; and he was greatly in want of money to prosecute his wars. He saw, at the same time, the incalculable importance of the country to us. He proposed to sell it all. He put this whole empire under the hammer. Mr. Monroe stretched his authority, limited to the smaller purchase, and concluded a treaty of cession. The credit is due to Jefferson of swallowing his over-strained scruples about the constitutional authority, and for clinching the bargain, and hastening through the measures that consummated the transfer of the possession of the territory to us. This measure of itself makes an epoch in American history.

It was not long before Jefferson found the rigid rule of construction which he professed while out of office, too stringent for a practical administration of the government. It is a singular fact, that every important measure of his policy would have been ignored by his own criterion of constitutional construction, to wit; that the auxiliary power must bear such relation to the express or specific power, that the latter could not be executed without it. The Embargo, for example—under what clause of the Constitution did that come? The power to regulate commerce? It was answered that this act was to *prevent* commerce, and that the power to regulate supposed the continued existence of the thing regulated; and that if it were a measure of hostility, there were *other* modes of warfare more direct, unequivocal and effective. And the Non-intercourse Act—it was neither a war measure nor a peace measure. It irritated, wasted and crippled like war, but unlike war, it conquered nothing but our own patience and resources.

We had, unquestionably, the most abundant cause for war with England. It was high time that the insolence of England was checked. It was time for us to show the nations of Europe that we had a national character, which we intended should be inviolate and respected. Half-way measures are inconsistent with the dignity of the government and the genius of the people. Essentially, a warlike and aggressive people, Jackson was one of the best representatives of the national character we ever had. To make the administration a galvanic battery, and send out, from the capitol, along all the nerves of official connection, the electric influence that arouses and animates a brave people; to gather up the national energies and hurl them, at once, like lightning, upon an enemy—this is the policy at once of resolution and of safety. This policy, we think, Jefferson did not have the boldness to pursue. Indeed, it was reserved for Jackson to demonstrate the terrible might of freemen, of great individuality of will, aggregating their strength into a single and common effort.

Jefferson, though he strengthened his party by adherents from the opposite, made no fusion. He still kept up his distinctive organization; and he was aided in this by the pressure of opposition from without; an opposition just sufficient to consolidate without embarrassing or compromising his party.

But that opposition became, after a while, mostly local and sectional. It lost its catholic character. Federalism degenerated into a factious opposition to the government. It lost its old prestige. It lost its *esprit du corps.* As it waned in strength, it grew sour, vindictive and turbulent. The flower and chivalry of the *ancien régime* had departed. And now, first coming upon the theatre, were the young champions of Republicanism, from the new States and the old, who, catching the later and fresher spirit of the times, charged hotly the waning squadrons of Federalism. The fresh Bluchers and Bulows, however, had nothing to do but to turn a defeat into a rout. The old conservatism was out of date. The world, passing a figure on the dial, had left it behind.

The policy of Jefferson was singularly politic. He was, as we have already remarked, one of the most vigilant and shrewd politicians of the age. He gave but few opportunities for assault; he never failed to seize and improve an advantage. He had the essential faculty of turning every thing to account; of giving an exaggerated appearance and appreciation to his own principles and movements, and of heightening the designs, miscarriages and practices of his adversaries. He had got them down, and he meant to keep them down. He kept alive the influences which had defeated them. Those things which made them unpopular before, he made more unpopular now. He avoided, as far as possible, new issues. He availed himself of all the imprudencies, the shifts, and desperate turns of his adversaries. Every one of his measures was a Republican measure; every opposition was Federal opposition. Even the general maxims of government, which all men approve, were made to appear as the distinctive tenets of his own sect.

But the most striking and inviting tableaux of party proceedings were the first measures of administration; abolishing internal taxes; pardoning offenders under the Sedition law; diminishing the patronage and expenditures of government; repealing the Judicial Bill with its host of Federal appointees;—these and other acts made up a list of popular measures, which promised most auspiciously for the new régime.

CHAPTER VIII.

Hamilton as a Lawyer—His Death—Personal Traits.

HAMILTON, during the greater part of Jefferson's first term, was engaged in the practice of law in New York, earning and building up that professional reputation which, even in a bar so eminent, placed him beyond rivalry. On the 11th of July, 1804, he fell, in a duel with Aaron Burr, at Weehawken, near the spot where his oldest son had fallen a victim to the same barbarous practice. It was not seen until death had removed him, what an immense space he occupied in the mind and heart of his country. The mournful tidings passed over the land, arousing the sympathies of all classes, and entwining his memory with remembrances of the heroic age of the confederacy, of which, next to Washington, he was the most vivid personation. Since the death of Washington, no similar event has ever created in the public mind such profound and universal sensation. Looking back upon his eventful and splendid career, and standing over his early and bloody grave, well might Fisher Ames, thrilling with emotion, exclaim, as, in rapid review, the stirring events and il-

lustrious personages of the past swept over his memory:
"My heart grows liquid as I speak, and I pour it forth like
water." Public horror and indignation, like an avenging
Nemesis, followed the honorable murderer as he fled, a vagabond and a fugitive through the land; speedily to be transformed into a maurauder and turbulent fillibuster, abhorred
and despised by all the world.

Whatever may be thought of Hamilton as a statesman,
his many virtues must be conceded. Jefferson himself acknowledged that he was honest, honorable and disinterested
in private life. He was not without fault. History has descended from its dignity to record his amour with a Mrs.
Reynolds. But the frankness of his acknowledgment carries
with it proof of the truth of his explanation. He was, at
least, as much seduced as seducer, and had the temptation
of Joseph, without, unfortunately, his invincible virtue.
Besides this, there rests no stain upon his life except the act,
more of weakness than crime, which destroyed it; and even
this last stain, under the circumstances of temptation, and
the perverted honor, which caused it, charity is almost
tempted to regard like

"A drop upon a vestal's robe,
The worse for that it soils."

He was ambitious, but we have Washington's authority for
saying, that his was only the ambition which prompted him
to excel in whatever he attempted; and this surely he did.
At forty, he had achieved more than any other man on the

continent has ever done at that age. In letters, in oratory, in statesmanship, in arms, in law, he was, if not first, yet not second to any man of his country in any one of these departments of intellect or service; while he stands alone in the distinction of wearing the wreath which blends all these honors in harmonious union. He was brave, generous, placable, magnanimous, gay and social of temper, frank, direct and unsuspecting; with no sordid qualities or littleness of mind; liberal in his bounties and expenditures; caring nothing about money; jealous of reputation; punctilious of honor; and fired by a noble passion for glory. He was full of energy and firmly fixed in his purposes; not sparing of labor, and had a remarkable power of application, and force and hardihood of will. No man was more constant to his friends or his principles, never deserting or compromising either; and no man had a greater faculty of attracting and retaining the friendship of others. We do not wonder that Hamilton thought Julius Caesar the greatest man that ever lived. There was no little resemblance between them in variety and kind of accomplishments; even somewhat in person; in energy; in the qualities we have mentioned; in ambition, though better tempered; in opposition to anarchy and popular turmoil, and, alas! what was to complete the parallel, in falling in the prime of life, by the blow of an envious and malignant Casca.

CHAPTER IX.

The Republican and Federal Parties—Characteristics of each—Jefferson's Democracy—Hamilton's Conservatism—Errors of both.

WITH Hamilton died the last hope of Federal ascendency. The WAR OF IDEAS, of which he was the leader on one side, and Jefferson on the other, may now be said to have concluded its first and most important campaign. What was the difference? In the dust and confusion of the field, and in the multitude of the combatants, with different banners, it is sometimes hard to see the original ground of conflict. We take it, however, to have been the same principle which has always divided parties and societies: the principle of *Conservatism* and the principle of *Progression*; the principle of stability and the principle of change; the principle which is more solicitous of keeping, than of hazarding what it has for the chance of getting more, and the principle which considers what it has as mainly valuable as capital for future acquisitions. The one principle owns prudence for its parent; the other enterprise. The one looks to the past; the other to the future. The one is sanguine and hopeful;

the other cautious and calculating. Conservatism affects security; Progress delights in achievement; preferring the turbulence and dangers of agitation to the calm which rusts genius, and dulls intellect, and invites despotism. These are the extremes of the warring principles which these illustrious men severally advocated, and which constituted the radical and organic basis of their creeds.

The war of the Revolution was the war of the people against the crown. Jefferson had taken the side of the people. He was for giving all authority to them. He was essentially a democrat. He was for practically transferring to the people all the powers of the government in every department, so that *their* will should, as far as possible, be the animating and controlling spirit of the government. He had seen the powers of government grossly abused, in many instances, by the crown and its satellites. He felt jealous of all governments, and was full of distrust of all who controlled them. His sympathies were all with the people. He was for a weak government. He thought the world governed over-much. Looking up the line of institutions, civil and ecclesiastical, he saw the road marked, as with milestones, by monuments of the monstrous cruelties and tyrannical excesses of government; the dark crimes, the inquisitions, the gibbets, the Bastiles, the graves of martyrs; the people crouching in ignorance and servility, despoiled by robbers in the garments of priests and kings, and princes rioting in splendid palaces, built by the hands of pillaged labor. It was a dark and gloomy picture. He attributed all the evils of society to bad government. Accordingly, when the new government superseded the old, he did all he could to give effect to the popular principle. It must be confessed, that in radical democracy, he was far ahead of his age. Perhaps he went too far. Seeing all these evils prevailing when kings were on top, he thought too sanguinely they would all cease by putting the people on top. We think that, if not opposed to the Federal constitution, he was not cordial to it. In another place we may advert to this point; but certainly, after the new government had been formed, he opposed most of the acts which demonstrated its power. Indeed, if we were to take his *casual dicta* on such matters, for his matured convictions—his objections to the extradition of criminals, his seeming sympathy with Shay's rebellion, and with the Whiskey Boys, and the like—we should be apt to suppose that he was an enemy to *all* government. But this supposition is contradicted by subsequent developments. His jealousy of the Federal government had a different cause from that of John Randolph, and others of the Virginia school. It was not founded in Virginia feeling and State pride. It was based on his dislike of power, wherever lodged, or by whomsoever wielded. It did not dissociate the power of government from the tyranny of government Hamilton, from a different stand-point, took a different view. He had opposed the British government, because *we* were denied its blessings. He considered that government an almost perfect plan of civil rule. He thought the end of government was to secure life, liberty, property—

4

in fine, the rights of the citizen; that these rights were in as much danger from the passions of the people, or of portions, or individuals of them, as from the crown or the rulers; that a strong government was necessary to protect these rights; and that a weak government led to anarchy, and anarchy to despotism. And looking up the past, he saw, by the light of history, amidst riot, confusion, turbulence, and tyranny, the failure of all experiments of government in which the people bore a principal share of the power. He saw, too, what was natural on the breaking up of a camp of unpaid soldiers, and the first attempt to bring to the discipline of government those whom the camp had made licentious and poor, signs of anarchy and insubordination around him.

Both of these great men were friends of liberty; but they differed as to the best means of attaining and securing it. Jefferson was a Republican, upon grounds so broad as to embrace within his theory all nations and all people. He seemed to think that man every where, and by the mere force of his humanity, was fit for self-government. Hamilton doubted if man, any where or under any circumstances, was fitted for self-government. We think both erred. That political affairs require skill, judgment, intelligence, and integrity of character all concede; and we know that, in the masses of the population of other countries, these qualities do not reside. The experiment of self-government has signally failed with them, whenever it has been tried.

But we think it was the error of Hamilton that he looked to other people, and not sufficiently to our own;

that he relied on history instead of observation; that he did not give sufficient effect to the peculiar circumstances which impressed so distinctive a character upon our people: their lineage; their familiarity with the rights secured by the British constitution and the charters; their tuition; the long struggle they had gone through; their few and simple wants, requiring few rulers and little government; their happy isolation, away from the contiguity of older societies and other countries; their actual participation in the transactions of government; the knowledge of men which the times had brought home to them; the practical equality which had all along subsisted between the members of communities, homogeneous, and with little disparity of fortunes or great diversity of interests; the fact that royalty had struck no deep roots in the soil, and that there was no aristocracy of exclusive privileges and distinct interests; and that republicanism was only one step in advance of the former system as *to us;* but, more especially, the individuality of will, and the self-respect which distinguished the Anglo-Saxon breed, with their maxim, "GOD AND MY RIGHT;" and then, the quantity and cheapness of land, giving every man the means of pecuniary independence, without which there can be no other independence, and the rural character, and dispersed and uncrowded condition of the people. These are some of the considerations which, we think, in view of the universal call for Republican Institutions, should have determined the statesman upon an unhesitating and confiding trial of the experiment.

Hamilton thought, as reported by Mr. Madison, that the British Government was the best in the world, "and he doubted much whether any thing short of it would do in America. He was sensible, at the same time, that it would be unwise to propose one of any other than a republican form."

We think this intimation unworthy of Hamilton's intellect. The establishment of the British constitution here, was simply an impossible thing. The interests, of which the British form was a representative, did not exist here. We had a homogeneous community, which did not there obtain. *Here* was no landed interest, with its dependants and particular claims, to serve as a balance between the crown and the people. The aristocracy of England had been built up by ages, constituted a great estate of the realm, and was able, if imposed on, by its wealth and dependants and connections, to bring the kingdom into peril of overthrow. Here a mushroom aristocracy would soon die out by contempt for its weakness, and general odium for its privileges; and it would have no influence besides its votes.

A constitution is made for a people, not a people for a constitution; and the folly and futility of building up a class of people in order to get up a constitution properly balanced are so manifest, that it would seem to strike the plainest apprehension.

Hamilton advocated in the convention this project: A President, to hold office during good behavior; a Senate of the same tenure, with power to declare war; the President to have the veto on State laws about to be passed; to appoint the governors of the States, who were to have vetoes upon the acts of the State legislatures.

It is said that Hamilton's views were considerably modified during the progress of the discussions in the convention; and that he was finally for fixing the executive term at three years. He gave a proof of his sagacity, by declaring, in opposition to the frequent recurrence of presidential elections, that every question would be sunk in the greater inquiry, Who shall be the next President?

But, notwithstanding the almost monarchial strength he wished to infuse into the new constitution, upon its adoption in its present form, he gave it his warm support; and he contributed as much, probably, as any man to its ratification. Having become the basis of government, he often declared that he intended, with whatever distrust of the success of the experiment, in good faith, to give the constitution a fair trial.

We think it the fault of the two parties, which, for opposite reasons, objected, in whole or in part, to the constitution, that they endeavored, wittingly or not, to give such construction to it as accorded with their ideas of what the constitution ought to have been, rather than what it meant, when construed according to the usual and recognized rules.

To the Republicans is due the credit of exploding the latitudinous construction, which deduced from the "*general welfare*" clause unlimited power; while, when in office, they have been compelled themselves to explode the hide-bound rules of construction, which would have denied to the government a claim to any thing better than the name.

The objection of Jefferson to the constitution, that its President was " a bad edition of a Polish king,"—an inferior sort of elective monarch—thereby breeding the evils of elective monarchy; and the exaggerated importance he seemed to attach to prefixing a bill of rights to that instrument, are not regarded as proofs of his unquestioned sagacity. We think, too, that he mistook the whole framework of the constitution, when he supposed it to be a thing of *majorities*, and when he wished to see the democratic principle introduced into, and paramount over, every department, even the judicial. We think he could never have retained that opinion, if he had heard Mr. Calhoun's luminous speech in reply to Mr. Clay, on the Veto Power—a speech, which may be safely pronounced, one of the profoundest expositions ever made of the true character of the constitution.

CHAPTER X.

Jefferson as a Statesman—Individual Freedom—State-Rights—The "General Welfare" Clause—Consolidation—Personal Freedom—Liberty—Free Popular Government—State-Rights Doctrines—Their Influence.

JEFFERSON, having won the victory in the great civic battle, was entitled to wear the laurel. Whether all of the practical measures of administration which he favored were *freer* than the opposite, it is not of any great importance to inquire. The general sentiments he proclaimed, and the grounds upon which he placed himself before the country, the spirit and tendency of his teachings, were for the largest freedom. The people adopted his views; and individual acts, while they may be of some influence in advancing or thwarting a great organic principle, are obviously of infinitely less importance than the principle itself; as the casual acts of a person are usually of less consequence than his character.

Jefferson, as a statesman, must be considered in two aspects; as teaching the principle of individual freedom, and the principle of State-Rights. The results of these two principles may *possibly* be the same; but the doctrines are different. It would not, however, *seem* to be inconsistent to contend for the most rigid doctrines of the State-Rights school, and, yet, to hold the least popular doctrines in the administration of the State government. Accordingly, South Carolina, in her local administration, is the most conservative State in the Union; while, we know, she is the strictest in State-Rights tenets. Jefferson was for both creeds. We think, however, he will be longer remembered, and that his influence will be more effectual, in regard to the first than the latter of these principles.

He marked out, with more precision than any other man, the boundaries of State and Federal powers. If the line was not entirely accurate, it was distinct; and, as in other questions of boundary, it is better to have a wrong line than an open one. It is true he made it, by his definition, too narrow, but he modified his definition by his practice. Federalism, if carried out to the extent ultra Federalists desired, *must* have run into disunion. A consolidated government would be the most corrupt government on earth, and the most impracticable. It would be, indeed, an impossible government, and would soon fall to pieces by its own cabals and corruptions. But Federalism never could go on to the point of consolidation. The very first assault made upon the rights of the States, by extending the jurisdiction of the general government into the domestic forums, would be followed by armed resistance; and this would lead to a dissolution, if not of the Union, at least, of the government. Every one who has read the history of the country sees this. Georgia and South Carolina are only witnesses of what every State would do. The Federal construction of the "general welfare" clause was really, in effect, *the principle* of consolidation; for, under it, Congress could do what it thought necessary to promote the general welfare, that is, any thing it chose. The resistance of this dogma, therefore, met at the threshold a principle which might have been fatal to the government.

The Federal government, being derivative, and having only limited powers, must confine itself, of course, to those powers; and the legislator, like any other depository of power, if there be a well-founded doubt whether he has the particular power he is asked to exercise, is bound, in honesty, *not* to exercise it. No one has a right to do that, of the propriety of which he is conscientiously doubtful.

We think it the misfortune of the times, that, in the construction of the powers, and the settlement of the relations of such an anomalous system as our double governments, men leaned to the State or Federal governments according to their attachments or jealousies. Unquestionably, having established a government for the management of national affairs, and having retained the State governments for the management of domestic concerns, it was not intended that they should be rivals, but co-ordinates;—each master in its own jurisdiction; and the desideratum was, to keep each to its own track, and to give all due efficiency to each to enable it to accomplish its ends. A strong government, unless it gets its strength by usurpation, or exercises it with oppression, is not necessarily a tyrannical government. We do not see, therefore, what sound policy forbade the strengthening of the Federal Government within the circle of its acknowledged powers.

In respect to the other principle, the personal freedom of the citizen, Jefferson's sentiments and teachings have exercised a more marked influence upon the minds of the masses of his countrymen. The subtleties of constitutional construction, though no man had the faculty of making them intelligible to the common understanding so well as he, do not take hold of the minds, or impress themselves upon the hearts, of the people, like questions of personal liberty.

There was an apparent justice, as well as generosity, in his trust in the masses, in his doctrines of political equality and of the supremacy of the people, which moved the popular affections and convictions with the force of natural instincts. What the precise nature and effects of these teachings were, have not always been fully understood. There is a vague declamation afloat about liberty, which conveys no true idea of what it is, or what its uses are. The advantages of a free and popular government are not chiefly, we conceive, in the direct and immediate blessings it conveys, or the evils it averts. So far as the body of the people are concerned, the *Habeas Corpus*, probably, is of little direct moment; not one in ten thousand would ever use or miss it; and so of speedy trial by jury, and other rights securing personal safety from the hands of the government. The great mass of the Russian people are, probably, safe from personal violence; and the impositions on that people, for war or governmental purposes, in proportion to population, are not greater, probably, than those *we* have borne within the last quarter of a century.

Wherein, then, is the essential general advantage of the popular system? We think in this: *It elevates the masses.* By making a man independent of external control, he becomes his own master. He relies on himself. He gets that individuality of will, which is the distinctive attribute of freedom and of manhood. With it comes self-respect. With these and the political power with which he is clothed, comes the respect of others. He feels his importance in the state, in his family, in his neighborhood. He becomes informed, more or less, as to those things with which he has concern. He associates with men with whom he can profitably converse and exchange views; he attends public discussions. The currents of intelligence, which circulate over the country, come to his mind. His port and bearing are those of a freeman. He educates his children. He sees them rise up to posts of honor and distinction. He strives to accumulate property, that their position in the world may be better than his own. He is thus a contented citizen. There is no cause of discontent. He cannot resist the government, because it is his own, and he has no cause of quarrel with it. He cannot rebel against the administration of the law. The functionaries, chosen mediately or immediately by the people, are but executing the laws the people have made, and can repeal. *Privilege is the preservative of caste.* Superior wealth, talent, information, or social position, with superior political privileges, would keep a chilling distance for ever between the higher and lower classes. But a community of privileges and rights, and the dependence of the higher upon the lower class for political elevation, repress pride, bring equality into fashion, and prevent the heart-burnings and jealousies which would otherwise prevail. It makes the population in a good degree homogeneous.

It is no answer to say, that by restricting suffrage we might have better laws. Probably, we might. But is it wiser to have better laws or a better people?

Nor is this principle of personal freedom, and this sense of it, elevating and redeeming influences only. They are also active and energetic agencies. The man free, and stimulated to activity, finds a thousand avenues of business and enterprise, that invite his talents. Instead of a few men thinking for all, each man is thinking for himself. From passive recipiency, his mind is awakened to energetic and independent action. The whole nation is thus aroused; the contagious influence of mind on mind obtains; and the immense volume of its aggregate thought and enterprise, starting from its millions of streamlets, pours forth its mighty current. Hence the advance of this nation in all material objects; for these are of the first necessity, and are the first care of every people; and hence will be, in due time, an equal advance in other enterprises of higher mental reach and attainment. From this same larger individuality, has come the remarkable contrast between our people and all others. Look at the French and Spanish colonies, cooped up in little towns, and sinking to the level of the aborigines around them; while the American pioneer, retaining his individuality and hardy virtues, armed with his axe and rifle, penetrates the forest; subdues alike the wilderness and its inhabitants; and, preserving his institutions, draws over the new land the physical and moral characteristics of the civilization he left behind him. And so, too, in war; having, unlike the common soldier, a character by which he is identified at home as much as by his face, and a self-respect he would die rather than forfeit, he conquers on every battlefield on which he fights.

We do not say that these observations are to be taken without modifications; and especially, we do not say they apply to all men, or to our own people even under all conditions. For we consider after all, that the chief proximate cause of our ability to maintain, even to this day, republican institutions, is, the facility with which our people obtain the means of support. And the great trial of *the experiment* will, in our judgment, come, when, in the Northern States especially, a great and lasting inequality of fortunes shall occur; when, in a single city, one man shall own ten millions of money, and a hundred thousand men not a cent. There will be no practical republicanism then; for, besides the evils poverty entails, the man who cannot call his bread his own, cannot call his vote his own. The extension of our territory, and the consequent cheapness of land, are the remedy, in part, for the great evil of over-crowded population and its concomitants—social divisions, undue influences and class antagonisms; and, happily, this evil will be averted from us for a long while; as long as our own land is cheap, or our neighbors' accessible!

We can trace these germ principles of popular rights to Jefferson. He planted the seed in the mind and heart of the nation, and it produced its fruit in due season. No man's influence has been so great as his in this country. Jackson's, though stronger, probably, at first, had more of will and less of principle for its base; and, therefore, will not be so lasting.

Jefferson's views of State-Rights will be received or not by the people, as they happen to strike or oppose the tone and temper of the public mind. Our people, eminently practical, aggressive, warlike, ardent and impulsive, never, when in pursuit of a great object, stop to scan logical niceties or solve subtle questions of political power. When they want a thing, they mean to have it, and have it at once. The public opinion will mould the constitution to suit itself. The people, if they had it not before, have already swelled out the constitution to be the representative of their own character. They have given the government strength enough to be terrible in war, honored in peace, full of energy, and commanding the respect of all men; reserving to themselves the right, or assuming the license, to beat it back, if it should venture across the limits of the state jurisdiction to attack any vital interest. Jackson, representing the *heroic and the energetic* of the American character, gave the strongest illustration of these predominant traits, in the administration which was made so faithfully the organ of the national temper.

We think that the doctrines of State-Rights, though sometimes ascendant, and seemingly received with favor in calm times, will not always, or even often, prevail, when they come in contact with the impulsive and eager utilitarianism and impatient wishes of the people.

CHAPTER XI.

Jefferson's Political Speculations—Their Influence—His Death—His Character—His Letters—His Published Correspondence—His Ana—His Influence in the State and National Governments.

AFTER the retirement of Jefferson from the presidency, he was busy in consolidating his fame; and it is scarcely too much to say, that, from his speculations while in retirement, the most important principles of government, which have come since to be adopted, proceeded. He returned home, with a reputation, contrary to his own apprehension, even greater than he brought to the presidency. His influence was unexampled; and it must be acknowledged, that its last prominent public manifestation was worthy of his best days. He originated and carried through that noble institution of letters, the University of Virginia. Regarded as a sage and oracle, as the apostle of a new and freer philosophy, men from all parts of the Union, and from the old world, came to pay him their homage. And the youth of the land, some of them afterwards called to proclaim his doctrines in the forum or the Senate, climbing the hill of Monticello, gathered into the Grecian portico that fronts to the east, and, sitting at the feet of the American teacher, like the disciples of the old Greek masters, listened, with reverent attention, until the sun went down, to the words of wisdom which fell from his lips.

He lived to see the influence of his name and doctrines the vital principle of nearly all the State governments of the confederacy; the party he opposed disbanded and annihilated; and its old leaders, his early rivals, only remembered as public enemies defeated by him, or their names kept alive as hyperboles to illustrate political heresy, corruption, and tyranny.

He lived to see the republic he had governed, crowned with the laurels of a second war triumphantly closed; already advanced to wealth and power and a respected place in the family of nations, and bounding on, with giant strides, to the first position in the world; and, at a riper age than is usually allotted to man he contributed, with poetic appropriateness, by his death, to the sanctity of that day which his pen had commemorated.

The intellect of such a man deserves a particular notice

One of the largest of Jefferson's faculties was his power of observation. His perceptive faculties were developed to an astonishing extent. He saw and took cognizance of every thing. Nothing, however minute, escaped his eye. He observed things in gross and in detail. He was an excellent mechanist. His fine perception seized, at once, the proportions of physical objects. It is said that he could detect at a glance the disproportion of any building in any of its parts and he was pained with a want of symmetry or order. He had an excellent head for business. He was familiar with its details. He had system, order, form, number, and all those valuable aids to the higher intellect, which these and the other lower faculties furnish. He kept and preserved papers with great care, and could readily find the sources of information. By these helps, he was enabled to accomplish a great deal within a little time, and at short notice.

He was a ready writer. To his pen he is indebted for much, indeed the greater part, of his reputation and success. Few men have written more. Except his State papers he did not print much of what he wrote; [and, perhaps, it had been as well, on the whole, for his fame, if his literary executors had followed the same example of abstinence from the press]. But his day was different from ours. The press was not then the powerful engine it is now. Comparatively few newspapers were published, and of these there were comparatively few readers. The influence upon the people was from the intelligent few. The men of a county were controlled by the man of the county; and a letter from Jefferson to that man, furnished the ideas and reasonings by which this control was effected and the public sentiment moulded. By his extensive correspondence, he not only communicated, but obtained, minute and reliable information of the state of public sentiment, and of the progress of political movements.

We have said that he was a very able writer. But the style of his correspondence was not, in all respects, the best.

It wanted, in its earlier exercises especially, freedom and ease. It wanted naturalness and grace. It was not harmonious, and it had a sprinkling of affectation, especially in the use of gallicisms, and new-coined, and not always happily invented, words and phrases. There was something of antithesis, but it was, for the most part, verbal, rather than of idea. It had, it is true, novel and felicitous turns and ingenious transpositions; but the style was alluvial, and, we suspect, originally far from easy or fluent. He had little wit, though his shrewdness was sometimes so pat, and the common sense so patent and vivid, that it looked like wit. But the worst defect was a want of humor. His letters, though good political or other theses, were not good *letters*. The light in them was the dry light of intellect. There was no transfusion of character into the written page. The letters of Lamb, of Byron, of Wirt, are as characteristic as their handwriting. They could no more easily be counterfeited in the style than in the chirography. The thinking in them is the least valuable part. They are transcripts, delightful epitomes rather, of their authors; as like the writers, so far as they go, as their daguerreotypes. Any man with Jefferson's sense could have written his letters. Indeed, with slight alterations, they could have been turned, at once, into state-papers or editorials.

But they were powerful state paper missives. They were full of salient points. They startled and fixed attention. They left something to remember. If rough, it was the roughness of the vice which better fixed the grip. He had an aphoristic turn, which gave a common thought the look of a profound one; and he had the rare faculty of saying things in such a striking way, that what he said became a proverb, and was received and repeated as a truism. The tone was positive and oracular; and the statement so plausible and comprehensive that all men understood it and most men believed it.

Hamilton's style was very different. It was easy to write and easy to read. It was compact, flowing, polished, musical. The sentences were well balanced and gracefully turned. It was that sort of style which art cannot make, but which art sets off and adorns. It blended strength with beauty, was just warmed by imagination, only enlivened by fancy, and showed the presence of a subtle discrimination in the nice selection of fitting words to express the exact shade of thought. It was adapted to all uses, like the athlete that can exhibit agility and grace in the dance, or do battle with heavy armor, or carry off huge burdens. Let the reader turn to Hamilton's letter to Laurens on the execution of Andre, and then turn to some of his controversial papers in reply to Madison, and verify what we say. We think that as a writer, combining *all* the various excellencies that give power and grace to the pen, Hamilton has scarcely had an equal on the continent. Not that he was probably as effective as Jefferson with the masses. Neither was Burke as effective as Swift.

Jefferson had not much imagination, but he had large invention and mechanical contrivance. He was, therefore, ingenious and full of resources. He was also copious of comparisons and illustrations; but these, though always striking and relevant, were mostly common-place, and sometimes coarse.

He was seldom eloquent in the highest sense of eloquence. The Lofty, the Impassioned, the Heroic, the Sublime were not with him characteristic qualities. The highest eloquence is the demonstration of the heroic. Such eloquence is, at last, but the self-manifestation of the heroic spirit, in its highest form. All heroic minds are thus eloquent, whenever the qualities that make them heroic are aroused and called into vigorous action. Eloquence, as Mr. Webster remarks, is of the man. It is rather the spirit of the man in operation. When such a soul acts, it is eloquent in deeds; when it speaks, it is eloquent in words. Chatham and Mirabeau, Demosthenes, Henry, Jackson, Clay, Calhoun alone in the Senate opposing the Mexican war, and Washington when aroused, as on the field of Monmouth, possessed this eloquence in an eminent degree; and when it is called into exercise, common greatness shrinks appalled and cowed before its imperial authority. It is the rarest and most infallible of the gifts and marks of greatness; for it displays, in a burst of passionate energy, the highest properties of man—great will, great courage, great intellect—the forces that command and subdue mankind. But for that other eloquence, which furnishes matter for convincing and persuading men to adopt our views or our projects, Jefferson may be accounted one of the first men of his age, as he was assuredly the most efficient in supplying the comprehensive texts and doctrinal axioms, which speakers and writers of smaller calibre elaborated into popular essays and speeches.

We come now to the quality which, we think, gave this illustrious personage his greatest efficiency, while, we conceive, it narrowed and marred his judgment. It was a faculty of mental exaggeration. Like all reformers, Jefferson was an enthusiast. Enthusiasm necessarily heightens the colors of the objects upon which it glows. It is the property essential to success. It gives triumph to the artist, the artisan, the advocate, the soldier, the orator, the statesman. Nelson, Jackson, Clay, all had it. It is not always associated with the divine faculty of poetry or ideality. It is found in the most prosaic natures. It is scarcely stronger in the raving poet glowing in his garret over his *aborted* poem, than in the cool Yankee tinkering upon his patent machine. It is especially the companion of invention and original intellect. It comes from a concentration of all thoughts, feelings, desires, in short of the whole mind and heart, upon the one object. That object becomes a world to him. The different parcels of the scheme expand into great departments; the accessories spread out into immense provinces. The eye, fixed on these things, grows microscopic. Great mountains loom up from mole hills; awful tempests blow in zephyrs; a prodigious storm rages in the teapot. All outside objects that approach the business in hand take their color from the mind of the projector; as all physical nature its hue from the sun.

Jefferson thought himself called to a mission. He had a great work to do. He was to be the founder of a creed, as lasting as the race it was to bless. He was to be " *The Apostle of Liberty.*" From Mahomet to Louis Napoleon, these founders of creeds and dynasties have carried with them a conviction of their destiny, almost as vivid as a consciousness of inspiration. Whether Jefferson, naturally prone to reject every thing savoring of superstition, had any such sense of a divine commission, we do not know; but his sanguine temper and implicit confidence in the people supplied very well the want of it.

To such men, all opposition is irksome, and all minor matters subservient to the great end to be attained. Every thing conducive to the end is important; all men, however unworthy, who aid in it, welcome and respected; all who oppose, suspicious and dangerous enemies to the state.

To this partisan bias and one-sidedness, we trace the earnestness and zeal of Jefferson. The *advocate* exaggeration, which proves so powerful an influence at the bar and on the hustings, to be effectual, must be realized by the mind that employs it; for deception comes most effectually from a man himself deceived.

It was this trait in Jefferson that transformed the harmless levees of Washington into the "forms," while the Federal measures of Hamilton were "the substance, of the British constitution;" the celebration of Washington's birthday was a fearful fore-shadowing of monarchy; Adams was a monocrat, essaying to bring the country over to the

British forms; Hamilton was not only a monarchist, but for a monarchy bottomed on corruption; the legislature was being bought up like cattle by Hamilton; Shay's rebellion was something little short of praiseworthy; the Whiskey Boys' *emeute* a mere frolic which the government was making itself ridiculous by sending out an army to put down; the judiciary was one of the most dangerous departments to civil liberty, and this, at a time when Georgia was shaking her fist in the face of the Supreme Court; and the Federalists were monarchists, seeking an alliance, on humiliating terms, with England. The opposition to a navy, as anti-republican; the project of bringing the judiciary into subserviency to the people; the notion that *all* men are capable of self-government; the doctrine that one generation cannot bind another to the payment of a debt; the moral legality of lotteries; the ascribing to Burr the design of separating the Western States from the Union, and adding them to the Mexican country, in order then to found a monarchy over the whole!—the charge against the Presbyterians, that they were " panting to establish an inquisition;" the charge that the religious sects wished a connection between church and state; the accusation against the Federalists that they sided with Burr on his impeachment, wished him success in his imputed treason, and would have joined him, if the prospect was favorable, in order to subvert the government and, in its place, establish their beloved project of British Monarchy; all these, and many more that might be added, are evidences of the extreme opinions which this state of mind generated, and of the influence of prejudice over an original and powerful understanding.

To the same influence may be attributed the coarse and gross injustice, which he did his contemporaries and others. Washington, though honest, was suborned to the arts and controlled by Hamilton & Co., and had not sense enough to see that he was made a tool of; Hamilton was the embodiment of political villainy and heresy; Adams, by turns praised up in the letters to himself, and denounced in the letters to others; Knox, the friend and companion of Washington, "a blabbing fool;" Edmund Randolph, vacillating and double-minded; Napoleon, a general, but without talent, information or statesmanship; John Marshall, a mountebank and trickster, and a corrupt judge, worthy of impeachment; Luther Martin, a co-conspirator of Burr and worthy of being indicted with him, ["it would at least muzzle the impudent Federal bull-dog"]; General Henry Lee, an eavesdropper, or something like one, "sifting the conversation of his (J's) table," and repeating with falsehoods, what he heard there; Paul, the Corypheus of rogues and roguery; some of the religious women of Richmond attending "praying parties in company with a hen-pecked husband," and addressing the Saviour in terms so amatory that they might be supposed to be addressed to an earthly lover; and that Jay and Hamilton sought by means of the treaty with England, to undermine the government. We have given these criminations, as we found them, on casting our eyes through Jefferson's correspondence, and might add, we doubt not, many more; but what we have given are, we think, amply sufficient for the illustration of our remark.

And yet the deduction which these facts would seem, at first, to warrant, that Jefferson was characteristically a malignant man, would do his memory great injustice. All who have known him agree, that he was a kind neighbor, and amiable in all the relations of private life. He appeared in social intercourse, to be singularly free from harshness and asperity. He was charitable to the poor, courteous to all men, ever ready to do a kindness or a service. He was generous and hospitable, beloved by his neighbors, a merciful and lenient master, attentive to the wants of his servants and solicitous of their comfort, even at the sacrifice of his pecuniary interests. He had many devoted friends, men as independent as himself, and capable of estimating character at its true value, and whose friendship could not be won by mere position or talent. He was, in a marked degree, the friend of young men, taking pains to serve, instruct and advance them; and he did numberless acts of disinterested kindness, for which he claimed no credit, and could have expected no recompense. No man can play the hypocrite in his own household, and for a whole lifetime, among the daily observers of his life. It were easier to be what he seemed, than to have seemed, against all his natural inclinations, to be, for all this time, what he was not. Besides, his public course, especially in all those parts of it the least probable of success, show him to have had at heart the happiness of his fellow-men. But all this general philanthropy is not inconsistent with the fact of particular enmities. We may observe briefly then, in half-defence, that politicians, beyond all men except play-actors and lovers, indulge in bitterness of rivalry and invective, and are most restive under opposition. There was much to excite this feeling in the high party times through which Jefferson passed. The principles were important. Great results hung upon public measures. *He* was assailed with intense bitterness. Moreover, it must be remembered, that these obnoxious passages in Jefferson's letters were not published by Jefferson himself, nor, probably, intended by him for the public eye; and that there is much difference between a declaration which a man makes to his friends, especially in the heat of momentary feeling, but little if at all influencing *their* opinions—forgotten, on both sides, possibly, as soon as written and read—and a public assault, wantonly insulting the feelings, and wounding the reputation of others. When we add, that the friends of Jefferson have exposed nearly his whole correspondence to the world, and have reserved scarcely any thing of his expressed feelings or sentiments for the privacy of friendship or of the grave (and what man could stand such an ordeal?) we have said all that occurs to us in mitigation of exposures, which, we confess, we do not think can be fully defended.

We think it a misfortune to Jefferson's memory that his correspondence, at least in its present shape, has been published. Besides furnishing to his enemies an arsenal of weapons for offensive warfare against his character as a man and a statesman; and besides the injustice done to others by this fossilizing of these seepings of party prejudice and personal resentment; besides these objections to this wholesale and unsorted publication, it must necessarily happen, in such a mass of speculation as Jefferson was daily in the habit of making on all subjects, that much that was crude, and much that was partial, in thought and expression, would come out. And, even apart from this view, it were better for such a man not to be too familiarly known. There was no danger of his being forgotten. He had left enough already to justify and to support through all time, the renown he had won. He stood so high that there was little hope of adding to his fame; and most of this new matter was of no essential service to the world; at any rate, such parts of it as were of permanent use, could easily have been selected, and the rest ought to have been omitted.

A great man is best seen in his great works. Romance is a maid of the mist; and we all have something of the romantic with which we surround the illustrious men of the past. A man seen through the haze is a larger man *for* the haze. A familiar approach removes the illusion. When we come near great men, we see other things than the great parts, which, like mountain-peaks, at a distance, we alone behold. Few men can bear the scrutiny. We know of but one; and that one, in the grand sameness of his character, the nearer you approach, and the longer you gaze, like Niagara, fills the mind the more with a growing sense of his vastness and sublimity.

It is certain, that, since the publication of his correspondence, Jefferson has stood less favorably before his countrymen, at least a large portion of them, than previously.

We have alluded to what we considered defects in the character of Jefferson—the want of reverence and of dignity. From these defects came, in a great degree, that independence of the judgments and authority of the past which distinguished him. The same characteristics produced other results. We allude to those shown by the Ana. It is unfortunate that those loose memoranda ever saw the light. Some of these notes are little better than gossip; some of them worse; and none of them are of any great value as illustrative of the history, or of the personages of the time, besides the author, and not favorably of him. Bozzy would scarcely have recorded some of them. Think of the great philosopher seriously writing how Hamilton and Adams and himself dined one day together, when Hamilton expressed the opinion that Julius Cæsar was the greatest man that ever lived; how Hamilton said, on another occasion, that the British government was bettered by its corruptions, solemn affidavit being prefixed to this account of the matter; how a Mr. Butler told him that, at some dinner-table in New York, Hamilton declared, there was no stability in any kind of government but a monarchy; that Mr. Lawrence took up the subject, and he and Hamilton had a pretty stiff quarrel, and, at length, broke up the company; that it was suggested that the thing should be confined to the company, &c.; how E. Randolph told him Lear told *him* that Washington swore a whopping oath when Humphreys entered the anti-room appointed to receive company on some show-day, and cried out, "*The President of the United States!*" how Beckly told him that Clinton had told *him*, that a circular letter of Hamilton's, favoring monarchy, was in the hands of some old militia colonel up on North River,—" Clinton is to go for it and will bring it to Philadelphia; how Mrs. Knox manœuvred to get a seat by Mrs. Washington on the sofa, in the ball-room, at Washington's birthday ball, and how she failed, the sofa being too short, &c.; how Washington got into a furious passion in a cabinet meeting, and swore by —— he would rather be in his grave than in his present situation, and would rather be on his farm than be emperor of the world, with a great deal more of such stuff.

But, notwithstanding these weaknesses and imperfections, it is worse than idle to deny Jefferson's claims to distinction as a man of powerful and original genius. That he committed errors, that his judgment was not always sound, that his passions were not always kept under the control of his reason and his conscience, may be safely conceded, without at all impairing his claims to a large share of the reasonable admiration and appreciation of the world. Posterity will award him his proper place between the position assigned him by his enemies, and that given him by his idolaters. He erred, in measures of government, like all other men, probably not oftener or more grossly than any other great political reformer and modern statesman; not so often as Napoleon, Pitt, Fox or Burke. His influence over the intellect of his party, was the greatest ever before wielded by any statesman in the Republic, over the opinions of his fellow-men. He had the merit of being before his times. He was one of the earliest and most steadfast champions of popular doctrines. He started the age onward in a new and fresher career. He spread over the land, in its length and breadth, an awakening, more inquisitive, and a freer spirit; and those ideas, like all received truths, have worked themselves into the character and produced fruits in the life. Let the reader turn to the proceedings of the convention that framed the Constitution, and then turn to the proceedings and speeches in any constitution-making assembly since Jefferson's time, and mark the difference between the tone of that body and of those that have succeeded it.

It is unnecessary to refer to particular measures to show what a great man is or has done. The influence of the whole life and character is the criterion. This is to be found in his case in the *Republican spirit* he aroused and emancipated, and set at work; and this spirit moulds the constitutions and laws as (if the phrenologists be right) the brain moulds the skull. Even some of those projects which were thought crotchets have gone into effect, in our day, and enter into the plan of government; and, probably, others, now laughed at and despised as empty vagaries, will yet be worked into the frames of our constitutions.

From his single influence and teachings, have come the schemes of the constitutions of almost every State in the Union; the constitution of his own being, with a single partial exception (the division of counties into wards), according to the plan he advised thirty years ago. And the Federal government, if not always conducted according to his principles, has been administered, since his elevation, in their name and in professed obedience to them.

CHAPTER XII.

Jefferson as a Popular Leader—His Inconsistencies—His Record of Private Conversations—Professor Tucker's Life of Jefferson—His Conduct in Burr's Trial—In the Impeachment of Judge Chase—His Sensibility to Slander—His Opinion of Newspapers.

THE extreme bitterness with which Jefferson was assailed by the Federal party, was partly political and partly personal. He was regarded with suspicion and with aversion. He was charged with insincerity, indirection and intrigue. He was, also, denounced as a demagogue. The spirit of the age was bold and heroic. It was marked by deeds of daring and chivalry. The virtues of the soldier, as in all times of danger, were peculiarly honored. Jefferson, though probably not deficient in personal courage, was not distinguished for it. He was eminently a politician, and pursued the arts and precautions which win party success, and hold the fruits of victory. Though bold in speculation, he was not bold in personal bearing. He had not the self-confidence and soldierly carriage of the camp. It must be remembered, too, that the Revolution found, and did not destroy, that broad social distinction, which then, much more than now, existed between the common people (the masses) and the gentry. Indeed, a state of war necessarily fosters caste, and widens the distance between the officer and the private; the gentleman and the plebeian. There existed, too, an *esprit du corps* in the army, which discriminated invidiously between the hero and the politician. There was nothing of hauteur about Jefferson. There was no foolish family pride, or pride of place or talent. He justly considered such pride a weakness. His sympathies were really with the people. He had associated much and intimately with them. He had found, as any one will find who makes the experiment, under rude exteriors, sterling qualities, denied sometimes to more cultivated intellects and refined manners; and more real intelligence and good sense, than aristocratic pride ascribes to the masses. Jefferson was wonderfully endowed with the politician's effective faculty of adaptation. This constituted the great charm of his manners. He knew men well. His penetrative curiosity made him acquainted, not only with individual men, but with societies, and with every branch of business, in all its details. He could easily interest himself in common topics; and it was no condescension with him to conduct a conversation on any subject connected with agriculture or the mechanic arts. He was exceedingly easy of access. He drew men easily, and retained them without embarrassment to him or them. His mind was cast in a popular shape. Though his tastes were a little Gallicised, they were, for the most part, simple and healthy. There was nothing in his manners finikin or Frenchified, as *we* understand the term; and his intellect, though speculative, was not refined, but rather coarse-grained and homely in its structure, as was the dress of his thoughts. Altogether, *he was a people's man.* It was natural that he should pay them attention. That attention was repaid by homage and devotion. The very theory he adopted, of their supremacy and title to it, required that he should give them this consideration. Besides, he looked to *them* for fame and appreciation. He had referred himself to *their* judgment for his renown, and relied immediately and exclusively upon *their* support for power.

We think the charge, therefore, that he courted the people, not more applicable to him than to any other successful politician, and no greater evidence of insincerity. The great fault of the Federalists, as party leaders, was, that they held themselves aloof from the people. If distance increases respect in some instances, it begets suspicion and distrust in others. In a republic, it is folly to omit those necessary attentions and efforts in the business of politics, which are essential to success in every other business. The politician, who is too fastidious for contact with the people, is more nice than wise, and ought either to have less punctiliousness or more of it; little enough to make himself acceptable to the people, or enough of it to keep out of the political ring. Jefferson was a great political manager, and, having popular ideas and principles, he adopted that policy, and put in motion that machinery, which were best adapted to give them success; and the same tactics have been practised by the various parties and politicians that have succeeded him.

We have said that Jefferson was not consistent. We do not, by any means, attach to this quality the importance attributed to it by many others. In a new country like ours, where every thing consecrated to unreasoning veneration by the old world, has been overhauled and re-examined with perfect freedom of past doctrines, and where the whole policy and the interests on which it bears are new; where so many questions are mooted, and such numberless speculations thrown out, it would be miraculous if *any* statesman should be so wise as to find no reason to alter some of the notions he first conceived of the government and its workings. A mechanist, who could, *à priori*, give the exact idea of the most complex machine, and could foresee precisely how the several parts would act and react under all circumstances, and could tell all its practical results, and the exact manner of its most easy and beneficial management, would not show a higher order of ability, in his line, than the statesman, who had been able to see at once the true nature, tendency and operation of our complex system, and what measures were best adapted to give it efficacy and to secure its objects.

But Jefferson, having indulged more liberally in speculation, and having expressed himself more freely, than any other man of his time, with many true principles, gave out more contradictory ideas than any other American statesman has published.

He started with opposing the Constitution. His first letters show his dissatisfaction in the strongest terms. He became reconciled to it. He was for four states holding off. He abandoned that idea. He was in favor of the assumption of the state debts. He was afterwards opposed to this, and says Hamilton tricked him into the project. As it was a public question, to be solved on public and general grounds, we do not see why he could not have decided it as well as Hamilton.

His whole administration was, as we have shown, in direct opposition to the principle of super-strict construction, upon which he organized opposition to the Federal party. Professor George Tucker, who can scarcely be suspected of prejudice against Jefferson, admits this, at least as to several of the measures of his administration. He announced the doctrine of Nullification in his Kentucky Resolutions. But, even under the Articles of Confederation, so low an estimate did he place on state-rights, that he declared the government would never get along until "the confederation showed its teeth," and administered chastisement to one or more recusant states. In the factious proceedings of the N. E. States (of which J. Q. Adams gave him particular information), taken with a view to secede, he pronounces the design treason; which it certainly was not, if a state has the right to secede at pleasure, or even in order to escape from an unconstitutional law, she being the judge of such unconstitutionality; for *they* declared the Embargo to be unconstitutional, and with some show of reason; by Jefferson's own rule of construction, with a demonstration of it.

He wavered to and fro on the subject of the navy until he seems, in his letter to Adams, not to have been himself aware precisely where he was He seemed to be not unwilling to take the feather, which Adams offered him (almost the only one left in his own cap) of being the father and protector of the navy; a claim to which he had about as good title as King Herod, after his decree, had to being the protector and father of the young children of his kingdom. He opposed not only the U. S. Bank, but the establishment of branches, as increasing the power, and duplicating the financial evils and the unconstitutional policy of the institution; and yet approved the bill creating the Branch at New Orleans.

He drew, or, at all events, approved of, the ordinance of 1787, inhibiting slavery north-west of the Ohio; and, in his letter to Mr. Holmes, on the subject of the Missouri restriction, argues in favor of permitting slavery to be extended on grounds of policy.

He opposed internal improvements by the General Government as unconstitutional, and yet approved the Cumberland road bill. He declared the opinion that the purchase of Louisiana was unconstitutional; but negotiated the treaty and approved it. At one time, in his messages, he speaks of disunion as an unmitigated evil; at another, he seems to think the separation of the states into two confederacies, Eastern and Western, as no evil at all.

He advocated and subsequently condemned the protective policy.

And when we come to his opinions of men, we find discrepancies, if possible, still more marked and decided. Bu to go into this examination would fill a volume. Indeed, into such a state of inflammatory prejudice had his mind passed with regard to particular individuals and parties, that we are forced to discard his opinions as to these as nearly worthless. It would be scarcely more unfair to take Lord Byron's "British Bards and Scotch Reviewers" as a fair criticism upon his literary contemporaries, than to take Jefferson's "correspondence" as giving a true estimate of the leaders of the Federal party, or even of some members of his own.

Jefferson's habit of recording and leaving for publication the colloquial remarks he heard, and those of which he heard, of some of his contemporaries, has been strongly censured. Professor Tucker, whose "Life of Jefferson" is to be commended for many excellencies of manner and matter, demonstrating an accomplished and powerful intellect, and abounding in much learned and able, and, for the most part, impartial criticism on public measures, undertakes an ingenious and elaborate defence of Jefferson against this charge. We think, however, that the learned Professor has scarcely discriminated with his usual acumen, in his vindication of his friend; and that the unconscious influence of his position, political relations, locality and personal feelings, led him to avow to the world doctrines, in regard to the ethics of private social intercourse, which, these disturbing influences withdrawn, he would have scrupled to have announced to his class from the chair of Moral Philosophy, which he formerly filled with so much dignity and ability, in the University of Virginia. We think it a sufficient answer to all the casuistry upon this subject, to say, that, by the universal consent of gentlemen, a private conversation imposes a silent obligation upon those who hear it not so to use it as to injure the persons participating in it; and, therefore, gentlemen speak freely under the idea that this rule will be respected. No reasons of presumed benefit to the public interest in a given case—certainly none in Jefferson's instances—to accrue from disclosures of this sort, are sufficiently strong to overbalance the positive and certain evils resulting from ignoring the inviolability of this principle. The confidence and freedom of social intercourse, and the peace of society, are interested in the observance of the rule; for social correspondence would be an evil, instead of a blessing, if every man were a spy upon his fellow; and if it were understood, that, as soon as the host had disengaged his hand from the embrace of his guest's, his pen was to be employed in writing down, for the public, whatever expressions the guest had unguardedly used in a free and friendly conversation. Besides, these expressions, whether of opinion or otherwise, are usually nearly worthless to the public, for any good purpose. A full account is not given of the whole conversation, or of sur rounding and germain matter; there is no cross examination; no room for explanation; no chance of denial or correction by the parties criminated; and then, consider the great temptation to overstatement; the liability to mistake in hearing, or understanding, or reporting; of which, there can be no better illustration than the positive denial by two of Jefferson's alleged informants (in the United States Senate) of facts reported by him, as communicated to him by them, and recorded in the Ana. And, even if we were assured of an entirely accurate report, we know that men's opinions, when spoken over their wine—often unpremeditated, often in the heat of disputation, sometimes from love of dogmatism or casuistry (as Dr. Johnson's) sometimes in mockery and satire, often in jest, and always without a sense of responsibility—are far from being invariably represented by their dinner-table observations. What a mess of opinions Boswell has made up for the illustrious moralist!

But Jefferson himself answers his biographer. In his letter to Washington, he stigmatizes the conduct of Gen. Lee as that of one " dirtily engaged in sifting the conversations of his table ; " and, we suppose, there can be no moral distinction between the sifting of these conversations by the host and the sifting of them by the guest.

Upon another subject Mr. Tucker is more impartial. We speak of the conduct of Jefferson in connection with the trial of Burr. Mr. Tucker disapproves of this conduct, though he speaks from tenderness to the character of his illustrious subject, more in a tone of regret than condemnation. We see no use of squeamishness or of false sentimentality, in reference to matters of official conduct, towards one who sets so bold an example of free and unmitigated censure of the acts of others. The interference of Jefferson in the trial at all, was wholly unauthorized and officious. He had a right to put down Burr's projects, and was bound to bring Burr to trial. He was right in seeing that the government was ably represented. This was the business of the Executive. After the court took cognizance of the case, the proceedings belonged to the judicial department. It was an invasion of the judiciary, and a most dangerous one, for the President to interfere in the trial. The President held in his hand the pardoning power. He should have kept himself aloof from the public excitement, and have preserved a judicial impartiality, in order to exercise that power, in case he was called upon to exert it, without prejudice. He should not have been closeted with the witnesses of the government. He should not have been the prosecutor, and more especially, *such* a prosecutor, carrying zeal to intemperance, and intemperance to the rankest injustice and coarsest criminations of the court and others connected with the cause. To bring Executive power to bear upon a prisoner; to let loose upon his head the influence of the patronage and placemen of the government, was to revive the worst judicial scenes of the days of the Tudors and the Stuarts. It were better that any criminal escaped, however guilty, than that he should be thus convicted; for the danger of immunity to crime, from the example of a malefactor's escape, is nothing to the danger of destroying the principle of personal freedom, for which all law was made.

We have no sympathy with Burr. He was guilty, doubtless, of *some* crime, for which he deserved punishment. We doubt if it were treason. We incline to think he was only a *Fillibuster*, in times so unsophisticated, that to be a Fillibuster was *not* to be a hero fighting under the commission of "Manifest Destiny." Out upon him! Let him fester and rot in his infamy! A man whose hand, yet wet with the blood of such a man as Hamilton, could write, from his skulking place, to his daughter, that, if she had an *ennuyant* lover, to advise him to try, as a relief, a *liaison* or a duel, was fit, without other crimes, for the execration *he* received. But he was an American citizen. He was covered by the shield of the constitution. He was entitled to a fair trial. If there was enough of manhood in him for him to be tried at all, there was enough to entitle him to be tried according to law, surrounded by its safeguards, and in the light of all of its presumptions and merciful intendments. The suggestion of the President in his letter to Hay, that Luther Martin, the counsel of Burr, should be indicted as an accomplice, as one effect of indicting him would be to "muzzle that impudent Federal bull-dog," is a fearful commentary upon all the texts that Jefferson preached of the jealousy and vigilance with which men in power should be regarded. There is no other commentary so strong in the annals of the government.

The impeachment of Judge Chase was another act of

party intemperance and prejudice, which stains the otherwise placable character of the Republican party after their triumph. The causes of complaint, that he had ordered a *capias* instead of a *summons* (which would have been but an invitation to the prisoner to leave) in the case of Callender, that he had "prejudged the law" of the case in the trial of Fries!—that he refused to permit the counsel to argue *to the jury* the constitutionality of the Sedition law; that he interrupted Mr. Wirt's argument by telling him that it was a *non sequitur;* that he refused to put off Callender's trial on some lying affidavit;—these grave matters kept the High Court of Impeachment in session for many long months, at an enormous expense of money and eloquence. It is but just to the Senate to say, that it acted with sense and dignity, and rejected the charges. Luther Martin made the prosecution a sufficient punishment of its authors; for he improved the occasion to the utmost to "pulverize" the charges and the managers. His speech in defence of the judge, was only equalled by Marshall's speech in the Jonathan Robbins matter. It presented nothing to be answered, and it left nothing to be added.

It is amusing to note the different sentiments and feelings which statesmen manifest towards great public principles or institutions, according to the different modes in which they affect them personally. We have shown with what favor Jefferson regarded Freneau's "free press,' when it was pouring out its opposition upon the first administration, and its lampoons on the President; with what fortitude he bore the inflictions upon Washington's patience and sensibilities; how he wondered that Washington had lost his "*sang froid*," when Freneau let loose his virulence upon him from the office of the Secretary of State. He seems almost to chuckle over the fury of the old chief, when, struck by these paper pellets, he writhed in agony, and, unable longer to endure them, his temper broke the bounds to which he was accustomed to confine it, and he gave utterance to that "tremendous wrath" which, according to Mr. Jefferson, sometimes possessed the old hero (as it did occasionally a later one), swearing by the Eternal, and denouncing hotly " that d——d rascal, Freneau," who had sent him three copies of his free paper, full of libels on him and the government, with the modest intimation that he wished them circulated under the President's frank! Jefferson seems to have sympathized a good deal with Callender, when under trial and in imprisonment, for libelling John Adams, and to have been a subscriber to his paper, indeed for a number of copies, besides helping him along with " material aid," in occasional sums of fifty dollars. But, after a while, the thing was reversed. The Federal papers grew as " viperous," probably more " viperous " even, than the Republican press; and poured out black torrents of fetid ribaldry and scurrility upon Jefferson. His private business, his domestic relations, every thing was descanted on. Even Callender turned against him, that " monster of ingratitude," and excelled even himself in low billingsgate and dirty vituperation. He drenched his old patron with showers of bilgewater and vitriol. Jefferson was thin-skinned. He was easily touched. He was morbidly sensitive to public opinion. He admits that he suffered more from a little censure than he enjoyed from a great deal of praise; and praise had a very pleasing relish for his palate. Indeed, as he says of La Fayette, he had "a canine thirst for popularity." He delighted in being called "THE PEOPLE'S MAN." He took much pleasure in circulating among them, shaking hands, inquiring about their families, crops, and so forth, and mingling with them in the frankest manner, on election days. It was *his* turn now to suffer. He did suffer in the acutest degree. His "*sang froid*" exhibited itself in this language about that "Great Palladium of Public Liberty"—the press.

"It is a melancholy truth that a suppression of the press could not more completely deprive the nation of its benefits than is done by its abandoned prostitution to falsehood. Nothing can now be believed which is seen in a newspaper. Truth itself becomes suspicious by its being put into that polluted vehicle. * * * I will add, that the man who never looks into a newspaper is better informed than he who reads them; inasmuch as he who knows nothing is nearer to truth than he whose mind is filled with falsehoods and errors. He who reads nothing, will still learn the great facts, and the details are all false."

This letter is another illustration of the *one-sidedness* to which Jefferson's mind was so prone, when his passions were aroused. For, as Mr. Tucker well observes, there is no newspaper, however mendaciously conducted, that does not print more truths than lies. Inferences and speculation are another matter; but even as to these, the sin usually is not so much that of false suggestion, as of suppression and bad logic; and the whole truth, in party papers, usually comes out when both sides are heard, as they are in political discussion.

CHAPTER XIII.

Hamilton—His Position, Influence, and Character.

THE career of Hamilton was probably the most brilliant in America. The impression he had made on the public policy, and the influence he had exerted over the history of his country, were, his age considered, as we have seen, unprecedented. At thirty-five, he had won a place among the public men of the Republic, if not the first in any one department of public and professional service, certainly the first in the aggregate of distinction in all these trusts. He had succeeded eminently in every thing he had undertaken. He stood, as a soldier, next to Washington; as a statesman, equal to any other in ability, and the first in influence over the public councils as long as he held office; as a lawyer, if not first, yet in the first class, and without a superior. Nor was he remarkable for proficiency or success only in particular branches of these various departments. He excelled in every branch of these diverse employments, and in all things connected with them, which could give efficiency or embellishment to his labors. As a statesman, his mind embraced the great principles of government, and the lesser details, not only in his own particular bureau, but in all others, and not only in the executive, but in the legislative branches. He was an eloquent and able debater; an admirable writer; remarkable alike for practical judgment and for executive functions; as a lawyer, ripe in learning, bringing comprehensive views of the philosophy of the law to the aid of accurate knowledge of its technical learning, and affluent in all those powers and accomplishments whereby judges or juries are convinced or persuaded. In the power of impressing himself upon his fellow-men, and of drawing to himself their affections and confidence, he was almost unrivalled. Indeed his enemies sought, in consequence of the devotion which was exhibited to him in so many quarters, to excite against him the jealousy of Washington, by suggesting a precedence to him, in the minds of his party, over his chief. In no small degree, this popularity and this influence were owing to his personal character and manly virtues. He was, as Jefferson acknowledges, honest, honorable, disinterested, frank and candid in all the relations of private life; but, with singular inconsistency, his great rival ascribes to him sentiments and practices as a politician, which favored and applied bribery and corruption as necessary arts of government. But we have shown that Jefferson's authority in such matters cannot be relied on; and we doubt if such an anomaly ever did exist, as a man characteristically bold and pure in private life, and, also, systematically corrupt and venal as a politician.

Nor did the influence of Hamilton terminate with his life. It is true that the impression he left on the masses was not as strong as Jefferson's. It is true that his name is not often quoted, because of the unpopularity attached to it, in part, by reason of some of his principles, and, in part, by the assaults made upon him by the Republican party. Yet the influence imparted to the government by his measures is still felt. He unquestionably strengthened the government, and gave it a tone of dignity, and power and respectability when it most wanted it, and which has survived to this day He turned towards the people the government in that phase which it still retains—the phase of a government able to execute its laws, and determined to maintain its dignity; clothed with the powers which enable it to stand forth as a national government, self-reliant and independent at once of aid and opposition. He contributed to give to the government the full measure of its powers. No one questions now that his financial system, though it may have been defective in some of its details, raised the government at once to a position of honor, and gained for it that credit which it has ever since so pre-eminently enjoyed. And from that credit and the public confidence it established, the country rose up immediately from its embarrassments, and started forward in the career of enterprise and energy that soon brought general prosperity and contentment. If he erred in seeking to give to the government too much power, it must be remembered that his enemies erred in seeking to give it too little. If he sought to make the new government do too much, it must be recollected that his enemies sought to prevent it from doing enough; and then it must not be forgotten that the measures in which he erred failed; so that their influence is not felt at this day upon the country.

Had his policy prevailed of resenting the first insults of France (insults, which it was left for Jackson, so many years afterwards, in some degree, to retaliate) we had been spared the profound humiliation we afterwards suffered, and the necessity of being kicked into a war with England, after our commerce had become the unresisting prey of Britain and France upon the ocean, to the extent of a hundred millions of dollars; while the national honor would have shone *then* with a lustre reserved for a far later day.

If Hamilton mistook, or was too independent to conform himself to, the popular mind, in some respects, he represented it better than his rival in others. He represented the character of the people in the boldness, energy, and decision of government, when great questions come up for solution, or great interests are involved. The Republican theory, however it may accord with truth in the abstract, that the Executive is to be looked to with jealousy, and the Representatives with favor, in the distribution or exercise of power, we know, from the experience of the government, is not practically acted on by the people.

Had Hamilton been President instead of Adams, it is highly probable that he would have crushed, at least for a time, the Republican party; or had he been the candidate in the election of 1800, it is nearly certain he would have been elected. The mismanagement of the campaign by Adams was the only safety of Jefferson; for the advantages the Federalists had got in the French difficulty, and the false position in which the Republicans had placed themselves, needed only *not* to have been counteracted to have secured the former an overwhelming triumph. Jefferson was elected, at last, by a majority of only seven votes; but once in power, his consummate tact and skill as a politician, combined with other causes, turned his victory into a sure and lasting ascendency.

Hamilton's influence, though more of class than Jefferson's, was not less durable. He addressed the mercantile, professional, trading, and military classes, representing a great portion of the wealth and talent of the country, especially of the commercial cities; and in his own state he wielded an influence and had a popularity almost unequalled; and, strengthened by the circumstances attending his death, he left upon the minds of his countrymen an impression of his power and his worth never felt since the death of Washington.

His writings have passed into the text-books of schools and colleges and politicians, and are quoted as authority in senates and courts of judicature, State and Federal, supreme and inferior; and, not less for their reasoning than their style, have become classics in our political literature, to endure as long as the institutions they illustrate; while his state papers are model compositions of their class.

What destiny might have awaited him beyond the great

eminence he had reached, is only matter for loose conjecture. But, as we have stood beneath the weeping-willow which mourningly droops over his modest tomb-stone, in the centre of the vast city, of which, in its infancy, he was the pride and benefactor—(the solemn stillness of his resting place, by the side of the great avenue, through which pours the fretted and boisterous streams of population, noting the contrast between the dead and the living man)—we have thought, that the heroic heart and massive brain that moulder there, could not have passed the long prime, which, in the course of nature, would have been allotted to him, without marking still more deeply the lines of his policy upon his country, and carving more strongly his own name upon its genius and character. For such a nature there is no pause and no repose. Activity is the condition of its charter of life. The strong energies and warm passions, the fearless and intrepid temper, the fever of the soul thirsting for glory, its glowing schemes and conceptions bursting forth irrepressibly into the life of action, could not have been content with a mere lawyer's fame and work. The excitements of statesmanship, and the glittering prizes of an eager and exalted ambition, are the stimulants that impel and the rewards that attract such a spirit. He had quaffed too deeply of the cup of power and renown, to be content, in his mid-day heat and prime, with a tamer beverage. But it was not a rabble popularity which he sought. He was prouder even than vain. His self-respect kept him from every seeming of servility to the leaders or the led. Indeed his foible was, an independence of even the allowable acts of conciliation towards superiors and the people. He desired that renown which follows in the wake of great talents and great services; that fame which is the sum of the intelligent and grateful appreciation of good men; which mingles itself with the lettered glory of a free people, and is blazoned on its historic annals, and on its monumental measures of policy.

Even in the presence of Washington, his high-toned self-respect did not lower its crest; nor did he suffer what he conceived to be his just claims to be disregarded by him. His tone, though deferential and courtly, was bold and manly and exactingly self-appreciative, in his address and bearing towards that chief, when his own character and feelings were involved.

The duel with Burr illustrates both the weakness and the strength of Hamilton. He was opposed upon principle to duelling. He thought there were higher claims upon his life than any Burr could set up. He had a large family dependent upon him. His pecuniary affairs were embarrassed. Great interests were confided to him by clients, which must necessarily suffer irreparably by his death. He had a lively sense of his importance to his country, and of his responsibility for the use of his great talents. He was sincerely affected towards religion. His early youth had been impressed by the teachings of pious parents, and especially by the precepts and example of his Huguenot mother. As a boy he was remarked for the purity of his life, and the evidence he gave at college of fervid piety; and his respect for religion and his sense of its value returned to him with a renewed, though a more silent, influence, in later manhood. And on his death-bed, as his thoughts wandered back to his island-home in the tropics, his halcyon youth rose up before him, with the face of the sainted mother, whose meek eyes, in that far-off time and home, looked down on her gallant boy, as softly as the stars above them shone upon the frolic waves of the bright and breathing sea. And when his wife was weeping bitterly at his bed-side, his consolation was,— 'Remember, Eliza, you are a Christian!'"

Considerations more worldly doubtless had their weight. He had reached the age when men take serious and sober views of life and its uses; when the prurient chivalry of the boy has succeeded to a better estimate of true manliness. He had promised himself important objects in the future. He did not wish to kill Burr; and he knew that Burr was seeking a pretext to kill him. Notwithstanding these weighty considerations he accepted Burr's challenge, with the premonition that the event would be fatal to himself, and with the determination that it should not be fatal to his foe. He was proud enough to derive no satisfaction from the applause of those whom he did not esteem; but he could not endure their scorn. Like the old Doge, he belonged to that proud class, to whom,

> "Dishonor's shadow is a substance,
> More terrible than death here or hereafter.
> Men, whose vice is, to shrink at vice's scoffing,
> And who, though proof against all blandishments of pleasure,

> And all pangs of pain, are feeble
> When the loved name on which they pinnacled
> Their hopes is breathed on; jealous as the eagle
> Of her high aery."

He was a soldier, and he could not bear the thought of ever seeming to be wanting in the soldier's greatest virtue. He thought, too, his future usefulness depended upon the acceptance of the challenge. And the fear of public opinion overbore his sense of right, as it did in the case of Clay. The defence of this moral cowardice by both is simply drivelling. It deceives no one. It had been more candid in both to have said: We fought from cowardice—from the fear of the scoffers.

CHAPTER XIV.

Hamilton and Jefferson Contrasted—Their True Greatness—Conclusion.

We have intimated that the characters of these celebrated men were as marked and as different as their politics. Hamilton was, besides the qualities we have ascribed to him, frank to imprudence in the avowal of his principles. Either he did not care for popularity, or, else, he did not look to it as a guide. Jefferson was more wary and circumspect. He had a sharp eye to the popular current, and a delicate touch for the popular pulse. He was consequently, beyond all comparison, the abler politician and the safer party leader.

Both were men of great activity and of great energy, and possessed of uncommon physical and mental capacity for labor. Jefferson's mind was more versatile and less continuous in its operations than Hamilton's. He was as busily occupied, but he changed his subjects of labor oftener. His invention was busier. He had more irons in the fire. He turned himself more readily from one thing to another. His mind was more fertile of schemes and projects. His curiosity led him to take cognizance of a vast variety of matters, political, personal, scientific, theological, agricultural, literary, mechanical, indeed of every sort; but the very number prevented a profound acquaintance with any, except, perhaps, those which more especially claimed his attention. He was, therefore, more intelligent than learned. He had more freshness and originality than Hamilton. His mind had been cut loose from all moorings of authority, and his thought expatiated over wide seas of speculation. His intellectual intrepidity amounted almost to audacity; but this was held in check by a timidity or a prudence, which made him cautious of putting new schemes or ideas into the form of measures. He was singularly self-reliant and devoted to his own views and reasonings; and, though not consistent, seemed seldom to know or acknowledge previous errors. He loved to govern, and did the thinking and planning for his party, who looked up to him with singular devotion and reverence. Without being the ablest, we think him the most original and plausible of his countrymen. His statement, even when on the wrong side, was better adapted for popular effect than the statement of almost any one else on the right side. He was a man of strong prejudices and ardent passions, and speaking from these, he addressed, with the greatest skill and power, the prejudices and passions of the masses. In detailed and finished ratiocination, in reasonings drawn out in artistic form, he did not so greatly excel; but in rapid and comprehensive statement, for force, plausibility, acumen and clearness, he was unsurpassed. He could not have sustained himself in senatorial discussion, written or oral, against

Marshall, Madison, or Hamilton; but in a popular paper, or, if he had cultivated oratory, in a speech, he would have made a better popular impression than either. Like Doctor Johnson, it is said, he conversed even better than he wrote. We can well believe it. His active mind, under social excitement, so original and so replete with information, with such versatility and variety, and so much tact, made him, as we know, from the reputation he has left, one of the first conversationists of the world.

He was more artificial as well as more original than Hamilton. He had to some extent superinduced a French character on his own, or intermixed it with his own; and yet, with such tact, that something of what seemed artlessness, was probably art. He was intensely worldly-wise; and a sagacious sense of his own interest in what he regarded the main ends of life, consciously or not, presided over or influenced most of his actions. He needed but the physical resources and accessories of Mirabeau to have made him the most marked man of his age.

He was a thorough-going party man, as much so as Mr. Polk, and understood—what no man on the other side knew—how to organize, build up, and consolidate a party.

It has been objected to Jefferson that the measures for which he gained so much credit with the people—the statute for religious freedom, and the acts abolishing primogeniture and regulating descents—were called for by the times, and required as a necessary adaptation to foregone measures. But this is not true as to one of those measures, for it was proposed long before it was passed, and was carried, at last, with difficulty; and even if true, the objection would only prove that it was a good blow struck in good time.

Jefferson, while his state-papers convey an idea of great philanthropy of character and a philosophic serenity of temper, yet discloses in his correspondence an apparent vindictiveness and prejudice which are unequalled among his contemporaries. To some of these ebullitions we have alluded. These intemperances have brought down upon his memory some severe strictures, impeaching the fidelity of his statements, and the sincerity of his character; some of which are unfounded; some requiring explanation; and some defying it. Though no man could use more gracefully the language of eulogy, he usually reserved his commendation for his party associates; while his liberality towards his opponents rarely exceeded a very cold laudatory modification of very warm censures. Indeed the whole tone of his mind was partisan, and though his intellect was large enough to originate and resolve great ideas and principles, they were usually the ideas and principles of his own side. He regularly opposed every thing on the opposite side, and supported and defended every thing on his own.

We think, on the whole, that it must be acknowledged by the enemies, personal and political, of Jefferson, that, to this illustrious tribune belongs a niche in the pantheon of the great men, who have, in whatever countries or times, appeared upon the earth; and that he must be classed among that small number, whose names and genius descend, along the course of generations, as permanent institutions and influences in the world.

But we think too, that the leaders of the opposing host were not worthy of the odium he sought to cast upon them while they lived, and upon their memories after they had died. Accuser and accused—once associates and compatriots in the work of the independence of America and of Americans—are now all gone to the bourne, where the mighty events—as *we* esteem them—of *this* mortal life are remembered, if remembered at all, but as empty pageants and flitting shadows. The memory of these august shades is all that is left us of them except their works; and the fame they have left is more our property than theirs. And justice to ourselves and to the truth of history, requires the declaration, that a nobler band of patriots, than those, who stood around the first and second administrations of the Government, never lived. If they erred about modes of administration, theirs was an honest error; and, inheriting our principles from the victors, we need not take them with the incumbrance of their personal or party prejudices; for the Liberty we hold, was it not bequeathed equally by victor and vanquished?—by Federalist and Republican?

There is enough of glory for them all! Honor to every hand that was raised in that holy fight! Honor to every tongue that spoke a word in season for the faith! Honor to the PEN, that drew the Declaration which pronounced us free! Honor to the LIPS, afire with Liberty, that seconded and supported its adoption! Honor to the stainless SWORD of the boy-votary, who, side by side with Washington, through the long war, strove to make that Declaration good! And honor in the highest, save to God, to the AUGUST CHIEF who was the presiding Genius over Camp and Council; winning our freedom in the field and perpetuating it in the cabinet!

At last, we have brought our weary task to its close. We return from the twilight, which envelopes, in gray shadows, every year growing thicker, the men and deeds of the HEROIC AGE, and we come back to the open light and bustling activities of this utilitarian day. We would fain hope our labor has not been quite in vain. It will not have been, if asperities, long indulged, and prejudices, lagging far behind justice, have been at all allayed or dissipated. At all events, our task, in part, has been a grateful one; and it was meant throughout to be impartially performed.

We have stolen out from the busy employments of this progressive time; from among the multitudinous material objects, which spring up, in rank luxuriance, around our free institutions; from the throng of men, the scream of the engine, the street roaring with the tides of life—to visit the quiet cemetery, where the patriarchs, the martyrs, and the fathers of the Republic repose; and, like "Old Mortality," with mallet and chisel in hand, bending over the tombs in pious reverence, have sought to remove the moss which time, and the mould which mistake or calumny have gathered on their names.

JOHN RANDOLPH OF ROANOKE.

CHAPTER I.

Introduction—Garland's Life of Randolph—John Randolph—Public Opinion of him—His Birth, Family, Education, and Politics.

An uncommon interest invests the character, and has settled upon the memory, of this eminent personage. This is usually the case with men of a peculiar mould. The natural curiosity which seeks acquaintance with the histories and qualities of distinguished men, becomes more keen and eager, when the elements of the *Strange and the Mysterious* enter into their characters. The dramatic interest which enveloped Byron, and which he communicated to the dark heroes of his romances (impersonations of his own passions) is a witness of this general feeling and sentiment. Unquestionably, there was something more than curiosity at the bottom of this interest, in the case of the noble lord. Sympathy had its share in the feeling; for the medium of his revelations of these strange and eccentric traits and developments, was a voice of eloquence and of passionate utterance, whose plaintive tones, and whose wild and daring freedom, addressed the most powerful sensibilities of the heart.

Whoever has seen a strong man bowed down beneath the weight of a great affliction, absorbed into oblivion of self by a passionate grief, knows how sublime a spectacle he presents, and what sympathy he draws from the beholders. The manifestations of genuine passion are always more or less interesting; but, when the whole man becomes the representative of the passion, the whole life a prolonged illustration of it, the passion becomes so pronounced and so prominent as to impress on the mind of the observer the most marked and lasting influence. Pride, self-reliant and self-sustaining, neither conciliating friendship nor dreading animosity, asking no sympathy, enduring in silence, shrinking from no danger or evil, although it chills approach, and offends egotism by a sort of silent assumption of superiority, yet always draws respect. It is a sort of regal passion; and when, not obtrusively nor in weakness, but in some indirect or quasi-confidential way, it discloses its own grief and affliction, it mingles with that feeling of respect a sentiment of human tenderness and kindness for a brother man, under the sufferings of our common nature.

Mr. Garland's work has been the medium by which the inner life of John Randolph has been disclosed to the world; by which, too, his real character and much that was mysterious in his conduct may be explained; by which the fearful struggles of his soul for peace, and the mental and physical agony and unrest he endured, have been revealed. The biographer has done for the memory of his great subject, something of that service and justice which Carlyle did for the memory of Cromwell. No man's fame more needed such an exposition of his real nature and history. Randolph has been, and is still, perhaps, much misunderstood. He was, during his troubled life, an object of marked distinction. In an eminent degree, he was, from curiosity as well as from the natural attractions of his genius, and, in no small degree from his eccentricities, "the observed of all observers." The eyes of the world followed him, wherever he went and in whatever he did, with the intentness of prying inquisitiveness, the more eager, probably, because he seemed anxious to shun the public gaze. The public voice sounded its loudest notes of praise, the more obstreperously, perhaps, as he seemed to despise its plaudits. But his was a fame and an applause singularly unmingled with regard, and even esteem. Men looked upon him, and with reason, more with fear than love. They regarded him, as a man bereft of the ordinary kindnesses and amiable sensibilities of humanity. Nay, he was considered as a merciless satirist, as an unfeeling bravo, wielding the stiletto of an inexorable sarcasm; torturing, like his Indian progenitors, from the love of inflicting pain, or from the lust of dominion; his heart filled to overflowing with gall and bitterness—with hatred of all good men, with scorn of all common men, with envy of all great men, and with malignity towards all of his race, who would not humble themselves slavishly before him. In short, the majority thought him the best specimen the age had produced of a genuine misanthrope.

As is usual with such men, public opinion decided variously as to his intellectual character. Some set him down as a madman, whose sagacity was only the cunning of a lunatic, and his brilliancy only those occasional gleamings of light which are fitfully emitted from the darkness of a madhouse. Others viewed him as a man eccentric, indeed, but whose acuteness of thought, deep insight into the motives of men and the affairs of government, and whose perspicuity and prescience were nearly miraculous. By the majority, he was thought to possess no claims to the honors of true statesmanship. They conceded to him brilliancy as a debater, and, some of them, efficiency as a Guerilla warrior, fighting along the lines and cutting off an annoying adversary; but they denied him solidity, plan, tact, judgment, and especially the power of constructing. He could not, they said, build up or sustain a party or a policy; but was an useful auxiliary in pulling down others or their work. And some were found who denied him even this small claim to consideration, and who declared that he was useful to no one except his enemies; like the elephants of Pyrrhus, whose *maladroit* movements were more dangerous to their allies than to their foes.

Much of the grossest part of this misconstruction has been, and more of it probably will be, removed. The time is fast coming when monsters will be out of fashion; when history will cease to manufacture men (it is not portraying them) out of one or two simple elements, infernal or divine; when people, no longer gods or devils, will be suffered to be again the men that God made them. Such creations of the muse of romance, not the less romance because labelled history, are not like those made in the laboratory of nature. *She* mixes the elements variously and curiously, sometimes, it is true; but still mingles the ingredients into one organized, composite mass, the whole of which is man; the individual differing always in degree from the rest, but being always the same in species.

On several accounts, John Randolph may be considered as among the representative men of our country—as belonging to and representing a phase of the period of the Constitution, and of that immediately succeeding; as a representative of the political-republican, and the social-aristocratical spirit; as a Virginian and Southron of the old regime; as a leader in the Congress during the last days of the Adams, and the first term of the Jefferson administrations; as the leader of the Republican opposition to the war and quasi-war measures; as a State-Rights leader of the strictest sect, adhering to the tenets of that sect even when they were abandoned by the fathers of the church; as a Democrat by party association, yet with English prejudices and affinities social and political; and, probably, even more characteristically, as a *Virginia Conservative*, abounding in love for his native state, and an unreasoning devotion to her interests, renown, customs, habitudes, and institutions, resisting all change and innovation in her organic law and ancient polity, and cherishing sectional prejudices as virtues.

Jefferson said that the politics of a man come from his temperament. Probably, this is no further true than that the moral nature of every man, in some degree, influences his opinions, especially upon subjects so nearly allied to, or mingled with, moral questions, as those of government. If, however, Jefferson be right, the peculiar temperament of Randolph, marked, as it was, by striking idiosyncracies deserves to be taken into particular account, in the examination of his opinions and history.

John Randolph was born at Cawsons, the family seat of his maternal ancestors, on the 3d of June, 1773. It is needless to say, that his family was one of the oldest and most distinguished of the old Virginia gentry. The mansion, like the proprietors, and, indeed, the families, of what may be called the old noblesse of the Ancient Dominion, has fallen into decay and ruin. It stood, at the birth of the last of the line, on a promontory, near the mouth of the Appomatox river, in lower Virginia. Within less than three years after his birth, his father died. His mother was left to him. She seems to have been, in every respect, fitted for the task of impressing and moulding a mind and spirit so much requiring maternal influence and restraint. The lady was, as we learn from Mr. Garland's work, a beautiful and accomplished woman, with many of the intellectual characteristics of her gifted son. She united to more versatile and showy gifts, a strong and decided intellect, and a religious character and temper. As might be expected, she was devotedly attached to her orphan boy, whose beauty, delicacy of frame and intelligence were calculated to excite even more than common tenderness in a mother's bosom; and he returned, in full measure, the affection she lavished upon him. She was married to St. George Tucker, in 1778; and, in her thirty-sixth year John, then fifteen years of age, was called to deplore her death.

Neither his constitution nor his taste fitted him, in youth, for athletic sports. His first reading—and it is this which exerts a marked effect on the character—was the Fairy Tales, the works of Shakespeare, and some books of history, among them, Voltaire's Life of Charles the XII of Sweden. Passionate, sensitive, proud, imaginative, quick, irritable, warm in his attachments, and strong in his dislikes, he seems at an early day, to have manifested the disposition which continued to characterize him through life. His earliest impressions were of the scenes of the Revolution. His mother had borne him in her arms from the marauding troops of Arnold, in that traitor's invasion of Virginia. His earliest teachings were from those who had participated, on the Whig side, in the Revolutionary struggle. His family were Whigs, distinguished for their ardor in the cause. They were, also, persons of wealth, family and distinction. They had agreed, too, in opposing the Federal Constitution. They were attached to, and much under the influence of, Mason and Henry, men, who, in such diverse gifts, combined as much talent and efficiency as any two men in Virginia.

Randolph, at the same age, at which Hamilton entered Columbia College, New York, became a student within its walls. He did not, however, long remain there. Shortly afterwards, he entered the college at Princeton. He witnessed the inauguration of Washington; attended the debates of the first Federal Congress; came within the influence of Jefferson, who was his cousin, and of other leading politicians, and was soon enlisted on the Republican side.

CHAPTER II.

The French Revolution—Randolph, in early Youth, a Jacobin—Burke's Pamphlet—Its Influence on Randolph—Points of Resemblance between Burke and Randolph—Randolph's Early Character—Death of his brother Richard and of other Relatives—His Physical Organization.

THE French Revolution and its influence on the foreign relations of this country, became the absorbing subject of national politics. Randolph, as with most imaginative young men, took the radical side; was, in his boyhood, as he expresses it, a Jacobin; but, very seasonably, Burke's pamphlet on the French Revolution came into his hands, and made a powerful, and, in the end, a controlling impression upon his mind.

The effect of a great author upon a young, plastic, and appreciative intellect is, perhaps, the strongest of all the influences which mould the character. Randolph, though easily impressed, was singularly fixed and stable in his principles; nor could the many-sided and magnificent English statesman have found a pupil, more intensely sympathetic with himself, or more appreciative of his writings, than the young Virginian. Acute, subtle, as full of fire and poetry as a bard, affluent of illustrations, quick of perception, yet deep in thought; with uncommon mastery of language; as fresh as the morning and as brilliant as its dew, in his conceptions and diction; and wide and discursive in his mode and range of speculation, the great ideas of the eminent Briton were to him as the kindred creations of a kindred mind. The structure of intellect was a good deal the same in both. A noble imagination, associated with high reverence, an imperious temper and majestic pride, gave a sort of baronial cast and unsocial aspect to the moral and intellectual temper of both the American and English statesmen. The same classic taste, whose purity nothing but the fierce heats of passion could corrupt (but which *they* did often corrupt), predominated in their speech and writings. The same moral and intellectual intrepidity was theirs, and the same utter and impatient scorn of what is low, vulgar, corrupt, venal or cowardly. The same passion for old things, the pride of ancestry, the reverence for establishments time had hallowed, for the old mansion, the old church, the old constitution, the old renown, the old paths trod by the old fathers, the old customs, the old heroes. Whatever prismatic hues seem to the eye of pride and veneration to hang, like an aura, over the past, were equally dear to the hearts of these proud and imaginative men. It may be wondered why, with these traits, they were Whigs, and not Tories. They were Whigs, in the ancient sense, because of their strong love of personal freedom—a love as deep and unconquerable as their pride; and because of their strong *caste* feelings; in other words, from devotion to their own rights and those of their order. We do not mean to compare Randolph with Burke. We do not mean to intimate, that there was an equality of gifts, in the bountiful dispensation nature had made to them. Nor do we mean to assert, that there were not points of strong dissimilitude. We limit the comparison and correspondence to what we have said.

It may well be supposed, that, to such a mind, so organized, and under such tuition, the callow Jacobinism of the boy did not long attach itself.

Randolph was not a close, laborious, pains-taking student. His early education was not systematic; nor do we think there was any error in this. His constitution was not hardy enough to withstand the severity of protracted mental discipline and continuous study. Nor did he require it. Nature is the best doctor, and the best teacher. A versatile, delicately-toned, ductile intellect should be left to the variety and relaxations, which its own organization invites. A race-horse should not be put to the work of a dray-horse. He had enthusiasm, a quick and sure comprehension, a nice and acute observation, and an uncommon memory, with great delicacy and refinement of taste, and a passionate, self-willed, and unconquerable temper. He *studied* whatever he read or noticed; and he read and noticed a great deal. His mind was active and powerful; and was obliged, by the very law of its existence, to be employed; and its thoughts, naturally and most profitably, took the direction most congenial with his tastes. The loading of his mind with what is called learning by the schools, beyond those things which he mastered, would have been but heaping and oppressing it with rubbish. His forte was his freshness, piquancy, originality, sharp sagacity, piercing insight, sparkling and biting wit, and brilliant declamation. To have made a formal logician, a man of facts and figures of him, would have been to spoil an orator and make a bore. But in history, politics, literature, the passing events, the characters and nature of men—all that qualified him for success in politics, (and much of this from merely hearing conversations of gentlemen at the table or the fireside,) probably, at twenty-one he was as well educated for statesmanship, as if he had taken all the degrees of all the universities.

At school, as in Congress, he was shy, reserved, unsocial, incommunicative, tolerating and practising no familiarity of manners, not opening himself to the confidence or acquaintance of other people ; but susceptible of warm attachments; loving the few friends whom he acknowledged, with a romantic tenderness ; extending to them an unreserved trust, and holding his friendship with knightly fidelity and loyalty. When about taking his place in the world, a severe affliction befell him. His brother Richard died. His loss was irreparable. Randolph was devotedly attached to him. He looked up to him, no less in pride and reverence, than in love. Richard was the elder. He possessed an intellect better balanced and more settled than his younger brother. He is said to have been, at least, equally gifted. His unqualified assumption of his father's debts, when the estate was legally discharged, and his manumission of his slaves and provision for them, in obedience to what he conceived his duty, show him to have possessed the noblest elements of character. From the slender materials for judging which he has left, we may take the estimate of his friends to be true, and believe, that, whether in respect of his talents or his virtues, Virginia had not, at that day, a son, who promised to contribute more to her honor, or the public usefulness. The bereavement of such a brother fell upon the young man with crushing severity. Probably, he never recovered from its effects. One by one, those nearest him, "who alone understood him," had been taken from him—father, mother, and now brother! Upon the last two, his proud spirit had concentrated its warmest affections; they were all the world to him; and when they died, life, even in its morning glory, seemed a dreary blank, to the youth seemingly so blessed by nature and fortune with their richest gifts.

A physical property must here be mentioned as bearing upon Randolph's character. He was as thin-skinned as an infant. His whole organization was delicate as a woman's; nay more delicate. His frame had a nervous sensitiveness, and a fineness of fibre, in harmony with the tone of his mind. The height of the figure, the dark flashing eye, the composed presence, the well-defined features, the elongated chin, and the shape of the head alone relieved his person from the appearance of effeminacy of character, of which no man was more free.

CHAPTER III.

Virginia at the date of the Federal Constitution—Contrast between the New-Englander and the Virginian.

IN order to understand the political character of John Randolph, it is necessary to look for a moment at the State, of whose character and politics he was for so many years a representative. This glance will help us to understand the reason why Virginia was the leader in the war for State-Rights, and has generally continued ever since to be a prominent supporter of those doctrines.

Virginia, at the date of the Constitution, was the largest of the States, both in population and in territory. Her proud and effective agency in the revolutionary movement is well known. So prodigious had been the extent of her territory, that it excited the fears and jealousy of the other States; and to appease them in a freak of magnanimity, she gave away the immense empire beyond the Ohio. To give still greater effect to the concession, she added or suffered the prohibition of slavery in the ceded territory; an act which must be regarded, we think, as even more flagrantly impolitic than the gift; and this, whether we consider the interests of the slave or of the master; or whether slavery is to be a permanent or a temporary institution. Like most foolish acts of generosity, it brought as little gratitude as profit.

The population of Virginia was very different from that of Massachusetts and of the other New England States. The difference between the Yankee and the Virginian was as marked as that between the Roundhead and the Cavalier, or that between the Churchman and the Puritan in the mother country; or, rather, the difference was the same. The iron men of New England came from old England as from the house of bondage. They fled from persecution, leaving behind neither attachments nor regrets. They were strongly touched with Republicanism in England. They soon became full-grown Republicans in their forest homes, which were, indeed, the *only* homes they had ever known. They were a race of men, stern, practical, ascetic, serious, devout, prejudiced, fanatical, fearing God, and without other fear; scorning the tendernesses and humanities, the elegant arts, embellishments, and refinements of polished and cultivated life, as weaknesses, if not denouncing them as sins; magnifying small frailties into huge crimes; carrying religion into government, and seeking to enforce religious duties and observances by the arm of temporal authority; pushing an inquisitorial spirit of tyranny and *espionage* into the families and affairs of the members of the community; harsh to visit punishment, and ruling in state and household by fear more than by kindness and love; men of large reverence, and high and conscientious, though often mistaken, sense of duty; of strong passions, the instruments of stronger wills; of fixed purposes, and of an energy and faith that never fainted in adversity, or quailed before danger and difficulty; obeying law with a prompt and reverential obedience; administering it usually with justice, and executing it always without mercy. Probably the world has never seen so efficient a breed of men; for the men of Lexington and Bunker-Hill were of the same strain with the men before whose unpractised valor, under Cromwell and Fairfax, the trained chivalry and fiery courage of Prince Rupert and his cavaliers went down at Naseby and on Marston Moor.

They had settled on barren rocks and on arid, stony hills. What of that? They have crowned the hills with villages, made the long coast gleam with gas-lit streets, like beacons on the shore, and the sterile soil to blossom as the rose. They brought but little outward wealth, but the wealth of mines was imbedded in their untiring labor, which was a godly virtue, and in their close economy, which was a saving grace; for even the business virtues were the offshoots and products of their religious zeal and character.

"Restless as the Vikings of old, in the gristle of their youth, they sent out their mariners to strike the whale in the Arctic zone, and to vex with their prows the waters of unknown seas." They soon laid the foundation of the largest marine in the world; and, almost before they were known to England, as worth either taxing or governing, they were competing with her for the trade of the Asiatic and African coasts.

They turned every thing to account, even the seeming disadvantages of soil and climate, of poverty and weakness. The sterility of the land drove them to the sea; their weakness to union; their poverty to greater labor. The rigorous climate hardened them to endure the added toil it required to afford them food and shelter.

Such were the mighty race of men, who were the founders of empire, and builders of states and cities in the northern portion of the Union.

Very different were the settlers in the Southern Colonies, especially in Virginia. This colony was settled by Englishmen, proud of their country, loyal to the crown and the bigoted King who wore it; loyal to the successor, who lost it with his life; and, on the change of dynasty, after the head of the first Stuart had rolled down the steps of Whitehall, keeping their faith, as long as they could, to the heir of his follies and his sceptre. The soil was grateful, and the climate genial; and the woods and fields abounded with easily acquired means of sustaining life. Large grants of fertile lands were made to favored subjects and colonists; which, under the strict entails, stricter than in England, and the law of primogeniture, as population increased, made the families of the proprietors wealthy. The principal interest was agricultural; and tobacco, coming into general use, and bearing a high price, became the staple which, for a time, yielded a large revenue. The labor on the estates was cheap; being that of servants, transported from the mother country, or that of slaves.

The slaves, that "stocked the new plantations," were sold cheap;—indeed, those engaged in the traffic could well afford to sell them at low prices, as they cost nothing but the trouble of stealing and transporting; or, at most, were bought at the coast, for a jackknife or a yard of calico per dozen; and, allowing for a loss of one half by death on the middle passage, the remainder would bear a handsome profit at one hundred and fifty pounds of tobacco apiece. Persons of family and wealth came out from England. Much wealth was thus brought into the colony, and much more was afterwards made. There were no large towns. Williamsburg, the seat of government, with a population of 2,000 souls, was the largest. The planters traded directly with Scotch and English merchants, who supplied them with merchandise, and took their crops, advancing them money as they needed it, and taking mortgages, as the debts begun to grow large, upon their estates. The Vice-Regal Court, with its elegance, and mimic forms of royalty on a small scale, infected the manners of the gentry, and kept up social distinctions among he different classes of the colonists; while the insular situation and retired habits of the planters on their estates, who made large quantities of provisions for which there was no market, made the rites of hospitality a grateful and inexpensive exercise. The planter had leisure, ease, money; and, in the absence of other excitements or occupations, amused himself with company, horse-racing, gaming, drinking, and such other modes of recreation as opportunity allowed. Literature was not much cultivated, except among a few, and even by them more as an accomplishment or a means of diversion than as a profession.

The established religion was the Church of England; and the ministers of it, selected more from regard to their own convenience than to the interests of religion, and from the orthodoxy of their profession than the piety of their practice, conformed, as much, at least, to the tone of society around them, as to the injunctions of their faith.

The Colony was essentially English—Cavalier-English. Their looks, their religion, their conversation, their commerce, their education, their manners were all English. The colonists cherished the kindest and proudest feelings for Old England. "They called it their home."

Gay, dashing, hospitable, careless, proud, high-spirited and gallant, loving pleasure and excitement, unused to labor or self-denial, there was but little sympathy between the Virginia planter and his more sour, thrifty, practical, shrewd and calculating neighbor of the north. They belonged to essentially different classes of men.

The effect of the institution of slavery was marked. It was seen in the pride, the individuality, the social spirit, the refined manners of the higher classes; and, with these, mingled other and worse effects on the character. The proprietors of the large estates lived in luxury and elegance Whatever wealth or credit could procure was gathered around them. Some of them emulated the style of the English nobility; and the wreck of many a noble mansion still gives evidence of the past state of its lordly master, though now, like him, mouldering in decay.

The feudal times and baronial manners of "merrie England" seemed revived upon this continent. Indeed, looking down, from his castle-like dwelling, over a broad sweep of wood, and water, and patrimonial fields, tilled by his hundreds of slaves, the old Virginian might well feel himself scarcely less of a lord than her Saxon Franklins, or her more modern Dukes or Earls. "Old times are changed, old manners gone." The revelry is silent in their halls; the halls gone to decay. The very site of their mansions is covered with stunted pines and sedge; and park, and garden, and field, and manor, long since worn out and deserted, are grown over with briers and the undergrowth of the returning forest, and never visited, save by the solitary sportsman in quest of the small game, which has taken shelter in the covert.

If caste has its evils, it has its peculiar virtues, too. These are the *esprit du corps*, the kindness and social courtesy, the gentleness of manners, the chivalry of bearing, the oint of honor, the homage to woman, and a nice regard for reputation. Where there was so much leisure, there was opportunity and taste for intellectual cultivation; and, at the bar, and in the public councils, a distinguished array of talent and eloquence was found. Indeed, at the opening of the Revolution, Virginia had more men of eminent character and intellect, than she or any other state has had at any other period.

CHAPTER IV.

The first Constitution of Virginia—Randolph opposed to equal Descents and Distributions—Virginia cherishes her Talent—Her State pride and jealousy of external power—Opposition to the Federal Constitution—Barely adopted by Virginia—Randolph subsequently against it—Strict Construction—Washington's Administration—Adams's—Alien and Sedition Laws—Callender's Trial—Opposition to Adams's Administration—Resolutions of 1798—Report of 1799—Madison—His Character—Patrick Henry joins the Federal Party—His Character—His and Randolph's Speeches at Charlotte Court-House—Henry's Eloquence—His Death.

THE laws, regulating descents and equalizing the distribution of property, were among the first acts of the new government of Virginia. These laws met with much opposition. Randolph seems to have been violently hostile to them. He thus speaks of them: "Well might old George Mason exclaim, that the author of that law never had a son." And again: "The old families of Virginia will form connections with low people, and sink into the mass of overseers' sons and daughters; and this is the legitimate, nay, inevitable conclusion, to which Mr. Jefferson and his levelling system have brought us."

The Constitution of Virginia was, in many respects, an

admirable one. Considered with reference to the times and people, it was, indeed, a wonderful performance. Though greatly in advance of the system which it superseded, it stopped far short of the popular requirements of the present day. It was the government of a class, though of a large class—the freeholders of the state; and the freeholders looked with implicit trust to the gentry.

The feelings of loyalty and of reverence, turned from the crown, were given to the new government and its rulers. The homage of the people descended upon the men in the state eminent for their talent and virtue; and Virginia, to this day, though with weakened force, has always cherished her talent with more pride and steadfastness than any other state in the Union, South Carolina, perhaps, excepted.

The principal part of the government of the colony had been done at home. The mother country, for a long time scarcely at all, and at no time very greatly, interfered in the usual and apparent acts of government; and when she did interfere, the colony had generally resisted the experiment.

Even in the revolutionary struggle, the alliance between Virginia and the other states, especially the northern, was not very close, and the contact of the inhabitants, as a whole, not frequent or lasting. The trade and intercourse between the southern and northern colonies before and immediately after the war, were small. There were jealousies, rivalries, and bickerings between them. There was, as we have said, but little sympathy between the Southron and the Yankee. The Southern people were very much an insular community, and completely homogeneous; cherishing the prejudices against " outsiders," which such a people are apt to feel.

It must be remembered, too, that, with such a people, there naturally existed great jealousy and distrust of any external power; for all such power, of late years, had only been seen and felt in its tyranny.

These considerations developed their effects, when the question of the adoption of the Federal Constitution came up for discussion. That Constitution proposed to establish a new government, which, in comparison with their own, looked like a foreign government. It cut down, as was said, the large, imperial State of Virginia, with territory enough for a kingdom, into a mere province or appendage of a great central government. It razeed her down in one, and that the most stable, branch of the government, to an equality with Rhode Island and Delaware; less in territory, and scarcely greater in population than one of her own counties. It took from the state the control and jurisdiction of its own liege citizens, with their lives and property, and transferred them to the Yankee. It transferred from her the characteristic and leading faculties of independent government, and created in favor of another sovereignty, paramount and mandatory obligations upon the people of the State; and put those people, directly and immediately under the power of the new, and, to a great extent, alien government.

As might have been expected, there was violent opposition to the Constitution in Virginia. Patrick Henry and George Mason led the opposition in the Virginia Convention; and, out of 168 delegates, but a majority of ten was obtained, at last, in its favor.

The stepfather and connections of Randolph sided with the opposition. He was himself, years afterwards, of the same way of thinking; and, had he been old enough to have engaged in political opinions, he would unquestionably have taken part with his relations.

When the new government started, it started, even under the direction of Washington, under circumstances which naturally drew to it suspicions and distrust. There brooded discontents in too many bosoms, not to make very slight causes the occasions or the pretexts for discharging them. Hamilton and his party led off a policy, calculated above all others, to bring them out. He was for making the new government felt; for impressing *energy* upon it, as its characteristic quality. The power of government had, in the past, only been known to the people of the South as another name for its oppressions. It is not easy for the common mind to dissociate the idea of governmental strength from the idea of despotism. Then came the exercise of the taxing power, a power always ungracious, and generally odious; and peculiarly hateful at a time when poverty and embarrassment made these forced contributions extremely onerous.

Although the people of several of the states preferred the new Constitution to the old articles, yet a majority, doubtless, would have preferred a Constitution of less power. And these would naturally be disposed to such a construction of the Constitution, and such a policy of government, as would limit its power to the standard they originally preferred.

The passion for liberty, so strong, yet so indefinite and vague, would come in, too, as a powerful auxiliary, whenever appealed to against an act denounced as arbitrary or as an usurpation. And, from the time of the Israelites, we know the inherent propensity in men to be dissatisfied with what *is*, and to believe and hope for something better in *what is to be*.

But the sentiment of reverence and of gratitude for Washington, and the general confidence in him, were so great, that, though with sadly reduced popularity, he stood the ordeal of two presidential terms. Adams, representing the same policy, succeeded. His whole term was a gauntlet, run through every sort of assailment and assailants. The Alien and Sedition laws completed his unpopularity in Virginia. These laws were extremely odious in the South. They were supposed to be levelled chiefly at citizens of Virginia, a state the foremost and boldest in opposition to the administration, and in denunciation of the Federalists. The Federal authorities arrested and tried in that state some offenders against the Sedition law—the infamous libeller, Callender, among them. The sympathies of the crowd are nearly always with a state-prisoner. Great capital was made out of the trial, by denunciations of those who sought to put down the liberty of the press, the freedom of speech, and all that. The Constitution was declared to be invaded, rightly so declared, we think; and Madison, who had been the ablest advocate of its adoption, was now prominent in the assault upon the law and its authors. The old anti-Federalists, almost to a man, opposed the Adams administration. The same views of policy which led them to oppose the Constitution, as making too strong a government, led them to oppose a strong and energetic administration, and a liberal construction of Federal powers.

The excitement in Virginia was intense. The Legislature, meeting in 1798, had expressed the strongest condemnation of the Federal doctrines of the day. Their resolves constituted the platform of the Republican faith; and, though they did not, at first, seem to meet with public favor elsewhere, ultimately became the recognized creed of the party; as the Report of the year following became its authentic exposition.

These papers were drawn by Madison, and are supposed to be among the ablest productions of his pen. Madison's accession to the Republican ranks was of great advantage to the party. His early antecedents had placed him not far from Hamilton, and very close to Washington, who seems to have entertained, for a time, a high appreciation of his talents, and, for his person, a warm regard. To Jefferson's influence over him is attributed, and, probably, with reason, the change which had come over his political character and relations. Cautious, prudent, pure of moral character, learned, thoughtful, acute and discriminating, with perfect command of temper, with marked facility and power of diction, and singular apparent fairness in his statements and reasonings, he was, by far, the ablest writer and debater on the Republican side. Indeed, he was the only one among them, who could, at all, compete with Hamilton, either by speech or with pen. Patrick Henry, called out by Washington, came forth, to the great disappointment of the Republicans, on the Federal side. It seems, that the old veteran had been smarting under the idea, that Washington had denounced him as a seditious mobocrat. He had made some carping remarks about Washington's *levees;* and, before that time, had opposed, with great vehemence and zeal, the ratification of the Constitution. Washington was advised of Henry's state of mind; and, through a mutual friend, removed this erroneous impression. Unusual pains were taken by both sides to conciliate the great Virginian; but the Federalists succeeded in winning him to their side; or, at all events, he attached himself to that party, and prepared to go into the conflict with his usual zeal and ardor.

In many respects, Henry was the most remarkable, and, Washington excepted, the most celebrated man of the Republic. His early identification with the Revolutionary cause; his prodigious influence in starting forward, and in arousing the people to undertake and prosecute that movement; the self-exposure he had made when, almost alone, he stood up against and defied the English rulers and ministers; his astonishing eloquence, which was a beacon-light of revolution, shining out above every thing and every one about him; and his civil and military services, were but some of the causes which gave him so prominent a position before the country, and so commanding an influence over the people. He was not merely regarded as the chief orator in a revolution, great and brilliant as this position is; he was looked upon almost as a prophet of Liberty, and a prophet foretelling and leading the way to great and exalted blessings. He was a man of wonderful sagacity, as well as of wonderful eloquence. His principles were eminently Republican. His manners and habits were plain, unpretending, kind and social, with a large, benignant and loving nature. Serious and severe of principle, and yet kind and tolerant towards men, he was a man whom the commons could readily approach, and yet a man whom familiarity did not depreciate. He was even more emphatically, in all respects, than Jefferson, *a man of the people*, and was as proud of the title; had appeared oftener before them, and in more imposing aspects and always as the representative of the rights of the masses or of the citizen; and his name and fame, passing from father to son, had become a sort of heirloom in every family of the State. He became one of those favored characters, whom an entire people agree to consider as the standard of excellence, and to refer to, in language at once affectionate and familiar, as the common favorite and guide. He had crowned many noble qualities with an ardent and unaffected piety; and had arrived at an age, when respect and love were mingled with veneration. He was very characteristically a Virginian of the middle class, with all the local prejudices of an insular patriot for a community among whom he had always lived. He had served Virginia and her alone, rejecting Federal offices of the first dignity, secretaryships, missions and embassies. He united, too, the habits and manners of the common people with the high-toned principles of the cultivated gentleman. He was one of those men of whom the people delight to talk. His sayings, his anecdotes, his witticisms, his sharp apothegms, his brilliant triumphs on the hustings, in the courts, in the deliberative assemblies, were themes of conversation at every fireside, and on every muster-ground and court-yard. Men followed him about wherever he went. His talents, his tastes, even his prejudices, adapted him for a great popular tribune. What would have been demagoguism in any one else, was only the expression of *his* natural feelings, sentiments and character. The old-fashioned honesty, and the homely virtues of the Virginia fireside found in him their representative and champion. New French ways, and modern refinements of manner, and modes of life, were his aversion. He had never read many books; but with two works, the noblest of God's works, he was as familiar as any one; and these were man and the Bible.

Had he taken the stump and canvassed the state, it is scarcely too much to say, that the Federalists would have carried every thing before them. But disease and age had palsied the old warrior's arm. He had fought, except one, his last battle. He came from his retreat reluctantly, at the urgent request of Washington, to announce himself as a candidate for the lower branch of the Legislature for Charlotte county, in order to be able to meet Madison in the Assembly.

John Randolph, then scarcely of the legal age, and bearing the appearance of a mere stripling, was a candidate for Congress, in opposition to Philip Bolling, a red-coated, choleric Federalist.

The spring term of the County Court, the time when, under the old *regime*, Virginia always brought out her best breed and blood of horses and politicians, witnessed the encounter, if such it could be called, between the old Republican-Federalist and the young aristocrat-Republican.

The news had spread far and wide that Patrick Henry would make his last speech on the first day of court. Schools were dismissed, business was suspended, men flocked from the country to hear him. At the appointed hour, proclamation was made that Colonel Henry (the title given him before the war, as he went to seize the gunpowder, when lawless men were led, as the proclamation of the old colonial governor had it, by *one* Patrick Henry, a seditious traitor)—that Colonel Henry " would make his last speech, at the risk of his life." Decrepit and feeble, like old Chatham in the House of Peers, leaning on his crutch, the venerable orator was lifted up on the rude rostrum, to speak to the survivors, few they were, and to the children and grandchildren of the large majority of those now dead, whom he had electrified, nearly half a century before, by the first essays of his marvellous eloquence. The speech, if we may trust tradition, was worthy of his summer prime. Indeed it won for him a new title to renown. Men thrilled and wept at his bidding. It seemed as if he possessed a super natural power over that large and sympathizing crowd; as if he could move, at pleasure, the pulses that beat in the veins of the thousands, who looked, lost and absorbed in him, into his speaking face. His magical oratory had destroyed individuality and selfhood in the masses under his spell, and made them, in subjection to common sympathies, seem but as one man; and that one psychologized and led captive, only able to feel, and think, and act, as the magician commanded. Making abatement for exaggerations, if we can believe any thing of the statements of opinions, facts and effects, coming from competent and credible men, themselves observers of what they relate, it may be questioned if a more eloquent man than Henry ever lived. He united all the elements of an almost perfect orator. He was enthusiastic, fervid, impulsive, but not rash, or extravagant, or fanatical. As M'Clung says of Clay, "Reason held the helm, while Passion blew the gale." His physical organization, as in every true orator, was admirably adapted to the expression of his genius. His moral and emotional sensibilities were quick, finely, yet strongly organized, and modulated, like a fine instrument, the voice to which they gave tone and utterance. His voice was musical, strong, various of tone and fitted for the expression of every variety of intonation and cadence.

His countenance serious, and almost dull when in repose, grew, under the excitement of speech, transfigured, and almost articulate with the emotions that thrilled his soul. The eye glowed or melted, was fierce in indignation, or tender in sympathy, or commanding in its imperial utterances of pride and dignity. Few men could stand unmoved the fixed gaze of that eagle eye, turned in scorn or defiance upon them. He did not so much possess, as he was possessed by, the spirit of oratory, when it moved upon him. It transformed his whole port and presence. He seemed another and a higher being under its inspiration. The awkward and slovenly air, the impassive countenance, the listless movement disappeared, as, rising with his theme, he soared, like a Hebrew prophet, to sublime heights of declamation and prose-poetry; and, glowing, inspired, irresistible, he commanded, awed, subdued, fired with passion, or melted with pity, the ductile subjects of his power. The specimens given of him by Wirt, are not always characteristic. Henry's style was pure Saxon-Bible-english. He spoke in no such scanned lines as "the next breeze, that sweeps from the North, will bring to our ears the clash of resounding arms." This is Wirt's rhetoric, not Henry's eloquence. The short, vigorous, pictorial sentences, winged with the fire of imagination, of the grand old man, were altogether different from these holiday, Eolian tunes. The difference between them is the difference between Homer and Tom Moore. The lines of Wirt resemble the words of Henry, about as much as the tinklings of the guitar resemble the bugle-notes before a charge; or as the carolling of a canary resembles the scream of the eagle, when he stoops on his quarry.

Henry fell back exhausted into the arms of his friends, after this great speech, amidst the most marked and striking evidences of its impressiveness and power.

Randolph rose, probably, to the surprise of every one, to reply. We do not suppose there was any comparison as exercises of oratory, between the speeches of the two. That the crowd, just released from, and still thrilling with, the eloquence of Henry, listened to him at all; that they listened patiently for three hours; that they were pleased and entertained all that time, and that the effect of the speech was to promote the personal interests of the youthful speaker, is praise enough for any man's first effort.

It seems that Henry listened to the reply. He did not rejoin. Probably, it was not expected of him. At the conclusion, he came to Randolph. He seems to have accosted him in a style resembling that which a father would address to a bright, but forward boy. Taking Randolph by the hand, he said: " Young man, you call me father; then my son, I have somewhat to say unto thee (holding both his hands), *Keep justice, keep truth*, and you will live to think differently."

Mr. Garland adds: " They dined together, and Randolph ever after venerated the memory of his friend, who died in a few weeks from that day."

They were both elected in April. But the death of Henry prevented that collision in the Legislature from which the Federalists hoped so much of benefit, and the Republicans apprehended so much of injury, to their respective sides.

CHAPTER V.

Randolph in Congress—His Political Creed—State-Rights—Opposes Adams's Administration—Election of Jefferson—Randolph and Hamilton—Excise Abolished—Policy of this—Acquisition of Louisiana—Impeachment of Judge Chase—Randolph as a Party Leader—His Unhappiness—Disappointed Love—His Friendships—Death of his Friends, Thompson and Bryan.

In December, 1799, Randolph took his seat in Congress. The Federalists were in nominal ascendency, but the old dynasty was crumbling, and the sceptre of authority departing for ever from hands that had shown themselves incapable, perhaps, unworthy of holding power.

The political character of Randolph was now formed, and formed for life; for, we think, it must be conceded, that he was one of the most consistent—*we* think *the* most consistent, of all the politicians that ever lived in the republic.

It becomes necessary to define his creed. He was a State-Rights man, and, *therefore*, a Republican. He was, by conviction, prejudice, and impulse, a strict constructionist. He opposed the idea of a great central power, which was to govern Virginia. He was therefore, opposed to the

Constitution; but the Constitution having been established, he endeavored so to construe it, and so to have the government it made administered, as to prevent the existence of this power; at any rate, to avoid any accession of power to the national government. He believed that the powers of the Federal Government were a mere delegation of powers from the states; and that the paramount sovereignty still remained with the states. The great monster evil of government, in his view, was consolidation. He thought that the great danger in the administration of our government, was this consolidation; that the Federal Government, was meant to be, or ought to be, construed as a limited agency, for a few, general, simple, external objects, and inter-state purposes; and that any power beyond these was an usurpation upon the rights of the states. How faithfully he adhered to these doctrines, will be seen in the sequel.

We think the expectation, that the government would long be administered in subordination to such doctrines, wholly illusory. Whenever the power was given to the government to enforce its own laws, such an idea was hopeless. The character of the government, which exhibited itself as the organ of nationality, would naturally conform itself to the character of the people; and the bold, aggressive, warlike, practical, utilitarian, eager, impatient race who constituted the mass of the republic, would mould the character of the government, whatever it originally was, to their own type and image; and such it has become.

Indeed, it so happens, that the measures, which have

given to the government its strongest national tone, have been the measures of the State-Rights administrations.

The State-Rights doctrine supposes a state of hostility or rivalry between the General and State governments; and that the danger is, that the General Government will invade the province of the state jurisdictions. When the Federal Government increases, the states decrease; for, what *it* takes, it takes from the states. The loyalty, respect, homage, affection, which are given to the General Government, are so many cords of attachment wrested from the states.

The wars, which the Republic has waged, have produced the strongest Federalism of sentiment and power. They have turned attention away from the state governments to the General Government. The eyes of the citizen and of the world are fixed on that government. The added patronage and money attract to it supporters more or less venal. The successes of the Flag hallow it. Patriotism becomes love for *the Republic.* The national Flag is reverenced as the symbol of *our* country, and the emblem of our power. We take pride in the *great* Republic, because *it is* ours. Who thinks of the poor states, unconsidered and unnoticed; or who, in time of war, calls himself a citizen of Virginia or Alabama? No; he is *one of the great American nation.* All the glaring external symbols of sovereignty are held out by the Federal Government—the flag, the army, the navy, the coinage, the forts, the arsenals, the docks, the customs, the light-houses. The successes of war are common triumphs in which state pride or agency is little known or felt. The soldiers, meeting in mass on the field, are placed under officers other than those of their own state; and thus a state of war, with its glare and pomp, with its military rules and summary proceedings—its unlimited powers, its excesses, forgotten in adversity, forgiven in triumph—all these things have an air and an "odor" of nationality which were unknown to the earlier ideas of the Republic. Besides, war is the highest executive function, and necessarily centralizes immense power in the hands that wield it. But we anticipate the narrative.

Randolph, upon his entrance into Congressional life, early took ground against the administration. The session of 1799, though marked with a good deal of excitement, was not productive of measures of a great deal of importance. The judiciary bill, and the measures for an increase of the army, in view of the difficulties in our relations with France, were the most important. There was but little talent in Congress. Randolph opposed the army bill, and made some intemperate remarks, not in the best taste, concerning the army, calling them mercenaries and ragamuffins. This excited the ire of a brace of lieutenants in the lobby, who insulted him at the theatre afterwards. Randolph complained to the President, who replied rather coldly, and communicated the correspondence to the House; but nothing was done, except a reference and report. The stand, however, taken by Randolph in the House at this session, drew on him the attention of the country, and gave an earnest of the distinction he was destined to attain.

The election of 1800-1 was decided in favor of the Republicans. But the vote being the same for Jefferson and Burr, the House of Representatives had, under the Constitution as it then stood, to decide between them. The Federalists, as the least of the evils, moved thereto, doubtless, in part, by the intrigues of Burr, preferred him. A long contest, with many ballotings, occurred. A furor of excitement prevailed. It was thought the government was in jeopardy. Randolph believed that it was only saved by the patriotism of Alexander Hamilton, whose powerful interposition with the Federalists was successful in prevailing upon them to withdraw further opposition to Jefferson; an interposition which, probably, was the instigation of Burr's malignant purpose in the hostile correspondence which, a few years afterwards, he had with Hamilton, under another pretext, and which resulted so fatally to the latter.

Randolph ever afterwards spoke of Hamilton in a strain of respect, and with a justice, which it would have been more creditable to Jefferson if *he* had imitated.

Randolph made his first speech in the next Congress, (which contained a Republican majority,) on the bill to repeal the judiciary act, which had been passed in the last moments of the late administration. This act provided for the appointment of a large and unnecessary number of Federal judges. The bill of repeal was resisted, on the ground, that the Constitution having fixed the tenure of the judges' office for good behavior, they could no more be removed by a repeal of the law, than by an act passed avowedly to remove them. But, it was answered by Randolph, and it seems to us rightly, that, if the former law was a nuisance, it might be abolished, *though the effect were* to displace the judges. He urged, that, if the object was not to put out the judges, but *bona fide* to repeal a bad law, under which the judges held office, the repealing law was not a violation of the Constitution. This, it is true, is delicate ground; for when the Constitution is made to depend upon the *motive* from which an act is done, it ceases to have any sanction; or, at least, the Constitution becomes indeterminate and variable, depending upon the state of a congressman's conscience or his own account of that state, instead of having written words and recognized rules of construction for the guide. Many of the Republican members seem to have thought that the repeal law was, at least, of questionable propriety; and, at all events, not a favorable commentary on the text, which the Republicans had announced, that all acts of doubtful constitutionality should be avoided.

Nathaniel Macon, of North Carolina, was chosen Speaker of the House, and Randolph appointed Chairman of the Committee of Ways and Means. He went to work assiduously in the important business of his position. His relations, at this time, with Jefferson, seem to have been cordial, politically and socially. He was prominently efficient, in the acts making provision for the payment of the public debt, for abolishing unnecessary offices and expenditures, and the other reform measures of the new administration. The great dissatisfaction, which the excise had produced, led early to the abolition of the internal tax. This threw the burdens of supporting the government upon the importations. We think it very questionable whether this measure, in the end, has not been injurious to the State-Rights party. It made the government sit too lightly upon the people. The masses of the people of any country *feel* the government chiefly in the taxes. The tax collector brings to vivid remembrance the costs of governmental luxuries. Under the new system the process of government is as easy as the process of breathing. Men, not knowing what they pay, nor seeing it in the bills they pay, forget that they pay at all. Indeed, under this chloroform process of extracting taxes, it was a debated point at one time, whether we had not, by the ingenious contrivance of a tariff, fixed it so that foreigners were made to pay our government expenses. Besides, to limit the power of the government, its expenditures must be reduced. If the people had annually to pay the tax collector, they would be apt to scrutinize the items in the bill, and to make themselves acquainted with the amount and course of expenditures. A direct tax on the people of the South to pay the manufactories of the North, for the protection and encouragement of their fabrics, would not have been laid, or, if laid, would never have been suffered to remain. A tythe-proctor in Ireland, collecting dues from the Catholic to be squandered in high living by the English heretical bishop would be about as popular. If, as Mr. Webster said, we are emphatically a debt-paying people, we are as emphatically a tax-hating people. The pocket sensibilities of the great

Yankee nation are morbidly acute. We think the State Rights politicians, who contended that the Federal government should be watched with suspicion, and especially those of them who desired to see it held, if not in odium, at least in less favor than the state governments, missed their aim, when, to purchase a temporary popularity, they removed a system, which would have been the occasion of perpetual complaints and discontents against the central power.

Soon came the question of the purchase of Louisiana. On strict State-Rights principles, this measure was inadmissible. Jefferson admitted it to be without constitutional warrant. He defended it on the ground of necessity; but the necessity was only a high expediency. It seems that Randolph went with him.

Then came the impeachment and trial of Judge Chase; which, we think, was a proceeding that owed its origin very much to the intemperance of party zeal; and which, both in conducting it and in its result, was a clear failure. Randolph was one of the managers before the Senate. His efforts there, though good specimens of oratory and rhetoric, were rather a foil than a match to the trained forensic skill, legal learning, and rough but strong logical powers of Luther Martin.

The relations of this country with Spain, arising from he conduct of the authorities of New Orleans in regard to the navigation of the Mississippi river, occupied a good deal of the attention of Congress and of the Executive.

On the whole, the first term of the Republican administration closed with honor, and largely increased popularity to the head of it, and with great benefit to the people. Randolph had greatly distinguished himself, not only as an orator, but as a business man; and, by his industry, intelligence, and zeal in the service, had raised himself to the position of the acknowledged leader of the party in the House. Young, admired, distinguished in high favor with the Executive and the party, a leading representative from the leading state of the Union, in closest correspondence and intimate relations with the President, and allied to him by blood, on a high sea-tide of party popularity, with a character pure and unsullied, and without many distinguished rivals in his own ranks, he might well have looked forward to the highest rewards of ambition.

But, notwithstanding all these things, he was not popular; at all events, he had made many violent and influential enemies. His manners were not conciliating. His pride was excessive. He neither permitted nor indulged in familiarities. His course was open, above-board, frank and independent, perhaps self-willed, certainly impatient of opposition, and not tolerant of contradictory opinions. He was not an out-doors legislator—the most effective of all politicians. He did not practise the arts of managing men. He had no adaptation to the dispositions of others. He was wanting in sympathy with his associates; in conciliation to his enemies. He had no concealments. He never affected any liking or respect when he did not feel it; and he had liking and respect for but few men. He had risen rapidly;

and the envy that always follows merit and distinction, was increased by the haughty manner in which he bore himself towards those who envied him. His wit was in his way. It was not genial or playful, but bitter and sarcastic. For the selfishness and meanness of interested politicians he had an utter loathing. He readily saw through the purposes and motives of men; and nothing so infuriates a base mind as the consciousness that its baseness is exposed.

Randolph was a bad party-leader. He was positively disqualified by nature from being one. We do not speak of leadership as it has often appeared in our day. *Any* man of spirit and honesty is disqualified for such a position. Randolph was more so than most men. He had as soon been a slave as a tool of a President or a party He had as soon worn the uniform of the penitentiary as the badge of official or party fealty. He had died before he could come into the political market, with his soul in his hand, as Whipple somewhere says, asking the dispensers of Federal bounty—" How much is this worth ?" But we speak of a leadership honorable in itself, and consistent with the claims of conscience and self-respect. He had not the temper for such a position. He had not the coolness, the tact, the knowledge of men, the compromising disposition, the forbearance, the conciliation, the sympathy, the power of making friends of the many, of drawing to himself the confidence and respect of others, the sober gravity and weight of character which befit such a place.

He had earned the immortal honor of exciting against

him a host of powerful peculators and ravenous leeches on the Federal treasury. The large list of prominent men, interested in indemnity for the repudiation of the Yazoo grant, was banded against him. He had attacked that colossal swindle, in terms exhausting all the epithets of indignant invective. The Yazoo fraud stands to common cheatery as the expedition of Hyder Ali to the Carnatic coast, stands to a single robbery by a foot-pad. It was a gigantic, enormous, imperial fraud. It proposed to steal by the forms of legislation, through the bribery of the legislators, an extent of country, out of which states might be formed, passing through degrees of latitude and longitude; the descriptive lines being rivers, mountains, and sea-shore. Men of the first position in the country, in Congress and in the States, were largely interested in the business; and, it may be supposed, felt the keenest animosity against those who opposed the realization of this flagitious enterprise.

We turn, for a moment, from Randolph's political career, to glance at him in more private aspects. Randolph, from his youth, seems to have been unhappy. As he grew older, he seems to have grown more unhappy. A private grief weighed heavily upon him after his congressional life began. His correspondence shows the nature of this grief. He was attached to a young lady of Virginia, one whom he loved, as he expresses it, "better than his own soul or its author." The course of his love, as with most first loves, did not run smooth. Unlike most first loves, his passion, or its effect, never lost its influence upon his mind. Long years afterwards, in the dreary winter of his sad life, in the mutterings of delirium, he called her name. There is but little sympathy, amongst the mass of men, with the woes of lovers; and an affair of the heart, however grievously afflicting, like the tooth-ache, is more a matter of ridicule, than of compassion. But in a temper so sensitive as Randolph's, so morbidly sensible to pain; to a nature so proud, so passionate, so exclusive in the objects of its affections and trust, a love, once fixed, was a permanent influence; and the dissolution of such a tie would leave the heart, ever afterwards, desolate and bleeding.

He had, in youth, contracted an intimacy with a young gentleman of the name of Thompson. The friendship seems to have been unusually ardent and disinterested. Thompson was a man of gaiety and wit, and of fine social qualities, but dissipated in his habits, and infirm in his purposes. He had sunk low in his associations and reputation, in consequence of these irregularities. Randolph, however, did not desert him, nor did he abate, in the least, his attentions and interest in him. The letters written to this unhappy young man, do Randolph the highest credit. They show, in lively colors, the real nobleness of his soul. We have never chanced to see any letters which breathe a more delicate, a more ardent, and a more generous friendship. They show more than this. They show a love of truth, a loftiness of principle, and a courage and fidelity in discharging the more ungracious duties of friendship, which only a good and a great man could exhibit.

Randolph procured for him an office in Louisiana; and the young man, with many resolutions of amendment, started to go to that territory to assume its duties; but he died on the way.

Another intimate friend of Randolph's boyhood was Joseph Bryan, of Georgia, a mad-cap, frolicking, dashing, jovial, light-hearted, warm-souled fellow as ever cracked a bottle or a jest. These light traits were but the froth that stronger qualities threw to the top. Joe took to politics, got to be a member of Congress, and married a lovely girl. His loving heart now ran over with happiness; and, looking out on life as a long day of sunshine, he gives utterance to his joy after such a fashion that we feel almost as happy as himself in sympathy with his bliss. Alas! a year or two passed, and laughter-loving, warm-hearted, whole-souled Joe Bryan died; the lovely bride died, too; and two children were left orphans, one of them named after Randolph. Randolph became a father to the children, and John, his namesake, was years afterwards married to his niece.

It seemed as if a fatality was about him, that all to whom his heart clung, of the early objects of attachment, were torn from him.

CHAPTER VI.

Jefferson's Second Term—Our Foreign Relations—State of Europe—President's Conduct—Randolph Opposes the Administration—Denounced by his Party—Returns Home—Illness and Unhappiness.

THE ninth Congress commenced its session under the second term of Jefferson. So far affairs had gone on, every thing considered, smoothly enough. But now every thing betokened a stormy and troubled period. Our foreign relations were complicated to an extent never known before. Never was there a time which required more the higher qualities of statesmanship. With Spain, with France, and with England, our relations were of the most delicate character. Europe was in uproar and conflagration. One continuous note of hostile preparation and conflict resounded throughout the continent. Whole nations were in camp, and the memorable war for the life of dynasties and kingdoms was raging with a fury and determination worthy of the stake. The modern Alexander was seeking to complete the subjugation of the world. But one obstacle stood in his way. Twenty miles of sea rolled between his camp and England.

He could see, but could not reach, the last fortress of freedom in the old world. England was mistress of the seas. He looked out from Calais to the white cliffs of Dover, and gnashed his teeth, in impotent rage, at the little space of water that kept him from his spoil. Nelson had swept the French fleet and that of her allies from the water. Every body knew—indeed, either rival boldly proclaimed, that the war was a war for the extermination of the adverse power. Two nations, the first powers of all the world, hereditary and immemorial enemies and rivals, whose past histories blazoned, in every glowing page, the brightest achievements that art or arms had ever won; brave, chivalrous, ambitious, proud, vain, vindictive, jealous, burning with the imagined or real wrongs and insults of centuries, under their most renowned captains and statesmen, in the eyes of the world, and to the grief or joy of all generations to come, were to fight out the battle which was to determine their own fate and fame, the empire of the world, and the sway of all, or nearly all, mankind.

The man of destiny had carried every thing before him. His prodigious genius seemed even less than his prodigious fortune. His career was a history of prodigies. He took kingdoms as other warriors take forts. He ran up his flag over capitals, as other generals fly theirs over fortresses. His imperial banner hovered, like the wing of the Destroying Angel, over the great battle-fields to which he led his conquering legions. Monarchs sued at his feet, and great kings were proud to be his allies and subordinates. England alone, the prouder and the loftier in her heroic isolation, stood up against his progress and defied his power; and England was the most feared and the most hated of all his foes. She had resisted at once his arts of conciliation and his arms. She prepared herself for the conflict. Single-handed and alone, she held him at bay; firm and unmoved in her majestic port, against a world in arms.

In this state of things—England all powerful on the seas, Bonaparte all powerful on the land, each straining every nerve to injure the other, holding *that* to be the highest earthly object, the very purpose and only security of existence—it could not be otherwise than that neutral rights and nations must suffer detriment.

Upon Spain, our claims for redress and for settlement of vexatious difficulties, seemed first in time, and the most urgent in character. She had acted in a spirit of haughty and characteristic insolence. She was nearest to our territory. She refused to recognize a convention, signed by her own minister under the eye of the sovereign. She disputed our boundaries, menaced our frontier, and protested against our possession of Mobile. She had committed spoliations on our commerce; for which, after keeping our minister dallying at court for five months, she refused indemnity. In the language of Randolph, "Great Britain, indeed, had impressed our seamen, and advanced certain injurious principles of national law, which, if carried into their full extent, would materially affect our commerce; but that Spain, after having refused to make good her solemn stipulations to compensate us for former spoliations committed on our commerce, had renewed the same practices during the present war." She had not, it is true, impressed our seamen, but her cruisers " had plundered and sunk our vessels, and maltreated and abandoned their crews in open boats, or on desert shores, without food or covering." " Her Courts of Admiralty had, indeed, advanced no new principles of the law of nations, but they had confiscated our ships and cargoes, without the pretext of principles of any sort, new or old. She had, moreover, insulted our territory, violated the property and persons of our citizens within our acknowledged limits, and insolently rejected every overture to accommodation. With Spain all of our attempts to negotiate had died."

Such, too, seemed to be the views of the Executive. There would have been short work with Spain, had not other parties stood in the way. To have blown her out of the water, or run her off the land, would have been only holiday refreshment. But France seemed to back her; and a war with her would have been war with France, too; besides, in the confused and complicated state of things in Europe, leading, probably, to other difficulties.

The supremacy of England on the ocean, naturally made her desirous of realizing its advantages to annoy and cripple her adversaries as much as possible. The destruction of trade between France and her colonies and allies was one of the chief of these advantages. But the keen enterprise of our countrymen saw the opening, offered by this state of things, to a neutral nation, and became the dealers in and carriers of the subjects of this trade, under the protection of the American flag. Not only was a legitimate commerce carried on in this way, but the American name and flag, through a process of fictitious assignments, were fradulently used by belligerent owners of vessels. By these means, vast profits accrued to our merchants. Immense fortunes were made by our shippers. England was thus deprived of the benefits she had promised herself from her maritime ascendency. To remedy this, the orders in council were issued, which declared the whole coast from Brest to the Elb, in a state of blockade; the consequence of which was an interdiction of commerce with the blockaded ports, under pain of the forfeiture of the cargo and vessel. Bonaparte rejoined, by issuing his Berlin decree, by which England and her ports, and their commerce, were placed under a like interdict.

There were other questions with England. The denial of the right of expatriation, and her consequent seizure of our citizens, natives of Great Britain, and the search for and seizure of seamen in our ships, were subjects of complaint; indeed the popular and moving grievance that led to the war.

It were a very easy thing to have made terms with either of the belligerents; but this would have been war with the other. As it stood, we had good cause of war with both. We desired neutrality. We wished no entangling alliances. We desired to reap the rich harvest which a neutral position must have given us. We were after trade, not war—for money, not blood.

Unfortunately, we had no navy, or next to none. Had the Federal policy been pursued, and a navy, adequate to the exigencies of the public service, been provided, we might have protected our marine and our commerce on the ocean. Nay, England would probably have shrunk from encountering us on the sea, where, if not alone equal to her in naval force, we might, in conjunction with her enemies, have imperilled her supremacy. At any rate, we could have retaliated any assaults she might have made upon our merchantmen. From our mercantile marine, we could easily, and at short notice, have increased our naval force, to have answered any additional demand upon it by the war. But the spirit of party had left us without this right-arm of our national defence.

In this anomalous and awkward posture, what was to be done? If we sided with England, France would be down upon us; and if England should be subjugated, or withdraw from the contest, the might of the arch-destroyer would descend upon our unprotected coasts; and Spain, standing ready to assist from her adjoining provinces, would, possibly, deprive us of our large South-Western acquisitions. If we went to war with England, our vast commerce upon the sea would be the spoil of her navy, and our coast cities be imperilled; while we would, of course, lose the fruits of the neutral position we occupied.

But the spirit of our people was up for war. The old

hatred to England was still a dominant principle among the Republican party; and the old friendship for France, notwithstanding the excesses and despotism which she illustrated, was still a strong influence with our people. Besides, Jefferson's whole policy, in the early organization and history of his party, had been governed, as by a chart, by *enmity to England—kindness to France.* His popularity was based in good part on the hatred of the masses to England.

The impulses of the highest chivalry would have led Congress to have thrown down the gauntlet to England, Spain and France! It looks, at the first blush, like madness for a young nation to have done so; but as there could have been no concert between the belligerents, and either, going out to fight *us*, would probably have encountered the other, we do not know that it would have increased, a great deal, the danger; while it would have crowned the young Republic—it matters not what the result, short of subjugation, was—with a glory beyond all Greek and Roman fame.

The suggestion of a far-seeing, self-aggrandizing policy would have been an alliance with England, and a conquest, and seizure in consequence thereof, of the Floridas and Cuba, and the " re-annexation " of Texas and half of Mexico.

There was another course recommended by present safety, and great plausibility. It was that of Randolph: To prepare to meet and expel every encroachment by Spain upon our territory, and to protect our possessions; **and**, in respect to the others, to hold the maxim to apply in international as in municipal law—" *Inter arma leges silent :* "—to postpone a demand for satisfaction and settlement, for wrongs inflicted by the belligerents, until the parties got cool and sober, and the war in Europe was at an end; making preparations to sustain our demand when that time should come.

Jefferson, we think, was not the man for the crisis. He was not distinguished for executive functions, in times of difficulty and danger. His conduct in the Revolutionary war, when he was Governor of Virginia, is proof of this observation. He was bold of speculation, and an adroit and successful politician. But he was not intrepid and determined in action, when bold issues were to be met, and great responsibilities to be assumed. He had not Jacksonism enough in him to be a great leader in a war movement. In the present crisis, he had no policy. He had a vague idea that something ought to be done, without seeming to know precisely what. The Constitution, his position and the nature of his office required *him* to recommend measures to Congress. He recommended nothing intelligible and definite. He told Congress, he should execute *their* will with zeal. Congress seems to have had as little will as himself. There was but little talent in that body. There seemed to be no unity or agreement in the members. Every man had his own project, and no man a good one. There was no authentic or catholic creed, or chart, or leader.

On the Spanish question, the President said : " Formal war is not necessary : it is not probable it will follow ; but the protection of our commerce, the spirit and honor of our country require that force should be interposed to a certain degree; it will probably contribute to advance the object of peace. But the course to be pursued will require the command of means, which it belongs to Congress exclusively to deny or yield. To them I communicate every fact material for their information, and the documents necessary to enable them to judge for themselves. To their wisdom, then, I look for the course I am to pursue, and will pursue with zeal that which they shall approve."

Judge of Randolph's surprise, when the President informed him that the *means* here spoken of were two millions of dollars, which the President wished appropriated *for the purchase of Florida.* In committee of the House, Bidwell, of Massachusetts, construed the message into a requisition of money *for foreign intercourse.* If any doubt could remain, it would have been removed by Mr. Madison, the Secretary of State, who told Randolph, that France would not permit Spain to adjust her differences with us; that France wanted money, and that we must give it to her or have a Spanish and French war. In other words, that we must pay tribute to France for her consent for us to trade with Spain! The course Randolph took, in reply to this indirect and humiliating proceeding and its explanations, was characteristic. He boldly rebuked it. He rebuked the course of the President in seeking to throw the responsibility on Congress of doing what he secretly wished, and yet would not openly recommend; and he closed the interview with Madison, by abruptly leaving him, with the remark: "Good morning, sir! I see I am not calculated for a politician!"

Randolph spoke in the House with great force and power against the bill, appropriating this money, to be used at the President's discretion. He attacked it on principle. He exposed the disingenuousness of the whole proceeding. It was in the course of this debate that a Mr. Varnum declared that the bill, opposed as it seemed to be to the message, was in unison with the secret wishes of the Executive. Randolph attacked him with great eloquence and caustic severity. He denounced "this back-stairs influence, this double dealing, the sending one message for the journals and newspapers, and another in whispers to this House. I shall always," said he, "reprobate such language; and consider it unworthy of any man holding a seat in this House. I had before always flattered myself, that it would be a thousand years hence before our institutions would have given birth to these Charles Jenkinses in politics."

Such was the language of John Randolph on this occasion; and right bold and manly language it was, befitting the lips of an independent representative, in response to the secret dictation of the Executive. Randolph thus broke ground against the party in power; and, for the future, continued in opposition to the most important measures of the Jefferson, Madison, and Monroe administrations.

The President made no recommendation of specific measures to Congress, in reference to our relations with

England; but the tone and temper of the correspondence between the two countries, and the representations of our grievances in the messages, show that the present posture of affairs could not long continue. Something, it was evident, must be done. Neither consistency nor the outside pressure would allow the government to stand still; and the President was not prepared to go to war. The only alternative seemed to be, a middle ground, a sort of compromise between peace and war. If we could not resist, we could show resentment. If we could not fight, we might growl. Accordingly, Mr. Gregg brought in his non-intercourse resolutions, cutting off commercial correspondence with Great Britain. This was neither a war measure nor a peace measure, but something between both. Randolph vehemently opposed it. He was for war, direct and open, if we must fight at all. He said, " If war is necessary, let us have war. But while I have life, I will never consent to these incipient war measures, which, in their commencement, breathe nothing but peace, though they plunge us, at last, into war." He argued against it as a war measure, and against an offensive war, as contrary to the Constitution. " I declare," said he, " in the face of day, that this government never was instituted for the purposes of offensive warfare. No; it was framed (to use its own language) for the common defence and general welfare, which are inconsistent with offensive war. I call that offensive war which goes out of our jurisdiction and limits, for the attainment or protection of objects not within those limits or that jurisdiction. As in 1798, I was opposed to this species of warfare, because I believed it would raze the Constitution to its very foundation, so, in 1806, am I opposed to it on the same grounds."

As to the impressment of our seamen, Randolph thought that it afforded just grounds for indignant resentment, but he saw no reason for putting that matter to extremity now, more than at any time within the preceding five years.

It is one of the most singular facts of history, that, in regard to the policy towards England, there was no official recommendation or opinion, either of the President, or of the Cabinet, as individuals or collectively; and that the President declared openly that he had none!

The resolution of Gregg was modified, so as to exclude only certain enumerated articles, and not to make a total exclusion of all subjects of traffic. The bill, thus modified, passed; eighty-seven Republicans voting for, and eleven against it. The Federalists went against it *en masse*. The whole opposition was only twenty-four.

Randolph's course drew down upon him great odium from the friends of the administration. It could not be otherwise. A bolder and more unqualified assault was never made. The tone of it was as decided and as daring as the matter. There was no mincing of words, or hinting, or hesitating, or glossing over unpalatable truths. It was a vehement onslaught, and the eloquence, the ability, the boldness must have carried consternation to those in power, as well as indignation for the exposures he had made of their duplicity and want of courage. Jefferson says, in his letters, that Randolph "did flutter the Volscii" of the House for a while, but they rallied again.

A charge was made against Randolph, that he had taken this course in resentment against the administration for not appointing him minister to England. It seems, that some friend of Randolph's suggested his name, without his knowledge, to the President, for this appointment; and that the President declined to make the nomination. It is highly probable that such a circumstance would, if known to him, have excited the eager resentment of Randolph, whose vindictiveness was easily aroused, and very difficult to appease; and this fact may have lent some poignancy to his feelings in his opposition to these measures of the Executive. But we feel sure, that it did not induce the course he took. He acted, as he always did, in public matters, upon public grounds and from his convictions. His bearing was not that of a renegade. He did not turn his arms against his old principles, nor his back upon his old friends. He professed no toleration for, he made no fusion with, his old enemies, the Federalists. He was willing, after this trouble vanished, to act with the party where he could consistently do so. His course was in unison with the principles he had ever professed; and he gave such reasons for it as ought to satisfy any reasonable man that, if he were not right, yet he might well believe he was.

In this same session, the fillibustering proceedings of Burr were brought up for action. The Senate, in a tremor of excitement, on a verbal hint from Jefferson, passed a bill suspending the *Habeas Corpus*. Randolph opposed it in the House, and had a marked agency in suppressing so unnecessary a proceeding.

The session drew to a close. It terminated in scenes of disorder. A systematic attack seems to have been made upon Randolph, by the friends of the President, in the last hours of the session. Among others, the son-in-law of Jefferson, and a relative of Randolph, Mr. T. M. Randolph, assailed him with strong personalities. Randolph challenged him; but the affair was settled by an apology from the assailant, from his place on the floor of the House.

Randolph returned to his lonely retreat at Bizarre, with a title to the respect and admiration of his countrymen, purchased at the expense of all the favor he had won, and all the applause and position he had gained, from his party, and of all his hopes of promotion from its power and influence. He had preserved his independence. He had, consistently with Republican principles, upheld the rights and privileges of the Representative character. He had opposed principles, as he honestly believed, at war with the interests and character of the Republic. In a day, he found himself tabooed and ignored. He found himself covered with odium. He saw the fruits of long service wither beneath the blasts of executive hostility. The independence of a month had swept away the memory of the service of years.

He did not enjoy the quiet and repose of his retreat. A fatal disease, inherited from his parents, lurked in his system. He was prostrated by it. Indeed, during the last hours of the session, he was racked by horrible pains of body, to which the excitement and troubles of his spirit added torment. For long weeks, he lay upon his bed suffering unutterable misery. The lady of his early love and romantic passion married another. He had cherished her image as the idol of his soul. He had abandoned the hope of being united to her in marriage; but, it seems, looking away from grosser views, he thought that a Platonic relation might exist between them. The austere man, proud, exclusive, repulsive, had yet in his heart, cold and hard as it seemed towards the world, one spot, warm and bright— amidst boisterous seas, a little emerald isle, decked with flowers and vocal with melody, and inhabited by the fair being, whom he idolized as the ideal of all that was pure and bright of womanhood and beautiful on earth.

CHAPTER VII.

Difficulties with England—Monroe's Treaty—The Affair of the Chesapeake—The Embargo—Randolph opposes it—Jefferson against a Navy—Gun-Boats—Non-Importation Act—Madison's Election—Randolph prefers Monroe—War Measures—War—Randolph opposes it—Clay and Calhoun in Congress.

ANOTHER meeting of Congress. The difficulties with England became aggravated. The restrictions had worked no cure. They had hurt ourselves, but not the enemy. Monroe had signed a treaty with England in December, 1806. This promised a settlement of existing difficulties. Monroe was proud of it, and was felicitating himself upon the credit it would do him at home. But the Berlin decree coming to the knowledge of the ministry, the English commissioners added a note that, if France should execute that decree, and our government acquiesce, the treaty should be of no effect.

Jefferson boldly pocketed the treaty, and there it ended. The truth is, it had got to be almost as dangerous to make peace as war. The outrage on the Chesapeake unfortunately occurred about this time. It excited, of course, great exasperation. But an English minister was sent to disavow the outrage. Some technical punctilio was interposed to prevent any advances and explanations.

The people were hot for war, and for war with England. The "fierce Democracie" were boisterous and vehement for fight. The policy of England and France was driving us from the ocean. The advantages of a neutral position were being lost, while all the evils of proximity to the scenes of hostility were upon us.

The President now recommended an embargo upon our vessels. "France and England were told"—we quote from Mr. Garland—"that it was not conceived in a spirit of hostility to them, but was a mere municipal regulation. The truth was, however, and they did not fail to perceive it, that the whole object of withdrawing our commerce from the ocean, was to operate on those two nations. It was intended to starve France and her dependencies, and to break England, unless they would abandon their absurd pretensions over the rights of neutral nations. But when this happy result would take place, it was impossible to tell. For a measure of this kind to come home to the bosoms and the business of a great nation, must necessarily take a very long time. Indeed, it was reasonable to suppose that the desired object never could be accomplished in that way. The resources of England and of France were too great and too varied, to be seriously affected by a suspension of even the whole of American commerce. The event proved what, it would seem, a little forethought ought to have anticipated. After the embargo had been in operation for twelve months, those two nations were no nearer being forced into terms than they were at first; while their spirit of hostility was greatly exasperated.

"But what effect did the measure have on affairs at home—on the character of our people? Here it was disastrous in the extreme. An embargo is the most heroic remedy that can be applied to state diseases. It must soon run its course, and kill or cure in a short time. It is like one holding his breath to rush through flame or mephitic gas; the suspension may be endured for a short time, but the lungs at length must be inflated, even at hazard of suffocation. Commerce is the breath that fills the lungs of a nation, and a total suspension of it is like taking away vital air from the human system; convulsions or death must soon follow. By the embargo, the farmer, the merchant, the mechanic, the capitalist, the ship-owner, the sailor, and the day-laborer, found themselves suddenly arrested in their daily business. Crops were left to rot in the warehouses; ships in the docks; capital was compelled to seek new channels for investment, while labor was driven to every shift to keep from starvation.

"Sailors seeing the uncertain continuation of this state of things, flocked in great numbers to the British navy. That service which, in former years, they most dreaded, necessity now compelled them to seek with avidity. Smuggling was extensively carried on through the whole extent of our widespread borders; the revenue was greatly reduced; and the morals of the people were greatly corrupted by the vast temptations held out to evade the laws. It is difficult to tell on what classes of the community this disastrous measure did not operate. On the planting and shipping interest, perhaps, it was most serious. On the one, it was more immediate, on the other, more permanent, in its evil consequences."

These views are so sensible and so well expressed, that we will not weaken their force by elaborating them. It has been seen that the Executive denied that the embargo was a war measure. Upon his own principles, how was it constitutional? Under what clause of the Constitution, strictly or loosely construed, did it come? What specific grant would have been rendered nugatory without it as a means of execution? The effects of the measure upon the country were disastrous to the last degree. Well did Randolph say, "It was the Iliad of our woes." It ravaged and desolated like the march of an invading army. We punished ourselves, but England was not starved into concession.

With her navy sweeping the face of the sea, and gathering products from every clime, and tribute from every shore, it were as idle to expect to starve her by withholding our breadstuffs, as to attempt to bale out the ocean with a tincup. After trying it for a year or more, it was abandoned. The Legislature of Massachusetts, taking example from Virginia, declared it unconstitutional, and, the fiercest opposition to it having been aroused, threatened the integrity of the Union. Jefferson thought that it would have answered its purpose, if we could only have waited a little longer!

Randolph, with all his power and eloquence, opposed this measure.

The President advised that our ships should be kept from the sea, and laid up in dignified retirement in our own ports; a suggestion which, to our gallant tars, doubtless seemed like the advice to a man of spirit, to lock himself up in his house, for fear some ruffian might attack him on the street. Randolph held a different language. He advised the arming of the commercial marine, and to let it go out on the paths of a lawful commerce, repelling all force and invasion from every quarter.

Jefferson opposed the building of a navy, upon the ground that we would only be building ships for the British. He thought that gun-boats, to protect the harbors, would be the best provision for the protection of our coast.

How cruel was the injustice done to that little navy, planted with a niggard hand, and growing up in the neglect and under the frowns of the government, but which, in a few short years, won such trophies on the ocean, that Canning was forced to declare on the floor of the British Parliament, that it had broken the spell of the naval invincibility of England!

The non-importation act, of kindred nature to the embargo, though milder in its bearing upon our interests, succeeded that measure.

Jefferson's term was about expiring, and preparations

were made for the succession. Madison, late Secretary of State, was the favorite of the Republicans. Mr. Monroe was a rival aspirant. Randolph advocated his pretensions, and bitterly opposed Madison. A sharp contest was the result. But the Republican opposition to Madison had more talent than numbers. The result, as we know, was the election of Madison; and Mr. Monroe, after serving for a time as Governor of Virginia, was called into his cabinet.

The old difficulties with the belligerent powers of Europe continued to be the engrossing themes of political interest. At one time, a good prospect for peace seemed to open upon our relations. A law was passed by Congress, authorizing the President to proclaim a renewal of commercial relations with either of the belligerents, who should repeal its decrees as to us. Great Britain had promised to do this, if France would repeal her illiberal interdict; having only, as she declared, prohibited neutral trade to France and her colonies, in retaliation for the French interdict against neutral trade with her. France, accordingly, repealed her decrees so far as we were concerned, with this modification, however, that British manufactures should not be carried to her ports, &c., in American ships. England refused, on account of this modification, to repeal her orders, declaring that the true meaning of her proposition was, that when we should be restored to *all* our neutral rights by France, she would act in the same way. The effect of the modification will be seen at once; as, without it, English goods, accumulated for many years in her warehouses for want of a market, could be sold as readily through American ships in the interdicted markets, as if there were no war; and hence, Napoleon's whole restrictive system against Great Britain would be, in a great measure, if not entirely, countervailed. We answered, that so far as *we* wished it, the French interdict was removed, and that England was, therefore, bound to go *pari passu* with France.

Then came the called session of 1811–12, and a warlike message, and another embargo, to last for ninety days; and at the end of that time, to be followed, as was understood, by hostilities with England, if our grievances were not removed. Mr. Madison, it seems, was opposed to the embargo; but it was forced upon him. He wished the period for the conditional commencement of hostilities to be extended to the 4th of August. Had this course been adopted, there would, probably, have been no war; for, on the 23d of June, just five days after the declaration of war, a change having been effected in the British ministry, the orders in council were repealed, so far as they affected this country. But it was too late, of course, to arrest the war. All these war proceedings Randolph opposed. Whatever anticipated want of energy and efficiency—if there *was* any such want—existed in the Executive department, was more than supplied by the zeal and ability of the Legislature. The crisis had, as usual, brought out the great men. This Congress was a very different affair from the pliant, subservient tools that registered the edicts of the past administration. The leaders now were men of the first talents that have ever appeared on the theatre of public action. Henry Clay was in the chair of the House, John C. Calhoun in the chair of the Committee of Foreign Relations; and they were supported by a strong corps of auxiliaries:

Randolph had competitors now who could put him up to a strain of his great abilities; nay, who were, to say the least, full matches for him when at his highest mark of excellence. He was no longer the sun of the House, extinguishing all other lights by the effulgence of his blaze.

CHAPTER VIII.

Clay—Calhoun—Contrast between Clay and Randolph.

THE leading champions of the war party, in the House, were Henry Clay and John C. Calhoun. These men, now great historic names, were first appearing upon the national theatre. They were younger than Randolph in public service as well as in years. We think it unfortunate for all three that they attained eminence of position so soon. It had been better for their lasting fame, if they had risen by degrees into prominence, and had developed and matured, by slower stages, their powers of intellect and their political principles. They sprang, at once, almost from boys to statesmen. By a single leap, they vaulted, like young giants, into the first places of fame and influence. Doubtless, the enthusiasm and fervor of youth were important elements of success to leaders of a war movement; but it was next to impossible that a sudden elevation, like theirs, should not, to some extent, prove unpropitious to those studious habits, that cautious preparation, that philosophic judgment, and those matured and far-sighted views, essential to highest statesmanship.

Randolph's sagacity enabled him to take, at a glance, the measure of the young giants. "We shall have war now," he said, "those young men have their eyes on the presidential chair." If a harsh judgment, it must be confessed, this was a shrewd guess.

Throughout the prolonged discussions on foreign relations, Randolph and Clay seemed to be pitted against each other. For Calhoun, strange as it seems, Randolph had even less of courtesy and kindness than for Clay. Though Calhoun, to say the least, in the higher intellect, was fully equal to Clay, or to Randolph, he could scarcely be considered then, if at any time, a rival to either in oratory. His manner was senatorial. He was decorous in debate, singularly free from personalities, making no pretensions to what is called brilliancy, and indulging very sparingly in declamation. Clay was a more effective popular speaker. Calhoun was a great debater; Clay a great orator. Calhoun spoke from his intellect; Clay as much from his feelings. It was utterly impossible for two such men as Clay and Randolph to be friends, whether on the same side, or any other. There was too much will, too much impatience, too much ambition, too little yielding and compromising, too much equality of intellectual gifts, and too little congeniality of character and disposition, except upon points, where to be alike must lead to a difference. The rival positions of Clay and Randolph led to a good deal of bitterness of feeling, and to frequent, spirited and acrimonious sparrings, from which the Speaker's chair did not always protect the former. Randolph complained that Clay took the advantage of him, in putting a test question to the House, as to the war, and in so ruling points of order against him, as to cut off free debate.

The contrast between Randolph and Clay, will convey a clearer idea of the character of the former. These men were the most remarkable personages of the Congress of 1812, and were severally the leaders of their respective parties. We think, on the whole, that Randolph was not nearly so great a leader; not that the intellectual differences were so marked as other qualities, even more essential than great intellect, for leadership. Both were men of great eloquence, every where and in every thing eloquent. Both were men of high moral and personal courage; of chivalrous and gallant carriage; of instantaneous command of varied resources in debate; self-reliant; well-informed, if not learned, in all the information immediately connected with public affairs; and singularly gifted—as most popular orators are—with a happy facility in stating and reasoning upon facts. They seemed to have preferred this matter-of-fact mode of discussing public questions to subtle theoretic disquisitions, or to arguments based on abstract principles. But the character of their eloquence, as well as their manner, was very different. Randolph had more wit. Indeed, he was unequalled in this effective weapon of debate. He had too much of it.

It was not genial, but bitter, sardonic, sarcastic. It ran through and colored every thing he did, and every thing he said. It gave an edge to his most powerful arguments. It gave piquancy to his most beautiful statements. It prefaced, or rounded off even some of the most exquisite passages of his pathos. He had the rare faculty of condensing an argument into a single sentence, and he could distil that sentence into a biting sarcasm. In knowledge and skill in the use of language, too, he was Clay's superior, if, indeed, any American speaker or writer—for he wrote as well as he spoke—ever equalled him in his astonishing attainments and aptitude in this respect. He not only expressed himself clearly and fully, but his words were the most appropriate the English tongue afforded, for the expression of the exact idea and the exact shade of idea he designed to convey. This was not all. His exquisite and almost faultless taste embellished his opulent resources, and his sentences were musical, harmonious and beautiful. Yet his style was an Apollo, that exhibited masculine beauty only as the best form of health and strength. He had the rare faculty of painting a picture or a character by a single word—a faculty which Mirabeau possessed in so great perfection. His ideality was larger than Clay's. Indeed, he had enough of imagination to have written " Childe Harold ; " and he is the only man we have ever heard of, who could have written it. His fancy, also, was richer and more active. It is difficult to say whether Randolph or Clay had better powers of narration. Both were accurate. The narrative of both was vivid, clear and easy. Randolph was more piquant, fresh, racy, pictorial; Clay more close, compact, dignified and imposing.

Randolph's intellect had more cultivation. He drew more on the resources of others. His taste was more pure, and he had more comparisons, quotations, anecdotes, incidents, from the old classics and the new, from our own and foreign literature, especially the English plays and satires. Clay scarcely ever made a quotation or a classical allusion; and those he did make were usually close at hand, or had gotten into general circulation before he saw them. Randolph said more brilliant things, more uncommon things, more things that could not be said by any one else. He was always interesting and instructive.

Clay was sometimes vapid, and sometimes dull. It required a great occasion or unusual excitement to bring him fully out. The manner of the two was in striking contrast. Clay, irregular of feature, with nothing but a lofty brow and a bright eye to redeem his face from uncommon plainness, was commanding and dignified in his place, with features changing expression, with pliant ease, in sympathy with his feelings and thoughts. Both were graceful in gesture and action when speaking, though not remarkable usually for grace of movement. Clay's voice was unequalled. Full, musical, sonorous, flexible, never hoarse or obstreperous, though sometimes too loud for good taste, it was adapted to every subject and mood, and was especially potent in lofty and impassioned declamation, and in daring and indignant invective. In the mere carte and tierce of digladiation—in those passages of arms, in which personal matters made up the staple of the speech, Randolph had usually the advantage. In raillery, as galling as Canning's, in subtle irony, delicate and insinuated satire, covert scorn, and short and pungent witticisms, sudden surprises, ingenious turns, and sharp transitions from other subjects to a striking personality—in short, in all the arts of an accomplished satirist, Randolph was an adept. Clay was more direct, and less ingenious and flexible. He came at once to what he meant to say. He could not restrain his impetuosity, and put his indignation or resentment under the tuition of his art. Randolph was unequalled in one thing—in blending his sarcasm with his argument, so that he did not have to wander from the text to say bitter things. He rounded off the argument by some allusion or comparison, which was good as an illustration, and biting as a sarcasm. Randolph looked the embodiment of satire. Tall, emaciated, bloodless, the flashing eyes, blazing over the livid cheek, the skeleton finger, the proud and classic features, cold and unsympathizing, or flush with indignant scorn, the haughty air, the sneering lips, the sharp, bony face, and the keen, shrill, piping voice, slow, distinct, deliberate in its varied and most artistic enunciation, made up a manner which gave the fullest effect to intellectual qualities, so well answering to these organs of communication. There was nothing theatrical in all this, though Randolph was the most eccentric of men. His eccentricities, unlike most men's, so far from proceeding from vanity, came from a self-dependence and self-will, consulting his own taste and feelings, and almost wholly regardless of the taste and opinions of the world, if not actually scorning them. Probably, no other man of his time could express scorn with such withering effect. He felt more scorn than he uttered, even when his utterance was most extravagant. His pride was morbid—Lucifer-like. His dislike transformed the object into a thing of utter meanness and boundless contempt. It is galling enough for a man to feel that another man looks upon him with contempt; but to be under the basilisk eye of one who, in a tone of measureless superiority, looking the lord and master, barely condescends to treat the gentleman with the contemptuous recognition of a trembling culprit, and to administer to him judicial chastisement for his crimes, or impale him for his follies—to mark him out by his wit for the general derision, and coolly dismiss him to contempt, as an object worthy of no further notice—this is a burden which few men have the philosophy to bear with composure.

Clay had considerable humor. He had a good deal of aptitude for ridicule. But it was better natured. He laughed when he excited laughter. He had little propensity to sneer. Randolph's laughter—if he ever indulged in it—was the dry, short laughter of a derisive contempt. But Clay had the advantage in invective. There was frequently a coarseness in the Philippics of both, which marred their style. But Clay's invective was mixed with and colored by an honest, and usually a generous indignation. It was always associated with some high principle, which had been outraged or was excited by some act of cruelty or oppression, some flagrant desecration of a patriotic or moral duty, or by an unfeeling or unjust assault upon himself, his friends or his party. There was at least something human in it. Even when most violent and vindictive, it seemed a fierce explosion of uncontrollable wrath upon the head of the foe. Randolph's was more like a cold-blooded torture at the stake, or a deliberate pressing of the red-hot branding-iron into the smoking and hissing flesh of his writhing victim.

Clay's eloquence was better adapted, on the whole, for popular effect. His sympathies were large and active, and with the masses. His opinion of men was higher. There was a frankness and generosity about him, that conciliated, in advance, the favor of the hearer. He addressed the better and kinder feelings and impulses, with unrivalled skill. He was plausible, even when not sound. He had the temperament that insures popular favor; sanguine, bold, confident, adventurous. There was something leonine in his gait, look, action. He came up to every question and to every antagonist, without skulking or hesitation. No man was ever freer from prevarication, indirection or equivocation. Even Gen. Jackson pronounced him "a magnanimous rascal." He had all the requisites of leadership. He was easily approached, practical, familiar; yet dignified, social, kind, generous, manly, bold, enterprising; of great skill in reading men; rapid in taking his cue; quick to see and seize an advantage; firm and constant to his principles and his party; and of a will and a spirit that could not be subdued or broken. He rallied a broken party, reanimated the hopes of the despairing, led on a forlorn hope as if assured of victory, and never knew when to give up or abandon a field. Though few men, if any man, ever equalled him as a party leader in debate, this was not his most effective position. While Randolph was preparing his arguments and sarcasms in his solitary room, or in company with one or two friends, Clay was going about from room to room, from mess to mess, from party to party, from man to man, countervailing all opposition; explaining arm-in-arm to this man; refuting an argument to that, as the cards were shuffled; in cosy confidence with another, over a glass of wine; prevailing by force of reason and persuasion, with the member from North Carolina—by force of will with the member from Kentucky; making himself, in this sense, "all things to all men that he might win some." There was a contagion in his enthusiasm which communicated his spirit to his friends. Personally, he was at this time very popular. It could not be otherwise. Like Fox, his principles in his hot prime were better than some of his practices; but, like Fox, his heart was warm; and his free manners were forgiven in favor of the strong and manly virtues and ardent affections, which were the basis of his character. If the hands went wrong frequently, the mainspring was always right. His vices were all warm-blooded vices, and these are of all faults the most easily forgiven; indeed, we are not sure, when in association with such lofty, generous and chivalrous characteristics as those of Clay, whether they are not elements of popularity.

What sort of chance could the aristocratic anchorite stand against such a tribune, especially before the rough backwoods legislators, now coming in from the new states, representing a population clamorous for war, as another name for patriotism?

We think Clay the more eloquent man of the two. He spoke with more enthusiasm, with more loftiness, with better adaptation to the hearts of men; and this is the most effective office of eloquence. It takes more than brains to make a man. To convince the judgment even, you must often do more than show it a good reason. You must enlist the heart, for it sways the brains. But it was not merely by appeals to the sensibilities of men, that Clay was eloquent. In the discussion of questions, mainly to be determined by facts—whether equal to other men in more abstract questions or not—no man of his day could meet him before a popular audience. His style, though carefully cultivated, was not the best. It had considerable clearness and beauty, but it wanted terseness, variety and vigor as prominent characteristics. It had, as his speeches read, something of monotony in the regular roll and measured flow of the Roman sentences; but this blemish was not perceived when, in delivering his speeches, his magnificent voice, and animated and varied manner, gave to his language new point and effect. He spoke best off-hand. His sudden bursts of passionate emotion, when freshly animated by some noble and heroic conception, swelled out his utterance and expression into the sublimest strains of eloquence. In this great and telling power, Randolph was wanting. In particular passages, he was brilliant as Curran and Grattan; in all, he was interesting, enchaining attention, gratifying an exquisite taste, imparting instruction, and frequently moulding conviction; but the permanent impression left was not so strong. He had no faculty of making men in love with his views or conclusions, so that they did not desire, and could not endure, opposition to them. And then the stream of bitterness which he poured through his speeches, was unfriendly to that moral effect which is the highest office of eloquence, by exciting and purifying the moral sensibilities, and making the triumph of the orator the triumph of virtue itself. He upbraided like an enemy, instead of rebuking like a judge. Randolph was irregular, episodical, wandering sometimes from his subject; but the episodes were so delightful, that, like some of the chapters of Cervantes, the reader regrets the return to the main story. Clay was often diffuse, but seldom strayed from the text. Old Dr. Speéce, of Augusta, Va., used to say he would rather listen to Randolph's nonsense, than to any body else's sense. Randolph, skipping over processes of reasoning, frequently struck upon views so deep, so subtle and penetrating, and so happily expressed, that they were cherished more than the most elaborate reasoning. He had the great advantage of a style, singularly pure, yet unique and picturesque; and so condensed in particular passages, that his sayings were long remembered, and had the currency of axioms. No speaker of his day gave his hearers so much to reflect upon, and so many things to remember. If his mind were not of the largest calibre, it may be doubted if he were ever excelled, by any of his countrymen, in the keenness and subtlety of his intellect, and the clearness and vividness of his conceptions, or in the almost supernatural sagacity with which he saw the tendency of events and the characters of men. The tissue of his mind was of Damascus fineness; the fibre close and compact. Though without the force and bulk of Clay's, it had more keenness, polish, and finish. When Clay and he came together, it was as the battle-axe of Richard against the cimeter of Saladin. And these men were now in violent opposition, and were to continue a course of bitter and defiant hostility until long years afterwards, when they became reconciled, under circumstances highly honorable to them both.

CHAPTER IX

Randolph's Speeches against the War—His Moral Heroism—Calhoun's—Randolph's Feelings towards England—Excitement against Randolph—Defeated for Congress by Eppes—Goes into Retirement.

RANDOLPH opposed the declaration of war with all his powers. His speeches on this question were the noblest and most eloquent of his life. He knew he was sacrificing every thing by this opposition. The public exasperation had reached its height. The policy of inculcating hostility to England as a virtue had brought forth its fruit. The equivocating and time-serving course heretofore pursued, could not be continued longer. The people, especially the warlike population of the interior settlements, demanded war; and men were now in Congress who were willing to take the lead in bringing it on.

Randolph's position was heroic. Right or wrong, he showed himself a man true to his principles, and ready to be sacrificed for what his judgment assured him was the right. He did not wish war at all, because he saw that war was adverse to our interests, and to what he regarded as the true principles of our government. He saw and deprecated the effect of an offensive foreign war upon the relations of the State and Federal governments. Above the clamors of the crowds shouting for war with England, above the yells and screams of the excited populace in public meetings, and the storm of fierce denunciations poured out against himself, was heard his shrill, piping voice crying out for peace.

As we look back upon this scene, we are reminded of a later example of the same lofty heroism. We allude to the day when John C. Calhoun, in the American Senate, pale, emaciated, his eyes glaring, and his frame quivering with excitement, lifted up his voice *alone*, in that august body, in opposition to the Mexican war; and, trembling with passionate patriotism, swore that he would strike a dagger to his heart, before he would vote for an unjust war, heralded in by a lying preamble!

But, more especially, Randolph did not desire war with England. He had no prejudices against England. He saw and condemned her faults. He did not justify her conduct towards us. But he remembered that we were of the blood and bone of her children. He remembered that we spoke her language, and that we were connected with her by the strongest commercial ties and interests; that, though we had fought her through a long and bloody war, yet we had fought her by the light of her own principles; that her own great men had cheered us on in the fight; and that the body of the English nation were with us against a corrupt and venal ministry, when we took up arms against their and our tyrants. He remembered that from England we had inherited all the principles of liberty, which lie at the basis of our government—freedom of speech and of the press; the Habeas Corpus; trial by jury; representation *with* taxation; and the great body of our laws. He reverenced her for what she had done in the cause of human progress, and for the Protestant religion; for her achievements in arts and arms; for her lettered glory; for the light shed on the human mind by her master writers; for the blessings showered by her great philanthropists upon the world.

He saw her in a new phase of character. Whatever was left of freedom in the old world, had taken shelter in that island, as man, during the deluge, in the ark.

She opposed the only barrier now left to the sway of unlimited empire, by a despot, whom he detested as one of the most merciless and remorseless tyrants that ever scourged this planet. Deserted of all other men and nations, she was not dismayed. She did not even seek—such was the spirit of her prodigious pride—to avoid the issue. She defied it. She dared it—was eager—fevered—panting for it. She stood against the arch-conqueror's power, as her own sea-girt isle stands in the ocean—calm amidst the storm and the waves that blow and break harmlessly on the shore. She was largely indebted, but she poured out money like water. Her people were already heavily taxed, but she quadrupled the taxes. She taxed every thing that supports or embellishes life, all the elements of nature, every thing of human necessity or luxury, from the cradle to the coffin. The shock was about to come. The long guns of the cinque-ports were already loaded, and the matches blazing, to open upon the expectant enemy, as he descended upon her coasts. We came as a new enemy into the field. It was natural to expect her, in the face of the old foe, thought by so many to be himself an over-match for her, to hasten to make terms with us, rather than have another enemy upon her. No! She refused, in the agony and stress of danger, to do what she refused in other times. She turned to us the same look of resolute and imperturbable defiance—with some touch of friendly reluctance in it, it may be—which she had turned to her ancient foe. As she stood in her armor, glittering like a war-god, beneath the lion-banner, under which we had fought with her at the Long Meadows, at Fort Du Quesne, and on the Heights of Abraham, Randolph could not—for his soul, he could not find it in his heart to strike her then.

The war was declared. An immense excitement reigned throughout the country. The session at length closed, and Randolph came back to his constituents.

He was to be opposed at home. It was a desirable consummation to defeat him and break him down. He was the impersonation of the anti-war party. His defeat would greatly strengthen the administration. Mr. Eppes, the son-in-law of Mr. Jefferson, had removed into his district, to become a candidate against him. No stone was left unturned. The most flagitious reports of British influence and coercion, among other things, were put out against him. The excitement against him grew intense amongst the people. He was threatened with personal violence in one of the counties, if he came among them to address the people. Proudly defying his enemies, he went through the canvass. He exerted himself as he never did before. For hours he spoke, and men listened to his burning eloquence, without moving from their position. It was all unavailing. His old constituents deserted him. He was defeated; and, without a murmur, he bowed his head to the stroke, and went into retirement.

CHAPTER X.

Randolph's Religious Sentiments and Conduct—Death of his Nephew, Tudor Randolph—Extracts of Randolph's Letters.

About this time (1814) a strong impression was made upon Randolph's mind by religion. As he grew up, and for some years afterwards, he was disposed to be skeptical, even atheistical. But, later in life, the old teachings of his mother came back to his memory and his heart. As troubles multiplied upon him; as, one by one, the objects upon which he had placed his affections were torn from him; as, day by day, he experienced the worthlessness of those things which are sought as the great ends of life and sources of happiness, he grew more and more anxious about the dread future beyond this life. This change, in great part, was the fruit of that keen observation of men which distinguished him. The only really happy men he knew were Christians. He was intimate with Moses Hogue, F. S. Key, and William Meade, three men distinguished for talent and attainments, but still more eminent for piety, usefulness, and tranquil and happy lives. He turned his attention to religious studies. In the solitude of Roanoke—to which he had removed from Bizarre in 1810—he could give an almost uninterrupted devotion to such studies. He seems to have become firmly persuaded of the truth of Christianity. His progress in this work, marks a most interesting portion of the history of this extraordinary man. He had his doubts and difficulties. Clouds encompassed him. Many things were dark and unintelligible to his mind; but he seems to have sought, in a humble and child-like spirit, for light, where alone it could be found. The account he gives of this change is so interesting, that we give it, in his own words, to that noble friend, Frank Key, whose friendship for Randolph is itself a guaranty, that Randolph was not the cold-blooded misanthrope his enemies have painted.

"For a long time the thoughts that now occupy me came and went out of my mind. Sometimes they were banished by business; at others, by pleasure. But heavy afflictions fell upon me. They came more frequently and staid longer—pressing upon me, until, at last, I never went asleep, nor awoke, but they were the first and last in my recollection. Oftentimes have they awakened me, until, at length, I cannot, if I would, detach myself from them. Mixing in the business of the world I find highly injurious to me. I cannot repress the feelings which the conduct of our fellow-men too often excites; yet I hate nobody, and I have endeavored to forgive all who have done me an injury, as I have asked forgiveness of those whom I may have wronged in thought or deed. If I could have my way, I would retire to some retreat, far from the strife of the world, and pass the remnant of my days in meditation and prayer; and yet this would be a life of ignoble security. But, my good friend, I am not qualified (as yet, at least) to leave the heat of the battle. I seek for rest—for peace. I have read much of the New Testament lately. Some of the texts are full of consolation; others inspire dread. The Epistle of Paul, I cannot, for the most part, comprehend; with the assistance of Mr. Locke's paraphrase, I hope to accomplish it. My good friend, you will bear with this egotism; for I seek from you instruction on a subject in comparison with which all others sink into insignificance. I have had a strong desire to go to the Lord's Supper; but I was deterred by a sense of my unworthiness; and, only yesterday, reading the denunciation against those who received unworthily, I thought it would never be in my power to present myself at the altar. I was present when Mr. Hogue invited to the table, and I would have given all I am worth to have been able to approach it. There is no minister of our church in these parts. I therefore go to the Presbyterians, who are the most learned and regular; but having been born in the Church of England, I do not mean to renounce it. On the contrary, I feel a comfort in repeating the Liturgy, that I would not be deprived of for worlds. Is it not for the want of some such service that Socinianism has crept into the Eastern Congregations? How could any Socinian repeat the Apostle's creed, or read the Liturgy? I begin to think with you, about those people. You remember the opinions you expressed to me last winter concerning them. Among the causes of uneasiness which have laid hold upon me lately, is a strong anxiety for the welfare of those whom I love, and whom I see walking in darkness. But there is one source of affliction, the last and deepest, which I must reserve till we meet, if I can prevail upon myself to communicate it even then. It was laid open by one of those wonderful coincidences, which men call chance, but which manifest the hand of God. It has lacerated my heart, and taken from it its last hope in this world. Ought I not to bless God for the evil (as it seems in my sight) as well as the good?

"Is it not the greatest of blessings, if it be made the means of drawing me unto him? Do I know what to ask at his hands? Is he not the judge of what is good for me? If it be his pleasure that I perish, am I not conscious that the sentence is just?

"Implicitly, then, will I throw myself upon his mercy; 'not my will, but thine be done;' 'Lord, be merciful to me a sinner;' 'Help, Lord, or I perish.' And now, my friend, if, after these glimpses of the light, I should shut mine eyes and harden my heart, which now is as melted wax; if I should be enticed back to the 'herd,' and lose all recollection of my wounds, how much deeper my guilt than his, whose heart has never been touched by the sense of his perishing, undone condition, This has rushed upon my mind when I have thought of partaking of the Lord's Supper. After binding myself by that sacred rite, should passion overcome me, should I be induced to forget in some unhappy hour that holy obligation, I shudder to think of it. There are two ways only in which, I am of opinion, that I may be serviceable to mankind. One of these is teaching children; and I have some thoughts of establishing a school. Then, again, it comes into my head that I am borne away by a transient enthusiasm; or that I may be reduced to the condition of some unhappy fanatics who mistake the perversion of their intellects for the conversion of their hearts. Pray for me."

In a subsequent letter, he tells Key: "In a critique of Scott, vol. xii., upon the Bishop of Lincoln's 'Refutation of Calvinism,' it is stated, that no man is converted to the truth of Christianity without the self-experience of a miracle. Such is the substance. He must be sensible of the working of a miracle in his own person. Now, my good friend, I have never experienced any thing like this. I am sensible, and am always, of the proneness to sin in my nature. I have grieved unfeignedly for my manifold transgressions. I have thrown myself upon the mercy of my Redeemer, conscious of my own utter inability to conceive one good thought, or do one good act, without His gracious aid. But I have felt nothing like what Scott requires." Again to Dr. Brockenbrough, himself, it seems, at this time, disposed to be somewhat skeptical: "I am no disciple of Calvin or Wesley, but I feel the necessity of a changed nature, of a new life, of an altered heart. I feel my stubborn and rebellious nature to be softened, and that it is essential to my comfort here, as well as to my future welfare, to cultivate and cherish feelings of good will towards all mankind; to strive against envy, malice, and all uncharitableness. I think I have succeeded in forgiving all my enemies. There is not a human being I would hurt if it were in my power; not even Bonaparte."

Another misfortune fell upon him in the death of Tudor Randolph, the son of his brother Richard, and the last of the line. Randolph had designated him as the heir of his fortune, and looked to him as the representative of his house and name. The few pathetic words of his letter to Dr. Brockenbrough, who had announced the death of the young man, which had occurred in England, explain the effect of this blow upon his heart: "Your kind and considerate letter contained the first intelligence of an event which I have long expected, yet dreaded to hear. I can make no comment upon it. To attempt to describe the situation of my mind would be vain, even if it were practicable. May God bless you; to Him alone I look for comfort on this side of the grave; there alone, if at all, I shall find it."

The effect of this calamity on Randolph is thus described by Mr. Garland: "Many said his mind was unsettled; that this dark destiny drove reason from her throne, and made him mad. In the vulgar estimation of a cold and selfish world, he was surely mad; the cries of a deep and earnest soul are a mockery to the vain and unfeeling multitude. David had many sons; Randolph had this only hope, *the child of his affections*. Yet when Absalom was slain, 'the king was much moved, and went up to the chamber over the gate and wept; and as he wept, thus he said, ' O my son Absalom—my son, my son Absalom! would God I had died for thee. O Absalom, my son, my son!' "

As might have been expected, this new religious influence became, for a while, the controlling principle in Randolph's mind. He was so organized that, when he was interested in any subject, he concentrated his thoughts and feelings upon it, until he became nearly monomaniacal. Hence the extreme vividness of his ideas. For a long while, the hours of his solitude—for he was the most unsocial of men—were given up to thoughts and speculations upon the exceeding mysteries of religion; mysteries which have baffled the most gifted intellects, which are too deep for human ken to penetrate, and most dangerous to the stability of the best-balanced mind to dwell long upon. The inquisitiveness of his mind was such, that he could not restrain it from such daring speculations. The affairs of the world became tame and insipid. He came reluctantly to the consideration of the most exciting secular interests. He had been elected to Congress again, by his old, and, ever-after, faithful constituents, who sorely regretted their desertion of him before; and the election was contested, yet he took but little interest in the contest. Even public life had lost its zest. He afterwards declared that Washington City was as lonely a solitude to him as the shades of Roanoke. *The* one great subject was still uppermost in his mind. But no peace followed. The miracle he spoke of had not yet been wrought. The light was still absent from his soul. He returned to Roanoke long afterwards (in 1818), and, suddenly, the light shines upon him. His eyes are opened! He hears the voice Paul heard! He now sees the rainbow painted on the lately frowning sky. After freaks of eccentricity; after bursts of petulance and unkindness towards those about him, which seem inconsistent with a rational mind, he writes these lines to Key. Was it madness or the *miracle* that prompted them? Let the reader judge:

"Roanoke, Sep. 7, 1818.
" Congratulate me, dear Frank—wish me joy you need not: give it you cannot. I am at last reconciled to my God, and have assurance of his pardon, through faith in Christ, against which the very gates of hell cannot prevail. Fear hath been driven out by perfect love. I *now know that* you know how I feel; and within a month for the first time, I understand your feelings, and those of every real Christian."

The following note by him is so full of sense and so characteristic, that we insert it entire.

" It is my business to avoid giving offence to the world, especially in all matters merely indifferent. I shall, therefore, stick to my old uniform, blue and buff, unless God sees fit to change it for black. I must be as attentive to my dress, and to household affairs, as far as cleanliness and comfort are concerned, as ever, and, indeed, more so. Let us take care to drive none away from God, by dressing religion in the garb of fanaticism. Let us exhibit her as she is, equally removed from superstition and lukewarmness. But we must take care, that while we avoid one extreme, we fall not into the other; no matter which. I was born and baptized in the Church of England. If I attend the convention at Charlottesville, which I rather doubt, I shall oppose myself then and always to every attempt at encroachment on the part of the church, the clergy especially, on the right of conscience. I attribute, in a very great degree, my long estrangement from God, to my abhorrence of prelatical pride and puritanical preciseness; to ecclesiastical tyranny, whether Roman Catholic or Protestant; whether of Henry V. or Henry VIII.; of Mary or Elizabeth; of John Knox or Archbishop Laud; of the Cameronians of Scotland, the Jacobins of France, or the Protestants of Ireland. Should I fail to attend, it will arise from a repugnance to submit the religion, or church, any more than the liberty of my country, to foreign influence. When I speak of my country, I mean the Commonwealth of Virginia. I was born in allegiance to George III.; the Bishop of London (Terrick!) was my diocesan. My ancestors threw off the oppressive yoke of the mother country, but they never made me subject to *New England* in matters spiritual or temporal; neither do I mean to become so, voluntarily."

His deep respect for religion, and its influence upon his life were never lost; but, plunging into the excitements of political life, the strong impressions and the resolves, sincere when made, as is too frequently the case, in a great measure lost or intermitted their power.

CHAPTER XI.

Randolph for Vigorous Prosecution of the War—His Letter to the New England States—Re-elected to Congress—Opposes the U. S. Bank and the Tariff—His Illness and Despondency—Monroe's Administration—Randolph Opposes It—The Missouri Question—His Letters to Dr. Dudley—His Will—Denounces the Slavery Agitation—Opposes the Bankrupt and Apportionment Bills—Visits Europe—His Impressions of England—Opposes the Greek and South American Resolutions—Opposes Internal Improvements—Opinion of Chief Justice Marshall—Opposes the Tariff of 1824—Visits England and France.

WE must go back to trace Randolph's political course. The war declared, and himself in retirement, he was, of course, unconnected with the public measures of the interesting session of 1813–14. But, though opposed to the declaration of war, he was for its most effective prosecution. He had no sympathy with, and gave no support to, the enemy. There was, to say the least, great discontent in Massachusetts. The minority of the Legislature charged the majority with designing a separate treaty with England, providing for the neutrality of the New England States during the war. Randolph, having been assured that *his* voice would find a favorable hearing in New England, pub lished a letter to dissuade the people from so unpatriotic a course. This letter is, in all respects, equal to the best of Junius; with not less of point and directness, and even more of grace and eloquence than characterize the writings of that master of satire. He thus speaks of Adams and Madison: "The name of this man (John Adams) calls up contempt and derision wheresoever it is pronounced. To the fantastic vanity of this political Malvolio, may be distinctly traced our present unhappy condition. I will not be so ungenerous as to remind you that this personage (of whom, and his addresses, and his answers, I defy you to think without a bitter smile) was not a Virginian; but I must, in justice to ourselves, insist on making him a set-off to Madison. They are of such equal weight, that the trembling balance reminds us of that passage of Pope, where Jove weighs the beau's wits against the lady's hair:

"'The doubtful beam long nods from side to side,
At length the wits mount up, the hairs subside.'"

The language contains few papers more eloquent with patriotism, or invective against England, or in defence of the South, especially of Virginia, than this remarkable letter.

On a threatened attack of the British upon Virginia, Randolph took the field, but the enemy did not then appear.

No man saw more clearly the effect of a foreign war upon state-rights, than Randolph. He said that the country would come out of the war without a constitution. According to the creed of *his* school, he was not far from the mark.

The war over, the project of a National Bank, opposed by Clay and Madison in 1811, and now advocated as necessary—the necessity being a result of the war—came up in Congress. The war party, headed by Clay, Calhoun, Lowndes, and others in the House, and by Madison in the Executive department, now sustained the measure. Randolph opposed the bill in all its stages. He seems to have been hostile to all new-fangled modes of getting along in the world without labor; and, as such, he considered banking and speculation. He cherished, with as much pertinacity as Franklin, the old-fashioned virtues of economy, industry, and personal independence. Debt he considered a great evil and disgrace, and a bankrupt as a great criminal. "Mr. President," said he, one day in the Senate, in the midst of one of his most brilliant harangues, "I have found the philosopher's stone—Pay as you go." He condemned extravagance, paper-money, and trading on credit as a sort of Jeremy-Didlerism, which government should discountenance. He thought the evils of the times originated in looseness of morals, and inveighed with great power against the corrupting influence, and the despotic power of the banks. It was in opposition to this bill, that he said, "If I must have a master, let him be one with epaulettes—something that I can fear and respect—something that I can look up to; but not a master with a quill behind his ear."

He denounced the connection between the Bank and the

government as "a monstrous alliance' This was long in advance of "the divorce between Bank and State," which was a party motto in our day.

This certainly is very plain talk: "Let us not disguise the fact, sir (said Randolph, in the House) we think we are living in the better times of the Republic. We deceive ourselves: we are almost in the days of Sylla and Marius: yes, we have almost got down to the time of Jugurtha. It is unpleasant to put oneself in array against a great leading interest in a community, be they a knot of land speculators, paper jobbers, or what not: but, sir, every man you meet, in this House or out of it, with some rare exceptions, which only serve to prove the rule, is either a stock-holder, president, cashier, clerk, or door keeper, runner, engraver, papermaker or mechanic, in some way or other, to a bank. The gentleman from Pennsylvania may dismiss his fears for the banks, with their one hundred and seventy millions of paper on eighty two millions of capital. However great the evil may be, who is to bell the cat? who is to take the bull by the horns? You might as well attack Gibraltar with a pocket-pistol, as to attempt to punish them. * * * A man might as well go to Constantinople to preach Christianity as to get up here and preach against the banks."

Equally decided was Randolph's hostility to the Tariff bill of this session, which though ostensibly, a revenue measure, yet contained the seed-principle of protection, that ultimately germinated into the policy, which scattered abroad over the land so much of excitement and discord.

Randolph's health, at this time, was wretched. It never was good. He used to say he had been sick all his life. At his best state, he never had more than partial exemption from pain and feebleness. Now, he was in a very low condition. He had many violent attacks of acute disease, bringing him —some of them—to the very verge of the grave. Several of these spells were long protracted. The vital organs were affected; and he had no doubt, and no room to doubt, that he carried within him a fatal disease. His disease affected his mind and spirits, and colored all objects on which he looked. He became a confirmed hypochondriac. His correspondence breathes the dreariest despondency. Every letter is but a dismal picture of the acutest mental suffering and depression. Doubtless, the solitude to which he condemned himself, contributed greatly to this state of mind. He writes: "My case appears to me to be peculiarly miserable; to me the world is a vast desert, and there is no merit in renouncing it, since there is no difficulty. There never was a time when it was so utterly destitute of allurement for me. The difficulty with me is, to find some motive to action, something to break the sluggish tenor of my life. I look back upon the havoc of the past year, as upon a bloody field of battle, where my friends have perished."

And again to Key: " For my part, if there breathes a creature more empty of enjoyment than myself, I sincerely pity him. My opinions seem daily to become more unsettled, and the awful mystery which shrouds the future alone renders the present tolerable. The darkness of my hours, so far from having passed away, has thickened into the deepest gloom. I try not to think, by moulding my mind upon the thoughts of others; but to little purpose."

Under the influence of such feelings, no wonder that he did many things—what hypochondriac does not?—which were attributed to mental aberration. But he was far from mad. Indeed, whenever he lost the idea of himself and his sufferings, and grew interested in any subject, his mind gave out the sagacity and brilliancy that had distinguished it of old.

We come to the "era of good feeling"—the administration of Monroe. Amnesty had been declared for all past political offences, or, rather, a complete fusion of parties, had been accomplished. Federalism, heretofore maintaining, here and there, a solitary post on the lines, or a local ascendency in some of its strongholds, had surrendered, on terms of honor; and the old strifes of party were banished from the public councils. The lion had laid down with the lamb and a short political millennium had set in. Beside the stalwart old cockade Federalist sat the French disciple of the secret societies. There sceemed to be peace, if not friendship, between the old combatants. Though Randolph, at one time, was the partisan of Monroe, or, rather, preferred him to Madison, he seems afterwards to have held him in as great, if not greater, disesteem than his rival.

The young war-champions were still leaders over the incongruous mass; and, riding on a full tide of popularity seemingly secure of being, at no distant day, wafted into the first places of power.

The agitation of the Missouri question brought on a fierce excitement. It was during the pendency of this measure, that a collision occurred, which affected inharmoniously the personal relations of Randolph and Clay. Randolph took occasion to show the backslidings of the Republicans, and the departure of the government from its early republican tack; and inveighed particularly against the inconsistency of Clay's course on the Bank, the Internal Improvement, and the Tariff questions. He complained that he could not command the attention of the speaker (Clay); and stopped, in the course of his speech, "in mid volley," to rebuke him for this direliction. Clay, however, denied the impeachment, and professed that he was paying all possible attention. Randolph complained to his friends that Clay's manner towards him was usually petulant or arrogant—sometimes both

He spoke of Clay's conduct in the chair, as a dictatorship. Probably, it was a little too much to expect of a speaker to listen, with the most exemplary patience, to such a tirade as Randolph could pour out for "four hours," in exposition of the Chairman's inconsistencies.

Randolph opposed the Missouri restriction with all his might as impolitic and unconstitutional, and he combated the famous *compromise*, with equal vigor In reference to the rejection of the votes of Missouri, in the Presidential election, which involved the question of her admission into the Union, and the power to exclude her, because her constitution excluded free blacks from the State, Randolph said :

"This is no skirmish, as the gentleman from Virginia has said; this is the battle where Greek meets Greek. Let us buckle on our armor; let us put aside all this flummery, these metaphysical distinctions, these unprofitable drawings of distinctions without differences. Let us say now, as we have, on another occasion (the election of Jefferson and Burr in 1801), we will assert, maintain and vindicate our rights, or put to hazard what you pretend to hold in such high estimation."

The great excitement wrought upon him by the Missouri question, and by the death of Decatur, to whom Randolph was warmly attached, somewhat unsettled his intellect, and caused him to commit some extravagant freaks, which drew upon him the charge of madness. His mind, however, recovered its usual tone, shortly after his return to Roanoke.

The advice he gave young Dudley, in a letter written about this time, certainly betrays no touch of insanity. It is difficult to find any thing in all literature more truly sagacious, or "common-sensical,"—to use a word of his own coinage—than Randolph's fine letters to his young friend.

In December, 1821, when just leaving home for Washington, booted and spurred for his journey, and his horses and servants waiting at the door, he sat down and wrote the will, which was finally established, after so long a contest in the courts. By this will, he manumitted his slaves—three hundred in number—and provided a fund for the purchase of a tract of land for them; a disposition, which, as it turned out, evinced more of benevolence than sagacity. But never did he speak more wisely or see more clearly into the effect of any movement, than when, as early as 1821, he reprobated the effect of the agitation of slavery by the Abolitionists, upon the interests of the slave: "I am persuaded" (he said) " that the cause of humanity to these unfortunates has been put back a century—certainly a generation—by the unprincipled conduct of ambitious men, availing themselves of a good, as well as of a fanatical spirit, in the nation."

We must pass rapidly over other measures in which Randolph vindicated his consistency to his early creed, especially his opposition to the bankrupt law, and to the apportionment bill. The last bill proposed an increase of the ratio of representation in Congress. It reduced Virginia from a first position. It marked the first step in the melancholy decline she has since experienced, from her ancient estate. He opposed it, too, because he believed a numerous representation afforded the best security for good government.

On the passage of the bankrupt bill, he went to Europe He visited England. As he approached the shore, the sight of Old England brought back "the olden time" to his memory, and he shed tears of delight. "Thank God," exclaimed he, "that I have lived to behold the land of Shakespeare, of Milton, and of my forefathers. May her greatness increase through all time!"

The tour promised to be highly interesting and beneficial to the gifted traveller. He started with a better knowledge of the localities and persons of note in England, than most visitors, and, indeed, than most intelligent natives possess.

He was received and treated with great attention and kindness, and left an excellent impression upon those with whom he came in contact. The refined and cultivated society of England was greatly to his taste; and he returned home with a large store of valuable knowledge, and many pleasant memories.

He returned in time to take his seat in the eighteenth Congress. The Greek and South American resolutions were taken up. The first expressed sympathy for Greece in her struggles with the Turk; and the other *resolved*, that we could not see, without inquietude, any forcible interposition of the allied powers of Europe, on behalf of Spain, to reduce the Spanish colonies, whose independence we had recognized, to subjection. These were very captivating themes. They were redolent of eloquence. In the hands of Webster, Poinsett and Clay, they were made the topics of a brilliant and glowing declamation. Randolph opposed these resolutions. He turned from the poetic side of the question, to its more prosaic aspect. He was the advocate " of a fireside policy"—of the principle of letting foreign nations alone, and not mixing ourselves up with them; waging no wild crusade for liberty. " Let us," said he, " adhere to the policy laid down by the second, as well as the first, founder of our Republic—by him who was the Camillus, as well as Romulus of the infant State—to the policy of peace, commerce, and honest friendship with all nations, entangling alliances with none—for to entangling alliances you must come, if you once embark in policy such as this." He concluded :—" For myself, I would sooner put the shirt of Nessus on my back than sanction these doctrines—doctrines such as I never heard from my boyhood till now. They go the whole length. If they prevail, there are no longer any Pyrennees; every bulwark and barrier of the Constitution is broken down."

The resolutions were killed off.

Next came the question of Internal Improvement. Randolph opposed this measure, as he had opposed all the others, with all his eloquence and vigor of argument. The bill passed, however, by a large majority.

Opposed to Marshall, as he was, and had ever been, and especially to some of the doctrines laid down by the Chief Justice in the cases of *Gibbons and Ogden, and Cohen and Virginia*, which were decided about this time, Randolph spoke of him in a very different tone and spirit from those of Jefferson. He said, " No one admires more than I do the extraordinary powers of Marshall's mind; no one respects more his amiable deportment in private life. He is the most unpretending and unassuming of men. His abilities and his virtues render him an ornament, not only to Virginia, but to our nature. I cannot, however, help thinking, that he was too long at the bar before he ascended the bench; and that, like our friend P., he had injured, by the indiscriminate defence of right or wrong, the tone of his perception (if you will allow so quaint a phrase) of truth or falsehood."

The tariff bill of 1824, came up, and, it is needless to

say, that Randolph exhausted all of his ability in opposition.

He sought relief from sickness and from the cares of public life, by another trip to England.

The second impression made by England upon him seems to have been quite as strong as the first. He said: "There never was such a country on the face of the earth as England; and it is utterly impossible that there ever can be any combination of circumstances again to make such a country hereafter as Old England is. God bless her!"

He crossed over to France, but he seems not to have been greatly pleased with the French metropolis or people.

CHAPTER XII.

Presidential Election of 1824—Election of Adams by the House—Randolph opposes the Administration—Elected to U. S. Senate—Proceedings in the Senate in relation to the Panama Mission—President's Message in reply—Randolph's Speech on the Message—His Expression "The Puritan and the Blackleg"—Duel with Clay—Third visit to Europe—Defeated for the Senate by Tyler—Elected to the House—Opposes the Administration throughout—Advocates Jackson's Election—Retires from Congress—Elected to the Virginia Convention to amend the State Constitution—Opposes all Innovations—Mission to Russia—Returns Home—Nullification—The Proclamation and Force Bill—Randolph denounces Jackson—Sustains South Carolina.

The presidential election of 1824 resulted in the return of Crawford, Jackson, and Adams to the House—no choice having been made by the people. Randolph seemed to have been almost indifferent to the result; if he had any preference, it was the barest possible inclination towards Crawford.

But when Adams was elected, through the great influence of Clay, then the most influential man in Congress, Randolph immediately took up arms against his administration. Doubtless, personal feeling had a good deal to do with this early opposition. Randolph regarded old John Adams with a cordial and unconquerable aversion. He visited upon the son this hatred. But the younger Adams had aggravated this sentiment by ratting over and carrying information—not too authentic, it was said—to Jefferson, of treasonable designs, on the part of certain Federalists of New England; and this communication had been used to the disparagement of the anti-war party, of which Randolph was the leader.

Randolph's dislike was mixed with contempt. He thought Adams not only a bad man, but a mean man; and very freely gave expression to this sentiment. Clay he disliked. They were old enemies. Clay had been all powerful. He had carried every thing before him. He had prevailed over Randolph in almost every important measure on which they had divided. He had more general popularity than any man in the Republic; though running, as he did, against men popular in particular sections, he did not receive as many votes as any of the three opposing him; yet he was the second choice of nearly all. Had Clay been returned to the House (and he came very near it), the probability is, that he would have been elected President.

Clay had committed the astounding blunder of taking office under the administration he had brought into power. That was enough to effect his ruin. Randolph had an opportunity to pay him off all old scores. Success had spoiled Clay's tactics. He had been the most successful man of his time; for he attempted more than any other, and succeeded in nearly every thing he attempted. His intrepid and enterprising spirit had carried him successfully over all opposition. He did not look about him, nor pause to weigh the consequences of his movements. He accepted the premiership. Suddenly a clamor was raised about his ears, which opened his eyes to the consequences of his position. The demonstrations of popular disapproval were too patent and unmistakable, not to awaken even *his* sanguine spirit to a consciousness of the fatal error he had committed. He saw it too late. He had tasted the forbidden fruit, and the gates of the political paradise were closed on him for ever.

Randolph had been elected to the Senate of the United States shortly after the opening of Congress. The President communicated a message to the Senate, on the subject of the Panama Mission. A motion was made in the Senate for a call upon the President for further information. Some further documents were sent in. Mr. Van Buren offered a resolution, that the discussion in relation to the Panama Congress, should be with open doors; and inquiring of the President whether there was any objection to the publication of the documents he had transmitted.

Randolph, taking the conservative side, as he usually did, opposed these resolutions; but they were passed.

The President answered the next day, leaving the question of publication to the Senate, and foolishly insinuating, pretty distinctly, that the motives of the Senate, for this departure from usage, were no better than they should have been.

Randolph took fire at this message, and let off a speech

of great bitterness and intemperance. He concluded his speech with this sentence: " I was defeated, horse, foot and dragoons—cut up, clean broke down by the coalition of Blifil and Black George—by the combination, unheard of till then, of the Puritan with the blackleg."

It is difficult to say whether the wit of this diabolical antithesis, or the charge it conveyed and endorsed, was more mischievous to the illustrious victim. The feather was nearly as hurtful as the shaft. Certain it is, that, like the arrow of Cullum Moore, this sarcasm passed through the mark. It was the very thing that was wanted by the opposition. It gave voice to a general suspicion. It authenticated a vague and irresponsible charge, and moulded the charge into the shape of current coin, stamped for universal circulation. Clay was already smarting under the charge. He was as proud as Randolph, of as pure and unsoiled honor as any man that ever breathed, and entirely conscious of his innocence. He eagerly resented this cruel attack; the more, because it came from an old enemy, who ought to have had more magnanimity than to have made it upon him, when he could not reply. He called Randolph to the field. Randolph answered the challenge.

The meeting of these remarkable men is suggestive. There stood on the banks of the Potomac, on that bright April evening, as the sun was declining behind the blue hills of Virginia, in the attitude of combatants, two men, around whom gathered, probably, a more stirring interest than around any other two men in the Union; and yet their political opinions and their personal history were as opposite as their persons, when they stood in their places. They were alike only in chivalry of bearing, integrity and independence of character, genius and pride. They had to all appearance met now to fight to the death with physical weapons, as they had met so often before, to do battle with the weapons of intellectual warfare. Their opposition had been unceasing. Probably, they had never agreed in one prominent public measure, since they were in public life together. Each looked upon the other as, if not the ablest, at least as the most annoying and dreaded opponent of his political principles and personal aims. They were, in early life, and to some extent, still, representatives of different phases of society. RANDOLPH, born to affluence; descended from a long and honored line; commanding all that wealth and family influence can give; with the best opportunities for education; accustomed, almost from infancy, to refined and intellectual society; the representative of the free-holders, and inhaling, with the atmosphere around him, the spirit of caste, which, in his circle, curiously intermingled itself, as in the English barons, with a love of freedom; aristocratic in many of his principles, and still more aristocratic in many of his practices; and CLAY, born in obscurity, of humble parentage—the first man of his family known out of his county—" the mill-boy of the Slashes"—without early opportunities or powerful friends; *rising*, at last, to be a deputy-clerk, and rejoicing in the rise; reading, in the spare hours released from manual toil, the rudiments of the law; going out into the backwoods of Kentucky, to find a "location" among the hunters and pioneers of that then remote territory, with but faint hopes, even in a breast not prone to despondency; seemingly unconscious of the talents and energies he possessed; aspiring to three hundred dollars a year, as the height of his good fortune; taking early a position at an able bar; rising rapidly to the head of it; soon going out into politics; mingling familiarly with the frontier population around him, and identifying himself with their character, habits, pursuits, and feelings; wrestling with the strong, though sometimes rough, champions for the favor of a vigorous, hard-sensed, patriotic and unsophisticated people; winning his way by his talents, and by a boldness as necessary as talents; literally fighting his way up over obstacles of all kinds, and men of all sorts and characters; first, in the State Legislature—then in the United States Senate—in the House—in the Speaker's chair—and now in the Cabinet; these were the two men, alike in splendid gifts of intellect, yet so unlike in character and circumstance, who now, weapon in hand, stood opposed in mortal combat.

The incidents that marked the meeting were characteristic of the men. Randolph refused to apologize or explain, because he conceived that he, a senator, was not amenable to demand for an explanation of words, spoken in his place, of the conduct of a Cabinet Minister; yet, with a singular inconsistency, he held himself responsible in the field. He seems to have gone upon the ground determined not to return Clay's fire; thinking that it was no violation of the anti-duelling laws of Virginia to be shot at, when no attempt was made by him to shoot. Randolph was one of the best pistol shots in the United States. Clay was out of practice; and the duel had been so arranged by the seconds, in their desire to avoid a fatal result, as to allow no opportunities for practising. *The word* was to be so given out as to force the shots as quickly as possible. When the mode of giving it was rehearsed to Clay, he requested it to be given with more deliberation, fearing that he should not be able to fire in time. Thinking that Clay's motive in this request, was a purpose to take his life, Randolph changed his intention of not firing, and determined, if he could, to disable, but not to kill his adversary.

Randolph's pistol fired accidentally before the word was given, the hair-trigger being set too finely. The shot fell into the ground, a few feet in front of him. This accident was embarrassing. Clay generously relieved the embarrassment, by exclaiming that the firing was evidently an accident, and begged that the affair might go on. The first shot missed. Clay afterwards interrupted the efforts to bring the matter to an adjustment, by throwing out his hand in his lofty way, and remarking, "Gentlemen, this is child's play." Clay's next shot cut Randolph's coat near the hip. Randolph fired in the air, remarking to Clay that he did so. Randolph then advanced and was met half way by Clay. The parties shook hands—Randolph telling Clay that he was in debt to him for a coat, and Clay expressing his

11*

gratification that he was no deeper in his debt. The parties afterwards exchanged cards and civilities.

This passage of arms was a brilliant vindication of a nice sensibility to honor, and of a generous and magnanimous spirit. It throws light on the character of Randolph; for though wanting in charity to men, and hasty and harsh of judgment, he was far from being cruel or implacable.

The session of Congress over, Randolph took his third trip to Europe.

In 1826, he was defeated by John Tyler for the Senate, and seems to have borne his defeat without a murmur. When his loved mother withheld her favors, he submitted like a docile child. He never electioneered for office. No one ever held himself more aloof from the position of a mendicant for place, or shrank, with more instinctive disgust, from the low hucksterings or the under-handed arts of the demagogue.

The administration of Adams was in a minority in Congress. The majority resolutely opposed its policy and recommendations, and, up to this time, successfully. Randolph had a leading, if not *the* leading position in the opposition; and his policy was full of tact. He was for letting the administration stand still in the middle of the sea, and to suffer it, with the leak it had sprung, slowly, but surely, to settle and sink; or, as he expressed it,—" Our play is to win the game; to keep every thing quiet; to finish the indispensable public business and go home." He imported the expression, " masterly inactivity."—first used, we believe, by Horace Walpole—which has been so much bandied about of late, and applied it to the policy to be pursued against the administration; which, opposed by various parties, would be strengthened by any definite creed or set of measures, on the part of its heterogeneous opponents. He was not for parrying but for thrusting—for carrying the war into Africa, by a vigorous assailment of those in power; for he knew full well that a merely defensive position is a losing game, in politics as well as in war.

Randolph was returned by his old constituents to the House. The same policy was pursued. Gen. Jackson became the candidate of the opposition. It was foreseen by all men that the old dynasty was going out. The election resulted in favor of the hero. Randolph retired from Congress.

For the last two or three years, his health became even worse than before. His constitution was a wreck. His mind had lost much of its strength and coherence. His speeches had deteriorated. They had become more rambling, desultory, disjointed, eccentric, extravagant. There were still vivid, lightning-like flashes—still passages of rare wit and beauty, lovely spots of sentiment, and bold original views; but they were often deformed by coarse vituperation, and weakened by repetitions and prolixity. He was incapable of the sustained power and elasticity, which distinguished him in better days.

The Virginia convention to form a state constitution met in 1829, and he was a member. He attracted general and eager attention. He was the cynosure of all eyes. In the assembly which brought together all the talent of the State— the Ex-Presidents, the Chief Justice of the United States, the names already become national—names then just rising into prominence—the first inquiry of the stranger was for Randolph of Roanoke. Shrivelled to a skeleton, huddled together in his solitary seat, the old veteran sat apart from the busy throng, watching with his keen, sarcastic glance, the progress of the proceedings, or moodily absorbed in his own gloomy reveries. He had dragged his shattered frame, with no pleasant feelings, into that assemblage. He had come, in the spirit of a pious duty, to the old commonwealth to which alone he professed to owe allegiance. He had come to ward off, if he could, the blow which threatened the destruction of the OLD CONSTITUTION, under which he had grown up, and which was the representative of all in the past, that was glorious and honorable of the land of his fathers. The attempt to despoil her of the charter, under which she had marched out to conquer her freedom, and under which her great men had been nurtured, inspired him with something of the fire of his fresher years. The olden day, to which he was so prone to refer, when Patrick Henry, and George Mason, and the Randolphs and the Lees held sway over the fortunes of the state; when the old families flourished; when the gentry gave law to the state, and the state to the confederacy, came back to his memory. He had always declaimed upon the degeneracy of the times; but he never even contemplated such degeneracy as the surrender of the state, to what *he* denominated, a rabble rout of non-freeholders; committing the honor and property of Virginia to the keeping of its poverty, improvidence and ignorance. He opposed *all* changes. Failing in that, he sought to limit as much as possible the alterations proposed, —to retain as much as possible of the spirit and conservatism of the old constitution. His speeches were the most interesting, and, probably, not the least effective, that were made in that august assembly.

And now, these labors over, and the new administration installed, an autograph letter from Gen. Jackson, couched in terms the most flattering and respectful, came to him, tendering him the post of Minister to Russia. And, alas! poor old man!—with the example of Clay, too, before him!—he accepted it!—accepted it, when, daily, he spoke of death as an expectant and not dreaded guest; when, nightly, the sweat of a fast-progressing disease was on his brow; when his mind was alternately flashing out in light and sinking back into darkness; when an Arctic winter was the climate to which the consumptive southerner was invited; when a strange people were to be the company for him, who could scarcely endure with patience the presence of a countryman; when patient diplomacy was to be the business for one who could not always restrain himself, even on ordinary occasions, from fitful bursts of vehement anger; when the forms and etiquette of a court were to be the clogs and fetters of the proud Republican, who had never known self-denial or opposition to his own whims, and whom no restraints of opinion could keep from breaking out into startling eccentricities; and when, emaciated to a skeleton, the exhibition of his person must have caused to his acute sensitiveness the keenest mortification. But this was not all. He was physically unfit for the duties of the post; and the office was to be almost a sinecure. He was now in the pay of the Federal government—a placeman—a " mercenary "—Randolph of Roanoke—like the rest! He had never known before any service, as he never acknowledged any fealty, to any other sovereign, than the Commonwealth of Virginia. He now put on and wore the Federal badge. He had scourged, with whips of scorpions, the placemen—the flunkeys—the *parvenus*—the hirelings of Federal power—and all office-holders were such to him. He had won his influence AS THE GREAT CHAMPION OF THE STATES, by never taking pay, or holding office, from the Federal Government. In one of his beautiful speeches, he said : " I will go back to the bosom of my constituents—to such constituents as man never had before, and never will have again, and I shall receive from them the only reward that I ever looked for, but the highest that man can receive—the universal expression of their approbation—of their thanks. I shall read it in their beaming faces; I shall feel it in their gratulating hands. Their very children will climb around my knees, to welcome me. And shall I give up them and this ?—and for what ? For the heartless amusements and vapid pleasures of this abode of splendid misery, of shabby splendor ?—for a clerkship in the war office, or a foreign mission, to dance attendance abroad, instead of at home, or even for a department itself?" He *did* desert them for this ill-fated mission. He closed the career of the GREAT COMMONER, with the diplomatic ribbon fluttering from his button-hole. He went out—did nothing—pocketed out-fit, in-fit, and salary, and came home to hear the shouts of derision, with which the old Federalists and the National Republicans were filling the air!

As might have been expected, the climate of Russia aggravated his disease, and precipitated its fatal termination. He became addicted to opium, and it contributed to those aberrations of mind, which now became more frequent and protracted than ever.

A year passed, and a new question agitated the land. The tariff of 1828 had been succeeded by that of 1832; and South Carolina prepared to resist. Randolph was in communication with the South Carolina leaders, and went with them in their course of opposition. That gallant State at last raised the banner of forcible resistance—for such it was. She passed her celebrated ordinance. Gen. Jackson issued his famous Proclamation. Randolph was, as he expressed it, " a Jackson man" up to this time. But he was so no longer. He was aroused to fury by this bold proceeding. True to his old principles, he could neither be purchased by gratitude for the past, nor by expectations for the future. He took the field against this measure. Too weak to stand, he took his seat on the hustings, and delivered to his constituents, at every court-house in the district, speeches against this Federal measure. He saw now what he had done. He had raised up a man, destined to exert a stronger influence against his doctrines, than all the Presidents in the Union put together.

In the name of State-Rights, in order to break down Adams and Clay, he had contributed to bring Jackson into power; and now, from *him* came the Proclamation, which ignored all the sanctions of State-Rights; which asserted the unqualified dominion of the Federal Government over the States, their laws and ordinances; and which shook the halter in the face of the sons of a State, who dared to act in obedience to the State authorities, in opposition to the Federal laws. No wonder Randolph raved. No wonder he spoke of buckling himself to his horse Radical, and plunging into the fight. Nor did these doctrines only appear on the face of the paper. There were, also, the warning and the threat. There were the obedient majorities in Congress. There were the Force bills; the soldiers under arms; the navy, waiting the orders to sail for the blockaded port; and not a single state to help South Carolina in her danger; and even she divided against herself. Worse than all, behind the Proclamation and the threat, stood the iron man, who knew no fear and no relenting, as immovable as a mountain, and as inexorable as death; and all around him, in the North, South, East, and West, were thousands of the friends of this great chief and most of his opponents, shouting out their applause of his proceeding and his doctrine. Randolph's keen eye saw at once the position of things: "If," (said he), "Madison filled the Executive chair, he might be bullied into some compromise. If Monroe was in power, he might be coaxed into some adjustment. But Jackson is obstinate, head-strong and fond of fight. I fear matters must come to an open rupture. If so, the Union is gone." He spoke of the Proclamation as the ferocious and blood-thirsty proclamation of our Djezzar Pacha.

He added: "There is one man and only one, who can save this Union; that man is HENRY CLAY. He has the power, and, I believe, he will be found to have the requisite patriotism and firmness."—What a commentary upon the sagacity of statesmen! Henry Clay, to put down whose "wild federalism" on some small police measures in the comparison, Gen. Jackson was elected, now appealed to to save the country from that degree of Federalism, which proposed to crush out the life of a State beneath the feet of a Federal army!

Randolph was not mistaken. Gen. Jackson was as firm as a rock. He was not a compromising man. He proposed nothing but unconditional submission to Federal law, or the halter or the bayonet. This was all he had to say. Clay stepped forward, seized his own cherished offspring, and threw it in the breach to save his country, as Curtius threw himself and his horse into the yawning chasm in the streets of Rome. And thus the political history of Randolph closed. It terminated where it began, in a contest for State-Rights. It began, by lifting his lance against Patrick Henry, and it ended, by turning its point against Andrew Jackson!

CHAPTER XIII.

Randolph as a Statesman—The Leader of the State-Rights Party—Contrast between his Policy and Clay's—His Consistent and Heroic Devotion to his Principles.

WE have signally failed, in the imperfect review we have given of the political career of John Randolph, if we have not shown him to have been something more than an eccentric orator and brilliant wit. We think that he was one of the most *consistent* statesmen the Republic has ever produced; and that he is to be regarded as the great leader and champion of the State-Rights party. The merit is his, if it be a merit, of governing his whole policy by the rudimental principles of State-Rights, as those principles were propounded on the organization of the party. He opposed nearly every measure—from whatsoever administration or man proceeding—in conflict with those principles. Their friends were his friends, their enemies his enemies. Witness his opposition to the Embargo, to the entire system restrictive of commerce, to the war with England, to all offensive war, to the Banks, the Tariff, Internal Improvements, the

Missouri Restrictions, qualified by the compromise or unqualified, to all foreign alliances or affiliations, to the Panama Mission, with its ulterior objects, to the Proclamation and the Force Bill; and his vehement support of all the affirmative doctrines and measures of State-Rights policy. Who else can show so clean a record? The answer is—not one! He went further. He was for the most abstemious possible exercise of power compatible with the carrying on of government, even when such power was unquestionably within the pale of the constitutional grants. He sought to restrict the governmental machine to its simplest and most indispensable workings.

But, it is asked, where are his monuments? Upon what great measure of civil polity can his friends lay their hands and say, "This is Randolph's work?" None, we admit. But, then, it must be remembered, that his policy was the policy of quiet, healthy growth, and governmental non-action. He might, if he now lived, point to the heaps of rubbish, the ruins of systems he had torn down, but he could not point to any thing he had built up; for his policy was negative and simply protective, not positive and erective. His policy was to protect the rights of the citizen, and thus to stimulate him to work out for himself and the state the highest results of civilization.

A contrast between his policy and Clay's illustrates the former. Clay thought the General Government a vast and mighty agency, which, made vital by the will of a free and energetic people, could accomplish, by its affirmative action, signal blessings to his country and the world. He desired to build up a mighty nation, whose power should be felt and acknowledged throughout the world. The AMERICAN SYSTEM was, through a National Bank, to afford a national currency, and to facilitate the transactions of commerce; Internal Improvements were to be the ties of a close commercial communion and personal correspondence between the different sections, and to bind the States together with bands of iron; the Tariff was to make us independent of foreign nations for the munitions of war and the comforts of life, and to build up vast storehouses of wealth for the country; the navigation laws were to foster an independent marine; the Panama mission to place us at the head of the continent, controlling and drawing its trade, and governing its policy; the public lands were to give to the States the means of improving their communications and educating their people; and a navy and army were to protect our commerce on the ocean, and command the respect of foreign powers. HE boasted that he was an AMERICAN CITIZEN, and was proud of the title, knowing no north, no south, no east, no west. Randolph, on the other hand, claimed to be a VIRGINIAN, owing his primary and only allegiance to that venerable Commonwealth, and acknowledging the Federal Government but as a limited agency, which she, with others, had established, for a few simple purposes. His doctrine was that that government was to be watched with jealousy; that it had an inherent proclivity to enlarge powers originally too strong; which enlargement would lead to the greatest possible evil, *consolidation;* for he regarded that as the worst species of foreign domination.

Such were the different views of these great leaders.

We think that Randolph was not only a consistent statesman, but A GREAT MAN. He possessed the indispensable elements of greatness—WILL AND CONSTANCY. No man had these high faculties in greater degree. Bruce, Hannibal, and Cæsar, were scarcely his superiors in this respect. His admiration of Patrick Henry and his confidence in him, were stronger than he felt for any other man; yet, when Henry supported the doctrines of the Federal party, *he* stood firm—nay, the first speech he ever made was to the crowd, yet thrilling with the eloquence of Henry. He was an ardent supporter, a personal friend, a blood-relative of Jefferson. When Jefferson abandoned—as he thought—his principles, Randolph stood fast. When Madison took the same policy, Randolph kept his place. When Monroe went the same way, he remained unmoved. When the whole Republican party deserted them, their desertion but quickened his zeal and strengthened his steadfastness. When the whole country rose up to second the leaders in their aberrations, Randolph was found firmly planted in his old position. When even his native State went over, he still lingered by the flag. His constituents rose against him, but they did not move him from his purpose. When Gen. Jackson, whom, more than any other man, he had contributed to bring into power, and who had rewarded him with office, turned upon State-Rights, he turned upon *him* the last energies of mind and soul left him, with the fury of a tigress, robbed of her whelps. He was, in 1806, the most rising man of his age, in the Republic. He had only to lie still upon the Republican wave, and be wafted into the highest places of the government. He saw the principles he had professed assailed by his friends, and he hesitated not a moment to oppose those friends, to the certain destruction of all his hopes. Nor did he oppose assaults upon State-Rights in a halting, compromising, hesitating spirit; holding open the door of ·conciliation, while he uttered his defence of his principles. No! he threw away the scabbard when he drew the sword, and defied all extremes of hostility, while he waged a warfare without mercy and without quarter. Let it be remembered, too, that this warfare was not a single campaign; it was not against a single enemy or dynasty; it was the protracted warfare of a whole life—against every single administration, from the first to the last, that assailed his cherished doctrines; and this hostility continued as long as he could lift a lance, or utter a war-cry.

No man had more individuality. He thought and acted for himself. He was afraid to meet no man. He never hesitated, not only to oppose measures, but to oppose men, not of the opposite party only, but of his own. His moral courage was equal to Luther's. Whatever danger, personal or political, to him or his fortunes, or his principles, was in the way, he fearlessly met. No combination could daunt him. No association of venal interests could inspire him with awe. Whatever he chose to say, whomsoever it might affect, he said it, and said it in the plainest English, and with the most cutting emphasis. He could neither be intimidated by his fears, nor bribed by his interests, nor, what is more common, seduced by his virtues. No friendship or sense of kindness could secure the perpetrator of an act of political or moral delinquency from his exposure. No personal or political obligation—if he ever acknowledged such—could make him blink, or waive, or deny a duty. He was a man of a scrupulous and religious veracity in word, act, and thought. Self-love, strong as it was, did not blind him to the truth; for he was as harsh a judge of himself as of others. The light of an ardent and dazzling imagination did not hide the cold, common-place, naked truth from his eyes. His allegiance to truth was marvellous. He did not hesitate to announce sentiments so unpopular, truths so unacceptable, so revolting to the multitude, that men of ordinary boldness would shrink with terror, from fear of being compromised by listening to them. He had no arts of concealment. He could not restrain his sense of disgust of men, or his contempt of them in their presence. If sometimes—pity that it was so—he was unduly harsh to humble men, he was free from the meanness of seeking to conciliate the powerful and the great.

If history gives us any knowledge of any other public man so true and loyal to AN IDEA, as this man was, we do not know the volume in which it is written. He was constant, throughout his long and troubled life, to this leading principle. Other men deserted it, others forgot it, others deviated, and, after a while, came back, others were converted to it; but, amid all fluctuations and backslidings—through evil and through good report—in adversity and in prosperity—through all changes of dynasty—alone or in whatever associations,

"Among the faithless, faithful only he."

He stood, like a light-house, solitary and alone, on the bleak coast; and, amidst the darkness, and the storm, and the whelming waves, with an unrewarded and self-wasting fidelity, he gave out ever the twinkling light that warned the heedless ship of state from the breakers and the lee shore of Federalism.

He preached State-Rights, as if his life had been consecrated to the ministry of those doctrines. Whenever he spoke—whatever he wrote—wherever he went—*State-Rights, State-Rights*—STATE-RIGHTS were the exhaustless themes of his discourse. Like Xavier, with his bell ringing before him, as he walked amidst strange cities, addressing the startled attention of the wayfarers, with the messages of salvation, and denouncing the coming wrath; Randolph came among men, the untiring apostle of his creed, ever raising his shrill voice, "against the alarming encroachments of the Federal Government."

Nor was he without his reward. The distinctive doctrines of his school, in their fundamental and primitive purity, were well-nigh lost, after the era of the fusion of parties in Monroe's, if not, indeed, under the "silken Mansfieldism" of Madison's administration. The old knights and cavaliers of the South were living, indeed, but were torpid; like—as we have somewhere seen it quoted—the knightly horsemen, in the ENCHANTED CAVE, seated on their steeds with lance in rest and warlike port, but rider and horse spell-bound and senseless as marble, until the magician blew his horn, when, at the first blast, they quickened into life, and sprang forth again to deeds of chivalrous emprize; so Randolph's clarion tones waked the leaders of his party to battle for the cause of their order.

But suppose he had no reward? Suppose all this labor and all this life were poured, like water, in the sand? Suppose he had followed, always, a losing banner? What then? Are we wasting ink and paper in recording the annals of such a warfare—the story of such a man? Are martyrs so common—is heroic constancy so frequent, and devotion to principle and love of truth such vulgar things, in this our age of political purity and sainted statesmanship, that a man, consecrating the noblest faculties to the service of his country, and following no meaner lights than the judgment and conscience God gave him, to guide his steps through a long road of trial and temptation, is unworthy of being held up for admiration and reverence?

CHAPTER XIV.

Randolph's Character and Death.

THE character of this remarkable man is a subject of various and contradictory speculation, and it may seem presumptuous to attempt any thing like a satisfactory analysis of it. He has had the misfortune which attaches to most men of fertile wit and brilliant powers. Men seem unwilling to accord multiplicity of gifts to any man. The same depreciating incredulity, which "shook its head at Murray for a wit," and which made Elizabeth pronounce Bacon a man of parts, "but not deep in law," has denied to Randolph, because of his showy qualities, the possession of stronger and higher powers. But, we think, that this judgment is partial and unjust. True, he had a most extraordinary endowment of wit and the lighter graces. He was, beyond all comparison, the wittiest man of his time. He overflowed with wit. He wasted more wit than men, characteristically witty, give out. Sheridan had not the same ease and flow of wit; the same tropical luxuriance of fancy; the same spontaneity, aptness and raciness. Randolph's wit was much more than humor. It was a refined, wire-edged and diamond-pointed COMMON SENSE; a sharp and shrewd sagacity, which, while it had the edge of sarcasm, had, also, the force of argument. Randolph had the rare faculty of interpreting for the crowd; of translating, in better and apter language, the thoughts passing in the mind of the hearer; who was delighted to find that Randolph was only thinking *his* thoughts. His verbal aptness was astonishing. When any thing was to be characterized by an epithet, he, at once, characterized it, by a word or phrase so striking and pat, that it created the surprise and the pleasure which are the most marked effects of wit. He had the same aptness of quotation. No man made the resources of others more subservient to his own purposes. He did not merely appropriate. He gave a new value to the quoted sentence. There was as much genius in the selection and application, as in the conception and expression of the idea. His ingenuity was very great. He had the faculty of seeing remote analogies and correspondences; and of accumulating around a dry, isolated, and uninviting topic, a multitude of images, facts, suggestions and illustrations. His memory was upon the same scale. It was comprehensive and retentive, taking in the whole superficies of the subject, and the minutest details. His information extended to a large variety of subjects. In polite learning, especially in the standard works of English literature, he was accomplished beyond most of the literati of his country; and his taste and appreciation of the latent and patent beauties and excellencies of the great classics were unsurpassed. Had he turned his attention to literature, as a pursuit, it is not going too far to say, that he would have enriched, not merely American literature, but the English tongue, with some of the rarest contributions made in his day, by genius to letters. He mastered history with like ease. He was supposed to have a more minute and accurate knowledge of geography than any man of his country; and he even committed the book of Heraldry of England to memory, and could repeat the annals of the noble houses of that kingdom, in their details. But, most largely developed of all his faculties, probably, was his quick, clear, and deep comprehension. His finely-toned and penetrative intellect possessed an acumen, a perspicuity which was as quick and vivid as lightning. His conclusions did not wait upon long and labored inductions. His mind, as by an instinctive insight, darted at once upon the core of the subject, and sprang, with an electric leap, upon the conclusion. He started where most reasoners end. It is a mistake to suppose that he was deficient in argumentative power. He was as fertile of argumentation as most speakers; he was only deficient in argumentative forms. His statements were so clear, so simplified and so vivid, that they saved him much of the necessity of laborious processes of ratiocination. Much that looked like declamation was only illustration, or another form of argument. He was too prodigal of illustrations; and sometimes his love of verbal felicities, of exquisite niceties and artistical finish of expression, led him into repetitions of what he had well enough said before.

He usually spoke without preparation; and his speeches depended much upon the state of his nervous system. He was, therefore, an unequal speaker; sometimes speaking with great felicity, and sometimes with diminished power; but seldom or never dull or uninteresting, though often erratic, eccentric and diffuse.

His vanity was not excessive. "He was too proud to be vain." He boasted that he scorned every thing merely "popular and eleemosynary." His ear did not itch for general applause; though he was solicitous of the approbation of men he loved and esteemed. His eccentricities proceeded, in a great measure, from the vehemence of his faculties and passions; from his disregard of the general opinion, and from the isolation of his habits and character. He had the advantage and the disadvantage of a want of caution; the advantage which an uncramped and unstinted individuality, and the freest use of his powers give a speaker, and the disadvantage of being betrayed into extravagance, and untenable positions, and needless offences against the opinions and tastes of his auditors.

To the account of his bodily infirmities, must be placed much of the acerbity and excesses of his temper. He was seldom in good health. His nervous system was extremely irritable. His disease was peculiarly annoying to the temper. So delicately-toned were his fibres and nerves, that he complained that he was "like a man without a skin." An east wind caused him the greatest uneasiness. He was a hypochondriac. His tastes were fastidious. He was easily disgusted with things inharmonious with his habits or mental condition. He was eminently unsocial, proud, reserved, uncommunicative. He could endure no associations that were uncongenial. He had no faculty of assimilation or adaptation. His firmness and self-esteem gave him such individuality, that he could not seem to be, or to act, except in subordination to his ruling qualities; which were inflexible laws to him. It was unfortunate for him, that his whole education fostered these characteristics. He was brought up in the lap of indulgence. He had never known self-denial. He was a spoiled boy. Left to himself early, he became "Lord of himself, that heritage of woe." He had wealth, attention, adulation, the means of self-indulgence, to come in aid of a temper naturally proud, self-willed and domineering. He was vindictive. He acknowledged and deplored it often. But he was neither implacable nor habitually cruel, nor unjust to his enemies. The spectacle of pain unmanned him; and it frequently turned him, in a moment, from rage to pity and remorse. His sentiments were naturally just, and he was occasionally capable of acts of magnanimity. The want of charity was his greatest defect. He had never learned to regard man as a brother. He had never considered himself as parcel of a general humanity. He was frequently neglectful, and sometimes indifferent to the feelings of others; at other times harsh and cruel; but, in many of these instances, his wilfulness or his impulses betrayed him into these acts, without his being conscious—so free was he from sympathy with other men—of the pain he was inflicting.

We think that he was an honest and conscientious man. The general tone of his mind was pure and elevated. He had a large sense of reverence, and an exquisite sense of the beautiful and good. He defended and supported his positions upon high moral grounds. He seldom or never pandered to the groundling and vile prejudices or passions of the mob. In some instances, he showed a morbid conscienciousness; for example, in the treatment of his slaves.

His affections, though not diffusive, were constant and vehement. For his friends, no man felt a livelier or deeper interest. He concentrated upon them the love due to the race. He seems, as a consequence of his isolation, to have personified his State-Rights principles and his native state; and he lavished upon them the devotion he extended to his few bosom friends.

We have omitted in our review, much of the private history of this extraordinary personage, especially a notice of the voluminous later correspondence illustrating the inner life of Randolph. His letters breathe the dreariest, dismalest state of feeling, of which any account is given in story. The darkness is cimmerian; the gloom and despair nearly those of the pit, over whose gates is inscribed: "There is no hope within." His life seemed a long sigh of hopeless pain —a long groan of intolerable agony. Sometimes he was insane. At other times, so miserable and dependent that insanity itself—the evil next to death, if not a greater evil—was scarcely a thing to be dreaded.

Who shall place to his account the deeds he did when in this state? Who does not regard him, even when considering his most harsh and unfeeling acts, as a man more to be pitied than blamed? and think that a harsher judgment would be imitating his own want of charity for an erring man, without his apology to plead for the imitation?

The solitude he courted was his worst enemy. The brooding mind preyed upon itself; and the bright intellect, like polished steel, was consumed by its own rust. He derived pleasure mostly from the exercise of his brilliant and active intellect; and from the most agreeable of these exercises—the social—he cut himself off by his hermit-like seclusion. Solitude, so necessary, at times, to ripen genius, and freshen and purify it for its loftiest efforts, but fostered *his* selfishness, and deepened his gloom, by his habit of brooding over his physical and mental maladies.

The causes of his unhappiness are patent enough. Apart from his other diseases, he was hypochondriacal, sometimes even to hysteria. Hypochondriacism is itself a dreadful disease, or, at least, the consequence of it. External circumstances, some of which we have noticed, had much to do with his unhappiness. He may be considered, too, during most of his life, an unsuccessful man. His political life was a series of failures, relieved, here and there, by an occasional success. He saw other men of less talent rising far above him in place and fortune. But the most effective cause of his unhappiness, he has given himself. It was "his ungovernable temper." His fierce passions had destroyed the balance of his character. Vindictiveness is more of a scourge to its possessor than to his enemy. There can be no peace of mind—without which there can be no happiness—where the heart is in perpetual warfare. He had brought down on himself a host of enemies. He never made a speech that he did not make more enemies than converts. The diabolical keenness of his wit planted wounds, for which he was never forgiven. He was as sensitive to pain as he was prompt to inflict it; and he felt in turn the suffering he caused. If he cut at his antagonists with a bold and trenchant blade, he received quite as many and as sharp blows as he dealt. He was no doubt, too, often called to suffer the retribution, which his conscience inflicted upon him, for wrong and injury, done often in the heat and impulse—for he was greatly governed by his impulses—of momentary excitement. He was not incapable, like some other politicians, of doing justice to his political enemies. Of Marshall, Hamilton, Rufus King, in some degree of Clay, Calhoun, Webster, even Jefferson and Madison, he spoke in later life, in terms, if not, as to all of them, of justice, yet in a spirit far from acrimonious; and even in language, evincive of at least a partial conquest of truth and charity over previous prejudice and ill-blood.

But it must not be forgotten, that, if disposed to be a bitter and harsh foe, he was an open one; not condescending to underhanded detraction; making no affectation of friendship, when he did not feel it, and saying the most publicly the most bitter things.

This harshness, pride, uncharitableness, and want o magnanimity, and of a pervading love for his race, are, certainly, great draw-backs from the fame of a statesman. Bu we must take greatness as we find it. Bedded in humanity, it comes to us, more or less, in association with human frailty. We may regret—but we cannot wholly condemn him for the defect—that the incorruptible truth and stern virtue of Cato were not associated with the clemency, generosity, and flowing affability of Cæsar; and that, to the constancy and intrepidity of Randolph, were not allied the suavity and gentleness of manners, which had made these sterner attributes to be loved as well as admired.

But few words remain to be added. The disease which had struggled so long for mastery with the unyielding, but seemingly so fragile form, was now making sure of its prey. It had been greatly aggravated by his sojourn in Russia; and now the pallid cheek and feeble frame, the tottering gait, and the seal of decay and weakness in the shrivelled and languid face, gave token that the power of resistance to its inroads was nearly gone. Another visit to England was concluded upon, as the last hope of relief. He sat out on his last journey. He reached Washington, and dragged his emaciated body, with difficulty, into the Senate-Chamber. Sinking with feebleness and the exhaustion of the effort, he caught the sound of Clay's voice, as the latter was addressing the chair. He asked " to be held up, that he might listen to that voice again." Clay turned, and saw him. Moved by his haggard look, with the death-warrant in his face, the magnanimous Kentuckian approached his old rival and foe. The interview was touching. All the past was forgotten, and the greetings of the illustrious commoners were kind and tender. They parted in peace and good will, never to meet again upon earth.

Randolph, in June, 1833, reached Philadelphia, whither he went to take passage from that port. He was too late for the Liverpool packet. He exposed himself to the inclemency of the weather, took cold, which aggravated his disease, and hastened its fatal termination. He was put to bed—his death-bed—in his lodgings, at the City Hotel. The idiosyncracies which had, of late years especially, marked his demeanor, distinguished the last hours of his life. The sudden bursts of petulance which disease wrung from him; the affecting kindness and tenderness which disease could not wholly take from him; the rambling conversation in the intervals of acute suffering, in some passages, as brilliant as ever—the last gleams of the sinking lamp; the groanings of remorse, which a review of his past life, at the bar of a stern self-judgment, drew from his contrite heart; the fervid prayer; the hesitating hope; the trust, qualified by self-condemnation, in the Saviour, whose name he professed; the concluding act, ere the curtain fell upon the last scene of earth, when, propped up by pillows, he called witnesses to his confirmation of his will, providing for the freedom and support of his slaves, and the last conscious words, which fired his eye and braced his sinking frame, as, speaking in this connection, he laid his skeleton hand strongly upon the shoulder of his faithful servant, John, and said with emphasis—" especially for this man." And then—this last charge upon his conscience off—his mind wandered away to the light, and the scenes, and the friends of the *Early Day;* and, the mutterings of the voice growing gradually fainter, as he passed on into the thicker shadows of the DARK VALLEY, the fluttering pulse stood still, and John Randolph of Roanoke was numbered with the dead!

They carried him back to his solitary home, and buried him—in death as in life, unsocial and isolated—in the forest of Roanoke. In the soil of the Virginia he loved so well, they laid the corse of her faithful and devoted son. They left him to rest, after the long fever of his troubled dream of life was over, in a humble and sequestered grave, beneath two stately pines. There let him sleep on! The gloom of their shade, and the melancholy sighing of the wind through their boughs, are fit emblems of the life which was breathed out in sadness and in sorrow.

ANDREW JACKSON AND HENRY CLAY

CHAPTER I.

Party Strife from 1835 to '45—Party Spirit—Jackson and Clay—Points of Resemblance—A New Country—Jackson—His Character, Public and Private—As a General—As a Party Leader—Adams's Election—Clay's Blunders.

THE mists of prejudice, which enveloped the prominent actors in the party-struggle, commencing in 1835, and raging for ten years, with almost unabated fury, are fast disappearing from the land. European tourists and statesmen have expressed their surprise, that questions of such little moment, as existed between the Whig and Democratic parties, should have so agitated the public mind, and so widely and bitterly divided the American people. It must be confessed that in Europe, parties are formed upon a wider base. Politics in Europe involve for the most part, to a greater or less degree, the foreign as well as the domestic relations of the nation; and the interests, not to say the fate, of other countries or dynasties. And even when the policy is more local in its character, it often involves more radical principles—the organism rather than the mode of administering a government, upon a commonly recognized basis or ground-work.

We have the inestimable blessings of a written constitution and of a republican system. We have the leading principles of government limited and defined. We are all Republicans. The rights of all freemen and the rights of all the States are equal. The powers of the Federal Government, and those of the State Governments, are marked out with such precision, that it is almost impossible to make such mistake as will vitally affect the scheme of their respective constitutions.

When we look back upon the fierce struggles through which the nation has passed, and recall the exaggerated declamation, the ferocious criminations, the bustling activities and the pervasive organization of party, we feel inclined to smile as we reflect that all this machinery and excitement were occasioned by a contest about a bank, a tariff, a distribution of proceeds of public property, and the like measures of police. At least these were the avowed principles. But it may be doubted if they were the real source of the party excitement. The zeal and violence of parties are not always measured by the magnitude of the principles or measures involved. When matters are trivial, they are magnified by the politicians, and are received by the people, in that exaggerated form.

The feeling of partisanship seems natural to man. The two main elements of it are sympathy and combativeness. After taking sides, the selfish and social passions are aroused, and grow warmer as the conflict goes on, until, in due time, the excitement spends its force, and first repose, and afterwards re-action ensue. Organization is itself a powerful fomenter of zeal and violence; agitation grows epidemic; mind acts on mind; and, as in a mob, by a sort of contagious excitement and a division of responsibility, men think and do, when aggregated, what each one singly would be ashamed of, or shrink from, as weak or wicked.

The most ignorant are the most prone to this passion. They go into a political struggle, as they take sides in a muster fight. They are drawn by clamor, like bees, as by an instinct. They cannot help it. They love the excitement. It gives employment to all their passions. It swells their importance. It gives them a sense of power. They are flattered by the leaders. They find employment in promoting the common enterprise. They become identified with it. A sort of free-masonry of feeling and affiliation grows up between the members. The jealousies and strifes of rivalry and opposition, party and individual, tend to wed them more closely to their own, and to separate them from the opposite party and its members.

Politics are the safety-valves that let off the discontent, and the surplus energies of our people. What the theatre is to the French, or the bull-fight or fandango to the Spaniard, the hustings and the ballot-box are to *our* people. We are all politicians, men, women and children; and, therefore, it is not surprising, that we should all be terribly excited on the eve of an election, even when the issues are not important. It does not cost us any thing to be excited, as it does other countries. We like the fun of it. There is no danger in it; for the steam being unconfined, the fiercest explosions of wrath are only the bursting of rockets in the upper air.

In the Whig and Democratic struggle it may well be doubted, whether the *personal* question were not the *substantive* one—the *who* rather than the *what*, the *men* rather than the *measures*. We do not speak in condemnation of parties, nor is it worth while to say any thing in animadversion of the undue excitement of party spirit. We must take the evil with the good. But while the principles which have divided parties are doubtless important, it is simply ridiculous to attribute to them, either in their immediate or remote effects, in their causes or their results, or in the mode in which they were carried or prevented, the degree of importance attached to them by partisans. The country could have gone on under either scheme, and the difference in its condition would scarcely have been noticed. Apart from, and rising above mere party questions, doubtless, were others in which the great men whose names head this article were conspicuously concerned, and which were well worthy of all the efforts made in their behalf. Such were the questions of the war with Great Britain, and the three compromises of 1820, 1832 and 1850, in all of which Clay was a prominent actor. Compared with these in importance, those questions which were peculiar to the respective party creeds (the Texas annexation question, in its principles and its ultimate effects, perhaps, excepted) were of little moment; the main and characteristic principles of republican government being equally conceded by both, and equally the basis of Whig and Democratic organization and profession.

But it was through these questions, and through this organization, that the characters of Jackson and Clay were impressed upon the country, and their weight and influence, in the formation of opinion, felt by the age in which they lived. That Jackson and Clay were great men, especially in that sense which defines greatness to be the power to control men and mould opinion or action, will not be denied; the degree of this greatness, absolute and relative, may be.

There were many points of similitude between these illustrious antagonists. As party men, they seemed to stand in irreconcilable antagonism. They were so in interest, in position, in feeling. Yet, with all this opposition, there was a striking correspondence between them, not only in character, but in many points of exterior resemblance.

Both were born, or received their earliest impressions, in Revolutionary times, or from the principles of the Revolution.

Jackson was the elder. But the spirit and genius of the Revolution, outlasting the period of actual hostilities, was equally the inspiration of Clay's awakening and fervid mind.

Both were denied the advantages of education. Both made a new country the theatre of their earliest exertions. Both were natives of the South, and emigrated to a new Southern state, with a population like that of the state of their birth. Both were dependent alone upon their own exertions, and equally independent of adventitious aid. Both were the architects of their own fortunes. Both chose the profession of the law as their first introduction to the public; and both, though in unequal degree, encountered the same opposition, and met with early success. Both displayed from the start the same enterprising spirit, the same obduracy and vehemence of will, the same almost arrogant defiance of opposition, the same tenacity and continuity of purpose, the same moral and personal daring. Jackson introduced himself to the practice by undertaking the prosecution of suits, which others, of a profession not used to quail before danger or shrink from responsibility were intimidated from representing. Clay enrolled himself, a boy, among the competitors of the strongest bar in Kentucky, and issued his writ against one of the most prominent and powerful of them, in favor of an obscure bar-keeper, at the certain cost of the defendant's deadly resentment; and defied that hatred to its extremest manifestations. Both early impressed themselves upon the community around them, and were distinguished for the same personal characteristics. Both rose at once to posts of honor and distinction; and at an early age enrolled their names, and to the last preserved them, among the first and highest of the republic. Both were men of quick perception; of prompt action; of acute penetration; of business capacity; of masculine common sense; of quick and unerring judgment of men; of singular fertility of resources; of remarkable power to create or avail themselves of circumstances; of consummate tact and management. Both were distinguished for grace and ease of manners, for happy and polished address, and for influence over the wills and affections of those who came within the circle of their acquaintance and associations. Both were of lithe, sinewy, and slender physical conformation; uniting strength with activity, and great powers of endurance with a happy facility of labor. Both were men of the warmest affections; of the gentlest and most conciliating manners in social intercourse when they wished to please; of truth and loyalty, and steadfastness in friendship; bitter and defiant in their enmities; of extraordinary directness in their purposes; of a patient and indefatigable temper in following out their ends, or waiting for their accomplishment. Neither could brook a rival or opposition; and each had the imperial spirit of a conqueror not to be subdued, and the pride of leadership which could not follow. They were Americans both, intensely patriotic and national, loving their whole country, its honor, its glory, its institutions, its Union, with a love kindled early and quenched only in death.

They both spent much of their long lives, from youth to hoary age, in the public service, maintaining to the last, with only the modifications which age necessarily makes upon the mental and physical constitution, the same characteristics for which they were at first distinguished. They lived lives of storm, excitement and warfare; each in point of real authority equally at the head of his party; in and out of office equally acknowledged leaders; and they died each full of years and honors, and by the same lingering disease; professing towards the close of life, the same religion; and leaving upon the country, at the death of each prosperous and peaceful, a saddened sense of a great and common calamity.

These distinguished statesmen owed much of their effective greatness to circumstances, and especially to their early settlement in a new country. A young community, unorganized and free, furnishes an open, unoccupied field for energy and intellect. It gives them a fair chance and an even start. The community is impressible to the former's hand. The intrigues of cliques, the artificial arrangements of an old society, and the pre-occupation of predecessors do not obstruct the way. The people, by the force of circumstances, stand in natural equality. They are as yet undivided into cliques or factions, or fixed to previous relations or parties, or bound down by ideas and prejudices to old men or old systems. The population of Tennessee and Kentucky in those days was a border people, full of enterprise, energy and boldness; men of warm hearts and generous temper free alike from wealth and poverty; independent in spirit, while dependent on each other for the reciprocal courtesies and benefits of neighborhood; and completely homogeneous in feeling and interest.

Such a community is eminently a practical people. Their ideas are about practical affairs. Their business is with the concrete. They have no time for refined theories or subtle disputations. Their business relates to the present and the material. Refined speculation comes with a refined and advanced society. What they have to do, they must do at once, and by the most expeditious and most effective means. To address them successfully, one must address their robust common sense, and their unsophisticated feelings. Bracing themselves up against difficulties and dangers, and forced to rely upon themselves for all things, the masculine qualities of heart and mind were early and strongly developed; and accordingly we find in the new settlements, the bravest soldiery which the war called into the field.

There was much to do. The wilderness was to be improved into a country; and a policy fixed providing for the necessities of a society that wanted every thing which government bestows, and to be divested of whatever governments repress.

As face answereth to face in water, so must the popular favorite answer to the genius and character of the people. Only a bold, frank, decisive man could rise to power in such a community. He must shrink from no danger; he must fear no responsibility; he must wear no mask; he must wait for no cue; he must be able to appeal to the strong feelings and the manly common-sense of the people.

Honesty of purpose, earnestness and faithfulness, and above all, a boldness approaching recklessness, were the qualities essential for leadership among such a people. Trained to grapple closely with every question, to apply to a measure the touchstone of its practical working, to look into the nature, motives and feelings of men as they were presented almost naked to the eye, and to see the springs and curious mechanism of the human heart and character, these great men had early schooled themselves in the most valuable learning of statesmanship, and mastered a knowledge, which all the books on statecraft and all the teachings of colleges could not supply.

The elaborate tricks and tinsel, the prettinesses of expression, the balanced sentences and glittering periods of oratory, much less the artful dodges and the slippery equivocations of a tricksy politician, would find but a sorry audience, before the stern countenances, and the keen, penetrating eyes of the hunters, assembled around the rude rostrum, in 'coon caps and linsey-woolsey garments, leaning on their rifles, their sun-burnt visages bent upon the face of the speaker, with an expression that indicated they were not to be trifled with. To come at once to the point, to seize the bull by the horns, to lead out boldly and roundly their propositions, to urge strong arguments in nervous language, to storm the enemy's batteries, to attack him in his strong-hold, to hurl at his head the merciless sarcasm, to cover him with ridicule, to denounce him and his principles in terms of fiery invective, to ply the warm appeal to the passions and sensibilities;—these were the weapons of a warfare which was only effective, when it was known that the hand was ready to wield, with the same alacrity, weapons of personal combat.

The habit of mingling freely with the people, brought the personal character of a public man in close contact and intimate acquaintance with them; and, in this way, he caught the spirit of the people, as well as communicated to them his own.

Though the circumstances of the two great rivals were so alike at the outset, their paths diverged in after life. The war with Great Britain and her Indian allies, furnished the theatre upon which both of them first became introduced to the nation; in different characters, it is true. The genius of each was eminently military and executive. Jackson was a statesman in the camp; Clay a captain in the senate. Clay had early come before the people as an orator and politician; and it was natural for him to continue to labor in that field when his country, at that time more than at any former period, needed his services in the public councils. It is known, however, that at so high a rate did Madison appreciate his talents for military command, that he was about to tender him the appointment of commander of the forces, and was only withheld from the proffer, by the call for his services at the head of the war party in Congress. It is impossible to know the result of such an appointment upon the public interests, or upon the personal fortunes of Mr. Clay. But it were a falsifying of all the calculations which men may make of the future, to suppose that such rare abilities, and such unsurpassed energies, would have been otherwise than successfully employed upon a theatre to which they were seemingly so signally adapted; and it needed but the *prestige* of the camp to have crowned a popularity and rounded out a fame, before which competition and rivalry must have hung their diminished heads. But this was fated not to be. The laurels of the hero were not to be blended in the fadeless wreath of orator, philanthropist, statesman, jurist, cabinet minister and diplomatist. Fortune could scarcely be reproached with injustice when, lavishing upon this favorite son the graces and accomplishments which lend a charm to social life, and all the qualifications and successes of every department of civil service, she refused to add the trophies of the soldier. Jackson's spirit, if not more active, was less fitted for the council-hall than the battle-field. His was not the elaborate eloquence of the senate. Swords, not words, were *his* arguments. His was the true Demosthenic eloquence of action. He had neither the temper nor the abilities to parley. He could speak tersely, vigorously, movingly, but his words were the brief words of command. Action followed speech, as thunder the lightning. He had no patience for the solemn forms, the dull routine, the prosy speech-making, the timid platitudes, or the elaborate ratiocinations of legislative debate. Sudden and quick in opinion as in quarrel, heart, soul and mind all mingled in his conclusions, and the energy that conceived a purpose, started it into overt act. With him, to think and to do were not so much two things as one. His eager and impatient soul would have fevered over a debate, on a proposition to declare war, or to provide means for prosecuting it, as the knight, Ivanhoe, on his sick bed in the castle of Front de Boeuf, writhed in helpless impatience, when he heard the clangor of the warriors storming the battlements for his deliverance. Like Job's war-horse, he scented the battle from afar, and, at the sound of the trumpets, cried ha! ha! The first man in resolution and daring in the community in which he lived, he did not so much rise to the command of the warlike troops, that flocked to the first standard unfurled in the young settlements, as the command naturally came to him; so, by native allegiance to greatness, the weak in distress and terror turn, through instinct, for safety to the strong. Putting himself at the head of his raw recruits, he moved upon the Indian camps and conquered, as easily as he found the enemy. His work was as thorough as swift. He did nothing by halves. A war with him was nearly an extermination. It was always a complete destruction of the power of the foe. He took no security from an enemy except his prostration. He closed the war at New Orleans by one of the most signal victories, every thing considered, upon record. But to do this, he assumed powers and responsibilities from which Nelson might have shrunk. But the event sanctified the means, if those were indeed equivocal. Arbuthnot and Ambrister were hung in Florida, notwithstanding the verdict of a court-martial; and the Spanish flag was no protection to those, who, under it, concocted designs against his country. His military career was short but brilliant. Without any military training or education, he discovered talents of the first order for arms, and brought raw militiamen to the strict subordination of the regular service. He was a rigid disciplinarian. He tolerated no license or disobedience in the camp. He could sit beside a sick soldier all night, and share his last crust with him, as with a brother; and shoot him the day after for sleeping on his post.

Jackson was an enthusiast; not a flaming zealot, but one of the Ironsides. He was built of the Cromwell stuff, without Cromwell's religious fanaticism. He had but little toleration for human weaknesses. He was incredulous of impossibilities. He was no patient hearer of excuses. Before his irrepressible energy difficulties had vanished, and he could not see why it was not so with others. He could not see why the Seminoles could not be driven out of Florida into the sea, as easily as he drove the Creeks into the Coosa. The spirit of a conqueror was his in a double measure. Upon the work in hand he concentrated all his powers, girded up his loins, strained every muscle, and put forth every energy of mind and soul and strength. He had no thought of failure. The world around was a blank to him except as the theatre on which he acted, and meat and drink, and air and light were only the instruments for success. Nothing was too costly an expenditure; no sacrifice was too great to attain it. With him, thus inspired, there was no such word as fail. Accordingly, there was no such thing as failure in his history. The man who, rising from a sick bed with a broken arm in a sling, could place himself before a company of insurgent soldiers leaving the camp for home, and, holding a pistol in the bridle-hand, threaten to shoot down the first man that marched on, had nothing to learn of human audacity. Men of nerve quailed before him, as cowards quail before men of nerve. When the storms of wrath passed over his fiery soul, there was something as terrible in his voice and mien, as in the roused anger of the lion. The calm resolution of his placid movements, in its still and collected strength, conveyed an idea of power in repose, like the sea, broad, unfathomable, majestic, awaiting but the storm to waken its tides, and lash its waves into the sublime energy, that hurls on high and against the shore the armaments upon its bosom.

He was ever the same. He did not rise to passion to fall back into lassitude. The same even port of firm, calm, dignified composure marked his bearing, when the gusts of passion did not disturb his serenity. His air of command was not broken by any familiarity. Serious and earnest in small things and great, there was no time when impertinence could break in upon his dignity, or feel itself tolerated by his condescension. Whoever looked upon him, saw one whom it was better to have as a friend, and whom it was dangerous to have for an enemy. He required of his friends an undeviating fidelity; he freely gave what he exacted. He could excuse or was blind to every thing in a friend except disloyalty to friendship; *that* with him was the unpardonable sin.

We consider Jackson and Clay as incontestably the greatest men of their respective parties. In this estimate, we judge of men as we judge of a machine, by what it can accomplish. That there were men of greater intellectual calibre than either, we are willing to concede; that in some departments of human activity, these would have far outshone the two leaders—for instance, as professors of colleges, or in literature—we readily allow; but in the practical business of statesmanship, or in any other business requiring the same sort of abilities—for whatever things energy, perseverance and courage can accomplish, they were the most efficient men of their time. Those who differ with us in the result, most probably differ in the premises. We regard the *will* as the man; as not so much giving individuality as being it. The strong will, therefore, is the strong man. The intellect is but the servant of the will, not controlling it more than any other servant may its master, but controlled by it; or, at most, is but the light by which the will may work; and is as inferior to it in true dignity, as the lamp is inferior to the man that reads or walks by its rays.

What better evidence have we of Napoleon's greatness, than that, in an age of great men, his pre-eminent greatness was unchallenged; and that, among the strifes of rivalry, the point of precedence struggled for was *below* him?

Who, in the Democratic party, could have carried away from Jackson, in a political contest, ten thousand votes? Who, in his time, could have made a respectable schism in the Democratic party? Much more, who would have ventured to *lead* a policy in the House or the Senate, before it had the Executive imprimatur? And at what period of the Whig struggle, would not Clay's defection have been equivalent to striking the flag?

It is a mistake to suppose that General Jackson owed

his popularity to his military services. Unquestionably, his military exploits were an element of that popularity. It could scarcely be otherwise among so warlike a people; especially with the soldiers he led to battle, and those whom they could influence, was this peculiarly true; and it is also true that, in the states in which his battles were fought, the mere circumstance of his fighting them made him a popular favorite. But mere admiration of a military chieftain as such, and mere gratitude for military services, could not have so impressed the heart or the imagination of the nation We see an illustration of this truth in the case of the conqueror of Mexico, the first of living generals, at once in the length of his career, and the number, importance, and brilliancy of his victories. The nation, although it appreciates and acknowledges his services, and feels proud of him, yet admires him coldly and at a distance; admires him as *he* admires the swords presented to him by legislatures, or as *they* admire the Paixhan guns he fired at the castle of San Juan. There is no *personality* in their idea of *him;* they seem to regard him but as a curious and effective military machine.

The deeds of the warrior were effective in Jackson's popularity, in drawing attention to, and in unfolding the character of the man; and it was *that character*, a knowledge of which was so evolved, that was popular.

We have already indicated in what this popularity mainly consisted; in what particular he stood forth pictorially, so to speak, before the people. He was marked out and distinguished from the mass of mankind as a substantive original, peculiar character, mainly distinctive in the sublime attribute of a powerful will, of a fervid enthusiasm; as the impersonation of energy and power; as the genius of the practical; and his character, otherwise severe and repellant, was softened and endeared to the people by warm passions and affections, and a genuine love of his race and his country.

The HEROIC ELEMENT impressed him strongly upon the mind of the nation.

It is of the nature of man to side with the strong. The influences which draw men are not the gentler or more loving qualities. Whoever has observed much of the conduct of the masses, knows that the hero of the crowd is a representative of the sterner qualities, rather than of the softer and more amiable. A daring robber on the gibbet excites more of vulgar sympathy than a suffering martyr at the stake. The bully of a muster-field always takes the shouts and attracts the homage even of those of the rabble, who are only spectators, from the man whom he has imposed upon or insulted, without provocation or mercy. The crowd must look up to a man before they will applaud him, much more before they will be governed by him; and they will look up only to those whom they fear, or, at least, whose qualities they fear. They only regard with reverence men who possess those properties which conquer or inspire men with awe. Courage is one of the most vulgar of virtues, yet the Romans prized it so highly that they gave it the name of *virtue*, as if it comprehended *all* virtue; and even now, in more cultivated times, and in the prevalence of gentler manners, it is that quality which is most respected among men. There is a mesmerism of will which works more powerfully upon men than virtue or intellect; a fascination of the eye which charms like the serpent.

Love wins. Power commands. But love is inspired for the most part only by personal relation, or in close proximity to the object of it. The man of a nation is but an Ideal; and we do not love the ideal. We can admire, we can reverence, we may have the image stamped upon our imaginations, and thus grow familiar with it. It may thus excite our enthusiasm. We thus become acquainted, so to speak, with great men; and thus honor, support, uphold them. But the merely amiable and quiet virtues will not impress them upon us. They must be painted in some stronger hues than water-colors. The vermilion tints and the great lines of the GRAND and the HEROIC are necessary to imprint the imagination with their characters. Men, to be popular, must be known; and a character like Jackson's could not but be known and felt.

We doubt if Milton's Satan would not be a more popular man, if he took the human form, than Fenelon; and, at least, in France, would not carry the suffrages of the masses in a popular election.

Take the case of Napoleon Bonaparte. He is the ideal of energy—energy incarnate. Did any name ever so impress the human imagination? Was human sympathy ever so drawn forth before as for him, when in his island-prison? More sympathy has been expended upon him than upon the whole martyrology. Did any man ever leave so vivid a sense of his being and personality upon the mind of the world? Why, his very name, the faintest shadow and memento of himself, turned French politics inside out, and established its representative as an institution of France. The Sultan's cimeter in the Eastern story, the shadow of which, at twenty paces, cut off an enemy's head, was nothing to the shade of the great Emperor, that, at a distance of a generation, cut down a kingdom, a line of kings, and a republic, and blazed out the way to a new empire and a new dynasty.

What a hold the great Marlborough had upon the admiration of the world in his day is well known; and yet, if the half of what Thackeray says of him is true, Falstaff might have set to him as a model and prodigy of decency, honor, and virtue.

We believe General Jackson to have been much misunderstood. He was neither a god nor a devil. He was worthy neither of adoration nor of detestation. Like every other man of strong and marked character and of positive forces, he had the centrifugal and the centripetal tendencies in a proportionate degree. He drew and he repelled according as the object was of like or contrary character, or as he conciliated or opposed the interests, purposes, or sentiments of others. It is the law of a soul highly charged with the electricity of passion and sensibility, to work in this manner.

Combativeness excites combativeness in others; pride, pride; as deep calls out to deep. No man had more devoted friends, and no man had more bitter enemies. He was a good hater. Dr. Johnson could not have had a man more to his mind in this respect; and he had rather conquer one enemy than conciliate two: He could forgive an enemy, but the enemy must first surrender at discretion. Like Tecumseh, he gave no quarter while the battle was raging; like Tecumseh, he never asked it; unfortunately for his enemies, he never needed it. But he never forgave a friend. He became reconciled to Benton, who had fought with him for life. He never could have become reconciled to Calhoun, whom he supposed, justly or unjustly, to have betrayed his friendship, or played double with him.

We have taken pains to learn the private character—the character as it was in dishabille—not draped up for the world to look at—of the man of the Hermitage. It was different from any thing many suppose. As a neighbor, Jackson was the soul of kindness and generosity. To the poor, he was as a father; to all honest to a punctilio, and, in money matters, as just and honorable as Franklin. Simple and frugal in his tastes and habits, he was unpretending and republican enough for a Swiss farmer; and yet neither avaricious nor prodigal of money. He neither wasted nor hoarded, was neither exacting nor negligent; was a discreet manager, without undue anxiety or driving energy. In his domestic relations, he was a model. He was a kind master governing his slaves more as a Scotch chieftain his clan, or a Hebrew patriarch his tribe, than as a driver, or as a planter holding lands and negroes, mules and ploughs as so much stock in trade, of value only as they were profitable. And in that nearer and closer tie of domestic life, something of romance, of a proud and knightly obeisance and homage, and devoted love, shed its unprosaic hues over a mind, whose characters were written in the strongest and most masculine prose of the sternly practical. More might be said in illustration of this observation, but more is unnecessary. Of kindred fidelity was his personal friendship. He could not do enough for his friends. He made their interests his own. He took charge of their fortunes. . He made their cause his cause, and their enemies his enemies. Truly did he say, in his last letter to Blair, that he had "never deserted a friend from policy;" and bitter was his scorn of his politic successor's desertion of the old thunderer of "The Globe." As sincerely did he make this protestation as he breathed the prayer that Blair "might triumph over all his enemies." He seemed to delight in promoting those to high offices, whom the opposite party despised, and was not deterred by the distrust or dislike of many of the most distinguished members of his own. But, it must be confessed, all this friendship was, perhaps unconsciously, the friendship of patronage. The spirit of his kindness was the spirit of a leader, or, at least, an air of imperial protection tinctured it. We are not aware that any personal friendship of his survived opposition to his measures or his ticket; and how many ceased with political agreement!

It were a bold thing to say that Jackson was the equal of Clay in many things. In many respects he was not. Jackson had no pretensions to oratory. His influence over men was as great, perhaps even greater, though this is saying a great deal. He was not a ready writer. He was scarcely able to write correct English on the commonest topics, as his letters to Lewis and to Blair testify. The man who could write the letter of which the fac simile is given in the Democratic Review, had a good deal to learn of the art of writing, and was certainly independent of his schoolmaster for his fame. He had no great deal of political information, and knew little of ancient or modern history. We apprehend he never was much of a student, and had no great partiality for letters. What he saw at all, he saw as clearly as any man, but he did not see far, nor was his vision wide in its sweep. He had remarkable sagacity, but it was a sagacity which related to the practical and the present. Men were his books, and he studied them closely and understood them thoroughly. He knew as well as any one what a man was good for, and to what use he could be put. If he could not do a thing himself, he knew, the next best thing, where to go to get it done, and when it was well done. Accordingly, he had able ministers, and the most powerful press that ever supported an administration. The only press that ever completely reflected the tone and character of an Executive, was "The Globe." It was a whole troop of cavalry and a park of flying artillery besides.

Nor did Jackson only know men in detail. He knew

them in gross. He thoroughly understood the genius of the American people, and knew what they desired and what they would stand.

His faculties did not sweep a large circle, but they worked like a steam-engine within that circle.

He lacked versatility; but this was so far from being a defect, that we doubt if it were not the secret of his wonderful success. It prevented a diversion of his powers and efforts, and concentrated them, as by a lens, upon those objects, which this singleness of aim enabled him to effect.

If we measure power by success, the palm must be awarded to Jackson. If we suppose politics to be a game of skill played for aggrandizement by politicians, the same award must be made. Jackson unquestionably was the ablest strategist. The letter to Monroe against proscription, if we suppose it written by Gen. Jackson, with the object of promoting his election to the Presidency, was a stroke of policy not unworthy of Talleyrand. The Federalists, long proscribed, and naturally desirous of again being admitted to consideration and office, were as yet unappropriated. They had abandoned their old organization, and had not enrolled themselves under any other banner. It was not difficult to see where gratitude and a sense of security and interest would carry them.

The election of Adams, by the House of Representatives, was turned to account, with all its incidents and surroundings, with admirable effect, by General Jackson. No one now believes the story of bargain, intrigue and management told upon Adams and Clay; but General Jackson believed it, and, what is more, made the country believe it in 1825. Adams was an unpopular man, of an unpopular section of the country. Crawford's friends were as little pleased as Jackson's with the course affairs took. The warfare upon Adams was hailed by them with joy, and they became parties to an opposition, of which, it was easy to see, Jackson was to be the beneficiary.

Clay's ambition or incaution betrayed him into the serious, and, as it turned out, so far as concerns the presidency, the fatal error of accepting office, the first office, under the administration which he called into power. It was, in all politic respects, a most inexcusable blunder. The office added nothing to his fame. It added nothing to his chances for the presidency. He was, on the contrary, to share the odium of an administration, at whose head was a very obstinate man, of impracticable temper, coming, by a sort of bastard process, into office; bearing a name which was the synonyme of political heterodoxy; and whose administration was fated to run a gauntlet, from the start to the close, through a long lane of clubs, wielded by the Forsythes, McDuffies, Randolphs, and almost the whole talent of the South. It was bad enough to vote for such a man. But Clay might have recovered from that. But to vote for him, and then take office under him, was suicide. A mere politician would have played the game quite differently. The Crawford vote was the vote to conciliate; and Crawford, in all human probability, would not live to be a candidate at the next election. One vote for him, would not have altered the result; while had Adams or Jackson been elected, Clay would have retained his chances for the presidency, and been uncommitted, with the advantage of the strength he had conciliated But, instead of this, he placed himself voluntarily in the minority, to bear the brunt of the assault of a majority that knew no mercy, and would give no quarter. When Adams was elected, opposition to him became the rallying cry of all the aspirants; and those, who were rivals before, now became confederates. Clay was, in all respects, too prominent as a man, as one of the actors in installing the administration, and as a member of it, to escape assault; and it turned out that, without the powers or honors of President, he had to endure the assaults and annoyances of presidential opposition.

Those assaults were not slow in coming. The public mind had laid fallow for some years, and was prepared for a bountiful crop of political agitation. Jackson raised the war-cry, and the hills and valleys, all over the land, echoed back the shout. A lava-tide of obloquy poured in a fiery flood over Clay. It seemed to take him by surprise. The idea that his voting for Adams, and then occupying the first office in his gift, seconded by the supports which the hypothesis of "*bargain*" found, or which were made for it, should originate such a charge, seems never to have entered his imagination. And when it came, he had the weakness to attempt to strangle it by personal intimidation, or to avenge it by violence.

The election of Adams, under such circumstances, was the making of Jackson. It filled up his popularity. It completely nationalized it. The State-Rights Party, to whom the name and lineage of Adams were enough for opposition, turned, at once, to the man who could best defeat him, and saw, at a glance, who that man was ; and the popular sympathy was quickly aroused in behalf *of the honest old soldier circumvented by two cunning politicians*.

CHAPTER II.

Clay's Party Tactics—Adams's Administration—Jackson's and Clay's Mutual Hatred—Charge against Clay—Jackson as President—Clay in the Senate—The War of the Giants—The "Spoils" Doctrine—The Proclamation and Force Bill—John Randolph—His Character—Jackson's Influence.

CLAY committed three capital errors as a mere tactician. He should not have become a candidate for the presidency. He was young enough to wait. His talents and his growing popularity had placed him " in the line of safe precedents." The presidency was coming fast enough to him. He stood no chance of election then, and a defeat nearly always weakens a candidate. He should not have allied himself to the New England influence; an influence never strong, then unpopular, and from which power was continually receding. He should not, above all, have taken office under Adams, We speak of these things as mere matters of policy, leaving out of consideration the higher questions of right and principle; though, as to two of these errors, there was no principle involved, which required a sacrifice of self-interest; we mean his candidacy and his acceptance of the premiership.

He had committed earlier a serious blunder, considered in the same narrow and selfish light. He had broken a lance with the Virginia politicians, and run a tilt at Monroe, on the question of Internal Improvements, involving a construction of the Constitution. So prominent had he stood in the ranks of the Republican party, by his services in Congress, in behalf of the war, and his agency in the treaty of Ghent, that the Virginia influence, still strong, if not longer exerted in behalf of one of her own citizens, (and it could not be expected that the Virginia market was to supply *all* the demands for Presidents,) might naturally be expected to go to one of her own sons. But Clay assailed, in no gentle spirit, the jealous character of a Commonwealth declining from the high position of her ancient influence, and the more sensitive, in her decline, of disrespect to her pretensions and authority. The Virginia doctrines, too, were progressive. What was orthodoxy in 1798 and 1816, was something short of it in 1825.

And Clay's opinions in regard to this measure and its principle, enabled the advocates of the Virginia doctrines to rally the Republican or State-Rights party against him; while the bold and imperious bearing of the great commoner, in the flush-tide of an ambition, which knew, at that time, better how to command than to conciliate, excited the jealousy of the colleagues and associates, who had, for so many years, exerted so controlling an influence on public affairs.

In the conduct of the canvass of 1827–28, Mr. Clay did not show any marked ability, as a manager. He made many speeches, and they were able and eloquent. But they were dinner speeches, addressed to but few, and those friends, and read only by few.

The course of Jackson was different. He said but little, but that little was to the point. The rough, unlettered honesty and vigor of his criminations were more effective than the polished sarcasm, the lofty declamation, and the elaborate reasonings of his antagonist. The policy of the Adams administration, calm, prudent, pacific and thoroughly conscientious and conservative, was not the policy to *win* favor and enlist support. It might have retained a popularity already won; but it was necessary, in order to sustain the administration, to stop the progress of opposing influences, determined to condemn and not to be appeased; and to throw in new elements, which might attract new recruits. A bold and spirited policy, with new ideas and large aims, was required, to draw off opposition, and to create fresh issues, upon which the administration and its enemies could join, with advantage to the former. The fiery spirit of Jacksonism could only have been fought with fire. The public mind craved excitement. One of those periodical epidemics had come over the country, before which a tame conservatism is driven like chaff. It is probable that nothing could have saved the Adams administration. It is certain that the healthy process of keeping the body politic on a quie regimen, and letting it grow, was not the prescription that suited a people thirsty for excitement and fevering for action. But the administration was fixed to a policy, which was to let the ship float, and keep the crew scrubbing the deck and scouring the guns. The opposition was fixed to none. There were many parties and sects opposed to Adams and his principles or practices; and all these were for Jackson. A very various opposition was melted down into a very vague Jacksonism. It carried every thing before it, as combinations usually do; and the star that never paled afterwards, shone out, the first and brightest in the political firmament, and shed disastrous twilight on Clay and his fortunes.

If these great rivals agreed in nothing else, they agreed in hating each other with uncommon fervor. They had early come in collision. Clay had attacked Jackson, in language studiously guarded, but still, in effect, strongly reprehensive. His speech on the Pensacola business was marked by great vigor, and more than characteristic eloquence; and, doubtless, in the frank habit its author had of saying what he thought and felt without mincing words, he had said things of Gen. Jackson's conduct, which, repeated with or without the usual exaggeration, were not particularly agreeable to his eager and passionate nature. But this might have been forgiven. It is certain that it was glossed over. The parties met and civilities were interchanged. When, however, the affiliation of Clay and Adams was consummated, a spirit of bitter, uncompromising, life-long enmity was aroused. Its course and its consequences we have partially attempted to sketch.

Clay had a great deal to forgive. Probably, his magnanimous and generous temper enabled him to forgive as much as any man. . He had use for all his energies in this department of Christian virtue. If any man could ever be justified in turning misanthrope, it was he. Jackson had dealt him a prodigious blow. He had struck him not only at the worst time for the victim, but in the most vital spot, and with a weapon himself had placed in his enemy's hand. Clay was at the age when men are most ambitious, and he was naturally one of the most ambitious of men. He had ascended the political mount with toil and labor, and saw before him the promised land glowing in the beauty of a lovely landscape, and gilded with the enchanted hues distance lends to the view; and to be hurled rudely and suddenly back to the foot of the hill, with a mountain of obloquy rolled upon him, was, certainly, no very pleasant experience.

Clay plumed himself upon his elevation of character. He had formed to himself a model and an ideal far above the vulgar standard of statesmanship. He had taken his type (he could not have taken a higher) from the brightest examples of the Virginia school, in the fresh and palmy days of her glory and greatness. His ambition was to fill a niche in the Pantheon, in which the Henrys, the Madisons, the Marshalls stood. His large love of approbation sought gratification, in the respect and homage of the moral and the intellectual of the land. He was a gentleman, and desired to stand high in the front rank of the gentlemen of the country. He loved general popularity, too, not wisely but too well. His strength lay in the lofty appeals he made to the higher and nobler qualities of the heart, to whatever dignifies and ennobles our nature, and in his withering scorn of the base, mean and sordid. He had but little skill and no inclination to address the prejudices, or to arouse the groundling passions of the masses; but those who have listened to his stirring and animated appeals to the reason, and the moral sense and the generous sensibilities of men, until every nerve thrilled at his bidding, know how strong was the power of that eloquence, which, equally in youth and in age, could sway senates and courts and people, as the moon sways the tides of the sea. To assail him in the source of his power, was to attack his very life's life. He found himself so assailed. He found the very idea of his existence associated with the idea of meanness.. He found his name the synonyme of intrigue, treachery and political knavery. He found the popular heart inflamed against him as a colossal cheat. The charge Jackson preferred against him could not be answered; for, in the tempest of indignation which prevailed, his voice could not be heard above the din of the elements. Jackson had piled on him mountains of infamy, which it required more than the strength of the Titans of old to upheave. A thousand presses rang with the charge; ten thousand orators echoed it from ten thousand stumps. He was the theme of hundreds of thousands of tongues, all busy in the work of acrid denunciation. In the council-hall, in the town meeting, in city and in country, at the church door, in the dram-shop, on the muster ground, by the fire-side, in the stage-coach, on the steamboat, on the busy wharf, at the log-raising on the remote frontier, his infamy was the engrossing topic of discourse. More than this: the leading issue of a presidential election was his corruption *vel non;* and the popular verdict, with almost unequalled unanimity, was against him; and what was worse, in the election with that issue, his native state and his adopted state both went against him.

As a mass of quicksilver attracts to it the vagrant globules, so the other errors of his free and unguarded life ran into and swelled this monstrous accusation. He had played cards, like Jackson and every other Southern gentleman. He was now set down as little short of a regular blackleg, who had turned his skill in that sort of cheatery into politics, and, in conspiracy with Adams, had cut, shuffled and dealt, on a stocked pack, General Jackson and the whole American people out of the presidency! It cannot be denied that, at this time, John Randolph's merciless sarcasm was the expression of a general sentiment; that he occupied the place in politics assigned to Captain Riley in private life, or to Overreach in the characters of fiction; and that sentence of virulent satire, condensing the venom of a whole brood of cobra capellos, "the union of the puritan and the blackleg, of Blifil and Black George," spoken, as Junius would have uttered it, conveyed the general sense at once of his conduct and his character. No wonder Clay called the sardonic satyr to the field, and essayed the keen marksmanship of splitting a bullet on him; the edge of his shadowy outline being nearly as sharp as his wit.

Gen. Jackson was not a man to leave a work half done. All his influence was exerted, and all his energies employed, to clinch the nail driven into Clay's character. The bold and constant denunciations of him by Gen. Jackson, were matters of knowledge to all who approached the White House. Clay found those who had been his warm friends, some of them his confidential and trusted ones, in the ranks of the opposition, not merely waging a political warfare against him, but the loudest and the bitterest in the assaults upon his character. It was a valuable lesson in human nature that was taught him; but the tuition charge was somewhat high.

It cannot be denied that the Southern statesmen looked upon Clay with something of jealousy and something of unkindness. Many of these were hereditary politicians; almost all of them were gentlemen, born, bred and educated. They seemed to look upon the Kentucky senator as a specimen of the parvenu, as a new man, as a hoosier, and a hoosier meant "half-horse, half-alligator, and a little touch of the snapping-turtle." He had come from the backwoods, at a time when they were a wilderness. He had passed through no college. His ancestral name was undistinguished. He had served no apprenticeship to any great man. He had been heralded and endorsed by no great name. Worse than all, he walked up to the first positions, asking no leave, conciliating no patronage, shunning no responsibility, soliciting no favors, acknowledging no precedence, and ready to assail all men and all questions that came in his way. He had risen with marvellous rapidity; first senator, then leading member, and in the first class of orators and statesmen, Speaker, commissioner to Ghent, offered the rôle of Madison's appointments, refusing it again under Monroe, candidate for President, and seemingly, though defeated for the present, on the highway to the presidency, if not checked in his forward course.

Besides, he had not borne himself very humbly, certainly not in a very conciliating spirit, to the Virginia influence, then the dominant influence in the House for brains and political accomplishments. He had given those politicians sundry raps on the knuckles; he had defeated their candidate for the speakership; he had opposed them on the internal improvement and tariff questions; and, with much of the sweetness of temper and frankness of Charles Fox, he had a cool, lounging sort of effrontery, a way of "giving a piece of his mind"—an air of deviltry gleaming out of his sparkling eye, before the chin lengthened into the earnestness and expressed firmness of his iron resolution—which was not a little mocking and annoying to the second-rate men of Congress, oracles at home, whom he encountered, and handled sometimes not very gently.

Almost without exception, these gentlemen joined in the clamor against Clay's imputed corruption; and, almost without exception, did they live to regret or to recant the charges they uttered. The rising talent of the country especially of the South, with probably a more justifiable prejudice, caught at the story, and made the stump ring and the press groan, with their callow and rampant sophomore philippics, before their porcupine quills had grown out of the pinfeather.

Clay returned to the shades of retirement, and Jackson stepped into the Presidential office. Never was an administration inaugurated more auspiciously, or started its voyage on a smoother sea or with more favoring winds; and, from the seat of power, its chief looked down, with grim satisfaction, upon his rival's prospects, clothed in true poetic hues,

> 'Darkly, deeply, beautifully blue.'

The high office did not change the iron man a whit, however he may have changed it. He was as much at home in the White-House as in his marquee; and wore the robes of office with as graceful a dignity as if his life had been passed in courts and cabinets. *Mens equa in arduis*, might have been his device, as Hastings' in India.

The calm delights of rural retirement did not long hold, in luxurious repose, the active spirit of Clay, then in the golden prime of his faculties. He returned in 1831-32 to the Senate of the United States.

And now began, in good earnest, the war of the giants. Each was in the place best fitted for the display of his talents: Jackson in the executive department; Clay in the great arena of debate, the American Senate. They were now, where they could be seen and their influence felt, by the whole American people. The administration of Gen. Jackson was spirited. His strong hand was felt at the helm. The tendency and character of his administration were to consolidate his party. He impressed his own individuality upon the government and the nation. His exercise of the power of removal and appointment inspired a new excitement into the irregular and torpid pulse of party action.

Clay made one or two moves on the board—and these unfortunate ones for his popularity—in favor of the Cherokees—against pre-emption to settlers on the public lands,—in favor of internal improvements and the Bank of the United States, and against the appointment of Mr. Van Buren as minister to England.

Another presidential election came on, and Clay again took the field against the old hero, and was signally defeated.

Gen. Jackson came into his second term, and Clay remained in the Senate; and now, for four years, the struggle was renewed with an earnestness, a bitterness and an ability which, brought out the energies of the two opposing leaders to their utmost power. Hitherto parties had been more personal than political. But now parties were to be formed with distinct creeds and well-defined principles, which, for a quarter of a century, would divide the country throughout its entire length. The spirit of Jacksonism was now to be seen in its full agency upon the country. The public mind was now prepared for the revelation to be made of it. The series of measures affecting the currency, beginning with the removal of the deposits, constituted the leading measures of contest. Never was the personal popularity of a man more thoroughly tested, the firmness of a politician tried more effectually, nor a popularity and nerve more triumphantly sustained. The veto of the U. S. Bank was nothing. It was rather unpopular even independently of the assailant's popularity. Money changers are not, and never have been, popular favorites, from the time they were driven from the temple. Corporations are not popular in republics. Exclusive privileges, money oligarchies, rag-barons, are phrases which catch the popular ear. Besides, their power is independent of the people. They are controlled by wealth, and wealth has no friend in envious poverty. Besides, charges were made against the Bank; and to make a charge against a colossal shaving-shop, is the same thing as to prove it. Proof is irrelevant and out of place. Moreover, the State-Rights party, who only tolerated the Bank from necessity, now that the necessity had ceased, opposed it. But the removal of the deposits was another thing. That was a measure of unequalled boldness. It involved the question of the powers of the different departments of the government. It brought into conflict the legislature and the executive. The Senate refused to sustain the measure. It rebuked the President and charged him with usurping power. The President retorted upon the Senate. He offered his protest. It was refused a place on the Senatorial records. The President accused that body of prejudging his case, and of trying and convicting him of crime unheard and without impeachment. He appealed to the people.

The course of the Senate was unwise. We think it unfortunate for the Whigs that Clay and Calhoun were there at all, able and powerful as were their efforts against the President. The popularity of Jackson was with the masses, and it was a popularity *against* them. The more conspicuously he stood out before the people, especially as the object of assault, and of assault by his personal enemies, the more the popular sympathies would side with him. *Their* attacks and proceedings carried with them the suspicion of malignity, or, at least, of prejudice and interest. There was something, too, in the contest of Jackson against the tremendous array of talent embodied against him (of which Clay, Webster and Calhoun were only the heads) himself standing in heroic defiance of the entire host —like Cocles at the head of the bridge—that was calculated to inspire admiration as well as to excite sympathy, with a generous, warlike and chivalric people. There were too many on one. The President stands as a personality—a warm and living man; the Senate as a corporation. The former draws sympathy as a man from men. The latter may excite terror by power, but does not win sensibility through feelings of a kindred humanity. Besides, the Senate is the aristocratic institution. Our idea of it is that of an army; of the destruction of the whole of which we can hear without emotion; while the portrayal of the sufferings of an individual excites our interest, and arouses our pity. It was impolitic to have put

Jackson on his resources—to have stimulated an activity, already sufficiently morbid. It were better to have "given him rope," and taken the chances of his betrayal into rasher schemes or projects, or of his leaving—a small chance—unfortified his positions. The question *must* have been made; and the great struggle should, at once, have been begun before the people, before the administration and its friends had foreclosed inquiry. Above all, the pretexts or grounds of crimination which he found in the conduct of the Senate, should not have been given him. The man of the whole people would beat the confederation of the men of the states, with any thing like an equal showing.

His first administration was aggressive, exciting, bold, daring; yet not rash, considering the head of popularity which brought him into power, and the small and feeble opposition he might expect to encounter. What he did, he did boldly; and much is forgiven in a free country to boldness. He vetoed the Bank bill, which pleased the State-Rights party, then a powerful interest; but he broke the effect of the veto in other quarters, by the intimation that some differently organized institution might meet with favor. He pocketed the land bill, broke up the cabinet, quarrelled with Calhoun, and kept up a pretty brisk cannonade on the Bank, then floundering and spouting blood like a harpooned whale.

But the leading influence on the country was the doctrine and practice of removals from office. He rewarded friends and discarded enemies. He gave out the idea pretty distinctly that it was worth while to work for his side, and very dangerous to the office-holder or expectant to work against him. In this way, he diffused his own spirit and energy through every department of the government, and into every section of the country; nor in this way only, but by his port, presence, bearing, enthusiasm, personal and official correspondence, and his earnest and decided expressions to all of the many who came near him, he excited the public mind in his favor, and seconded the efforts of an able press in his behalf. He had one advantage without which all this were of but little avail. He had the ear and the prepossessions of the people; and no man ever lived who could better address their passions, and apply the arguments, and ply the appeals which found approval, or would create an impression on the common mind. It is astonishing what one powerful and active mind, concentrating its energies on a single purpose, can accomplish. Jackson was the *boss* of the great political workshop, and he tolerated no idleness among the journeymen and apprentices. The great central will was felt at the remotest corners of the empire. The administration was a highly-charged galvanic battery, and the office-holders and aspiring politicians were the media, diffused throughout all parts of the country, by which the electric current flowed out upon the people.

As a mere party appliance, the spoils doctrine, as it is called, was and is (it seems to have been practically adopted by both parties) the most effective engine of party. It establishes communication all over the country; it gives an interest to thousands in the success of an administration; it secures a corps of supporters, besides furnishing them with the means of offence and assault; it makes the office-holder's place of business a party barrack, and himself *ex officio* drill sergeant and recruiting officer, and supplies him with the *materiel* for obtaining recruits, and instituting and perfecting organization. If it addresses the lower passions, they are the more active and energetic faculties. A man in politics may do a good deal from patriotism, but he does it by spasms and desultorily; while he will work all the time for money and promotion; and one or two active men and their tail can stir up a prodigious commotion in a community, if they will only do their best. The origination of this system was worthy of the genius of Ignatius Loyola.

The proclamation of the President against South Carolina, and the Force-bill, issued in accordance with its principles, was a severe and, in its result, a decisive test of Gen. Jackson's popularity. We have alluded to the enthusiasm with which the State-Rights party had supported him, and to the brilliant array of talent it brought to his aid. The Virginia influence had brought the *prestige* of the '98 doctrines and the statesmen of that school, to the hero's standard. It had supported Jackson, or at least, had opposed Adams and Clay, upon State-Rights grounds. Some purple patches of the old Professor of Rhetoric, intended to dizen out the commonplaces of one of his messages—something about " light-houses in the skies," and a toast about " ebony and topaz," which came pretty well up to the Scotchman's definition of metaphysics, neither the author nor reader understanding it—were taken, very much on trust, to be a covert assailment of the honored tenets of 1798. But what were these milk-and-water vaticinations to the strong meat of the proclamation? The proclamation denied the sovereignty of the States. It assumed the power of the General Government to treat a State as a revolted province, and to hang and quarter its citizens for high treason, if they, in obedience to State laws or ordinances, opposed the laws or authority of the Federal Government, within the limits of the State. Its principles unquestionably surrendered the State up to the mercy of the Federal Government; her very existence held at the tenure of the will of the national powers; saving only the right of revolution—a right, of which power is the predicate, and power the only arbiter to determine whether it exists in any given case. We wish the reader to understand that we express no opinion, as to the correctness of these or of any other principles or practices which have divided parties. We are only reviewing the history of the time, in perfect independence of partisan feeling. But, unquestionably, the heaviest blow ever struck at the State-Rights school, was dealt by the proclamation. It attacked those doctrines in the abstract and in the concrete, in the root and in the trunk, in the branches, in the flower, and in the fruit. Jackson dealt but little in abstractions at any time, but on this occasion the proclamation was but the reading of the riot act before firing into the crowd; or, rather, it was only a programme of proceedings, of which the first step was to be the blockade of the port of Charleston. If it be true that political or religious prejudices may, after long and incessant inculcation by generation on generation, be imbedded and ingrained in the mental or moral constitution, so that they become hereditary, like the instincts of animals, State-Rights doctrines ought to have been ineradicable, flowing in the blood, and mixing in the marrow of the Southern, and especially of the Virginian population. For, since "the reign of terror," never was a doctrine, which no one opposed, so eloquently and powerfully advocated, taught, expounded, and sworn by. The republican doctrine was affirmed and re-affirmed in every variety of expression, and with religious solemnity, year after year, and by every department of the State government, and by meetings of the people in every town and hamlet. It was the thirty-nine articles, to which every candidate for holy orders had to subscribe, before admission into the Republican church.

No wonder, then, that the leaders stood aghast at this bold proclamation. No wonder that *they* opposed it. No wonder that the Virginia legislature, trembling for the honored creed which had given Virginia her political prominence and authority, and a line of Presidents to the confederacy, should have been startled into opposition to this new reading of the constitution, which ignored all she reverenced and all she had taught. Tazewell and Tyler and Upshur, and Floyd and Gilmer, and a host of gallant and gifted men, took open ground against the President. There was another. He was away when this conflict between South Carolina and the President began. The bravest lance of all the Knights of the Temple was away, when " one blast upon his bugle-horn were worth a thousand men." He had gone, that proud and scornful despiser of office and placemen, that haughty contemner of the sycophants and hirelings of power; whose measureless contempt had been poured out in showers of vitriol upon sinecurists and dependents on official patronage, until elevation to office seemed to those, who followed the direction of his bony finger, to be the promotion of the pillory; whose strength, even more than in the vigor of his sarcasm, lay, as Samson's in his locks, in the immaculate disinterestedness of his politics, and in his romantic loyalty to Virginia, and her service, and her rights; and especially as against the General Government, which he regarded, as Hannibal looked upon Rome, as her sworn, hereditary, usurping enemy;—he, in a moment which he ever cursed as the darkest of his troubled destiny, had taken service under the administration. And where was this great Warwick, almost " the last of the barons," *now ?* He had borne a body, emaciated to a skeleton by consumption, to the hyperborean regions of Europe, with express permission to suffer the office to be subservient to his personal comfort and convenience; with a constitution fit only for a nursery; with an intellect racked, and, at times, unseated from its imperial throne by physical disease, and the exacerbations of a temper unfitted for the patient, coolly-arranged and wily plans of diplomacy; a presence and a person whose uncouth and eccentric movements only found apology and retained respect from those who knew him in the past, and knew the splendid abilities which lay behind that eccentricity and deformity: HE—of all living men!—HE went as a liveried sinecurist to the court of a despot, to exhibit himself to those whose language he did not know, and who did not know his, as a death's head at the pageant of the autocrat, to provoke the jeer or the more melancholy pity of a frivolous and half-civilized court!

But as the conflict thickened, which involved all he had ever cherished of political principle, he returned home again, weak and staggering, but with the old fire kindling into fierce action his sinking pulse.

Like Brian De Bois-Guilbert in the lists of Temple-stowe, the Cavalier of Roanoke came more to die in harness than to fight in the cause, and as the champion of his order. Right clearly did his voice ring out the old war-cry, and the lance, that had, in his boyish hand, struck hard and full upon the helmet of Patrick Henry, was now boldly aimed at the towering crest of Jackson.

Let us pause to do some meed of justice to this great man's memory. With all his faults and infirmities, great and glaring as these were, he was "the noblest Roman of them all." There was more of the true grit of manhood in him than in any man of his school Virginia ever produced. True, he was no democrat, and not much of a Republican, save in the name. Like Burke, his mind was that of a man of *caste*. He was a baron, but a baron of Virginia; a representative of the gentry, with all the ideas and prejudices of class; a Bramin of the Bramins. He was opposed to th Union, opposed to the Constitution, because it raised up a government and power greater than Virginia. It razeed Virginia from her imperial state. It allowed the Yankee to interfere with her affairs, nay even to control her policy. He wished to limit the power of the Federal Government—to un-nationalize it as much as possible—to recover by construction what she had lost by concession; and for his whole life was he consistent, amidst a deluge of inconsistencies in his associates. This was his polar star; and by it, wherever the winds or tides of passion or of circumstance bore him, he meant to steer, as his guide over the troublous sea of politics.

Beneath all the banners under which he had fought, in all the associations into which he had come; in the hours of triumph and in the days of adversity; in all moods of temper and in all transitions of mind; in every alternation of physical condition, there was *one* sentiment constant and unchanged, and that was *love of Virginia*. His imagination, fervid and poetic, dwelt lovingly amidst the scenes and the incidents of her past glory; for it was Virginia, as she was in her youth, in the days of her loosely-held colonial dependence—Virginia, as she was when, heroically, in the old English spirit, her planters, with the pride of the Barons holding council and dictating terms to John at Runnymede, rose to throw off the British yoke, yet preserved so much of the order and conservatism of English institutions, even in the very acts of resistance and revolution; it was the

Virginia of the freeholders ruled by the gentry, cherishing her talent and exulting in the virtues and renown of her great men, that won the affection, and drew out the reverence of her gloriously-gifted son. His veneration for her made her very defects seem virtues to his idolatrous eyes. She was a model. He resented, as little short of impiety, any alterations in her government or laws. Every proposition for reform he considered as an invitation to a desecration of the sacred labors of his fathers. As in a lover's eyes, so in his, blemishes apparent to all others were beauties. Progress was a name for ruin and destruction, and the desire to remodel her Constitution the idea of Vandals or Jacobins. It was his love for Virginia that survived the last, as it lived the strongest, of his affections. Like the Venetian exile's, his heart never beat for Virginia,

————but with such yearning as
The dove has for her distant nest.

But with what feelings could he think of the government which, according to his idea, was before too strong, enlarged into the colossal structure of almost imperial power and grandeur; the state governments playing, like satellites, around the great central sun?

Jackson had got between the politicians and the people. It is true, to a limited extent, that they had introduced him. It is true, that they had contributed to impress him upon the public mind. They had been profuse of eulogiums upon his character. They had exhausted commendation upon him. But they could not recall the impression they had made, and they had made him greater than themselves. They had a good deal mistaken their own power and popularity, after Jacksonism came into fashion. They thought they had made *it*, when they were but made *by* it. They were floating upon it as drift-wood, while they vainly thought they were giving motion to its resistless current. Its proud waves would not be stayed at their bidding, but dashed to destruction, amidst the rocks and breakers, those who sought to turn and buffet the raging flood.

Many politicians experienced the truth of this observation. Many, who before the Jackson era, had flourished as pachas in their local demesnes, found to their sorrow, that they had raised up a Sultan, who could bow-string them at pleasure, for a word of contumacy or an act of rebellion against his authority. Nor was it different with principles. These had been the shibboleths with which they had passed the disputed defiles of politics; but now they were nullified by a new watch-word. The political conjurers found the old cabalistic phrases of "State-Rights," "Reform," and the like, superseded by the modern cry of "Hurrah for Jackson!" Jackson had got into the hearts of the people, and the unreasoning affection for the man was stronger with the masses than the wise words of the politicians' argumentation. Principles are hard to understand, but sympathy and passion work their way without troubling the brain for thought or research for facts. The first are spontaneous productions; the last only come after cultivation and labor. The masses prefer the indigenous articles.

CHAPTER III.

Removal of the Deposits—Jackson's Critical Position—His Iron Nerve—Removal of Duane—The Whig Party—Union of the Purse and the Sword—Difference between the English and American Governments—Jackson's Charges against the United States Bank—His Issue before the People—The Conduct of the Bank—Biddle—His Blunders—Commercial Distress—Jackson's Tact—His Appeal to the Farmers—Effect of the Deposits on the State Banks—Increase of Banks and Paper Money—Error of the Democratic Party—Jackson's Triumph—The Monetary and Speculative Excesses of 1835-36—The Specie Circular—Its Effects.

It has been thought strange, that even a popularity, so strong and so consolidated as Jackson's, could have withstood the powerful opposition arrayed against him, upon the bold measure of the Removal of the Deposits from the United States Bank. Calhoun's coalition with the National Republicans, was certainly something gained to the opposition; but Calhoun and his congressional friends brought more talent than numbers. It might have been supposed, too, that the character of the measure, succeeding, as it did, other measures strongly federal, would have brought against the President the influence of the State-Rights party. This was the case to a considerable extent.

Many, who did not desert the President on the question of the Proclamation, but who were cooled by that measure, deserted him now. But the State-Rights party had opposed the Bank; and it was not easy to persuade the people, who go for results, and do not very curiously scan the means, that any conduct towards a rotten, corrupt, and unconstitutional bank, was not proper, or, if improper, deserved severe reprehension; and, thus, the aid of those who made such admissions, was not very great.

The first impression made by the opposition was encouraging to them. The speeches in the Senate were echoed back by the proceedings of public meetings, all over the country. There seemed to be a general uprising of the trading and mechanical classes, especially in the large commercial cities.

They passed resolutions disapproving of the removal of the deposits, and petitioned for their restoration. Memorials, with innumerable signatures, were gotten up to the same effect. The times grew hard. A great pressure occurred in the money circles. Clamor and excitement reigned in Wall street, and on the Exchanges of the Atlantic cities; panic and consternation took the place of confidence and contentment amongst the tradesmen; failure upon failure succeeded; the banks ceased to discount, and some of them closed doors; the business of large towns languished and declined; and thousands of workmen were thrown out of employment. The friends of the President deserted him by regiments. The politicians turned pale, and hesitated, and looked for a soft place to fall down upon, or broke into open revolt. The enemies of the President took heart, and made a bold assault upon him and his course. Committees from the cities filled the lobbies of the Senate and the Representative Hall, and waited in formal state upon the President. All would not do. He stood like a rock, unshaken and unmoved. He did not arouse himself to meet the crisis. He was always ready for it. He was but the calmer for the storm. They told him all who traded on borrowed capital must break. He knocked the ashes from his pipe, and calmly remarked that all who traded on borrowed capital *ought* to break. He heard with sober attention all they had to say, and merely observed, that his mind was made up.

Nothing but Jackson's nerve saved him. If he had flinched or sought to conciliate opposition, or to compromise with the Bank, or even had he contented himself with a defensive attitude, he would have lost the day. The Senate was against him, and the tone of Clay was triumphant, exulting, and full of confidence and hope. But the very boldness of the measure was Jackson's protection. The courage that leads a man into danger is his best shield against it. Jackson had taken the responsibility. He had come out from behind all entrenchments. He exposed his whole front. He had done a bold thing boldly, and in the light of day. Like a brave man who goes out on a dangerous expedition, he refused to ask any one to be the companion of the enterprise. He hazarded every thing. So far as appeared, he could make nothing by success. He might lose every thing by failure. He was not sure of his own party. Indeed, his Secretary refused to obey him; the Congress of his friends had pronounced against him on the propriety of the removal, and, indeed, it seems, he had little confidence that they would reverse that judgment; for he did not wait for the few weeks to elapse when they would assemble again. The Bank was still a powerful influence. It had many Democratic friends in Congress. It would make a fierce struggle, and seek to regain, in resistance to this movement, the ground it was losing under the veto.

Jackson saw the whole ground, and was prepared for the worst. It was the boldest and most hazardous enterprise of his life. He stood alone, or with only Blair and one or two other friends at his back. He had in "*The Globe*," though, good backing as far as one man—himself, in his way, a host—could make it. He ordered the Secretary of the Treasury to remove the deposits; but Duane refused. Here was a new difficulty. If Duane resigned, the President could appoint another man in his place. But Duane would not resign. Jackson removed *him;* and having made up his mind to carry this measure, he would have removed all the officers in the government, if they had stood between him and his purpose.

When the WHIG PARTY was formed, it was a critical period for the President. It not only combined new element of opposition, but the name—and "names are things" in politics—was an old and venerable one, and around it gathered many associations of the most stirring interest. It was based, too, upon the old principle, which, as well in England, as in our own country, had marked the line of division between the advocates of executive prerogative and power, and the champions of popular or legislative privilege; and it was claimed, with at least a color of truth, that, in these bold measures, affecting the money of the nation, the legislative department, to which its custody and expenditure belonged, had been invaded by an act of the executive, which assumed the control and disposition of the public treasure. It was charged that the President had, by his conduct, fulfilled the definition Patrick Henry gave of a tyrant, by uniting in his own hands the purse and the sword. It remained to see what effect would be given to this revival of the old English and American revolutionary name, supported, as it was, by this plausible title to it, on the part of the enemies of the administration.

It is true that the great characteristics of English parties, running through so many centuries, and still dividing them, were the rival principles, one of which sought to limit the power of the executive, and to give power to the legislature, and the other, to strengthen the executive, at the expense of the legislature. But, it must be remembered, that our Constitution is widely different from the British form. The throne is independent of the people. The king is neither elected by the people, nor, within the constitution, removable by them, nor responsible to them. His interests may be adverse to theirs. His power, whenever increased, derives its accessions from their liberties and rights. The commons are their only representatives. But, in our form, the presidential chair rests upon the same basis as the seat of the member of Congress. The President stands even nearer to the people than the Senator. He owes his official existence to the people; he holds office for a limited term—practically he is disqualified from holding it for more than eight years; he came from the people, and he goes back, like any other citizen, to live and die amongst the people. He is, before his election and after it, an object of peculiar interest. He must have been known, and favorably known, to his countrymen. He is talked of, his character and merits canvassed, his history, and services, and qualities, discussed in every neighborhood, nay, at every fireside, in the Republic. He stands forth, therefore, in bold relief. He comes accredited to the people by the popular endorsement, and by the *prestige* of success. It is vain to talk to a confiding people, whose affections are, at least, as strong as their judgments; who are not politicians, and who do not look forward from abstract dogmas to far-off results, that it is their duty to be jealous and suspicious of him whom they have just trusted with the highest proof of their confidence and regard.

It is very true that the sentiment of liberty has grown with us into a passion. But liberty is a very indefinite term, and conveys a very vague meaning, until some overt act, coming home to the people, gives it an interpretation. That sort of liberty, which is invaded in the small beginnings—in the cautious encroachments of tyranny, feeling its way gradually to ungranted and unlawful dominion—the seed-acts, from which spring up, at a distant day, a harvest of errors and precedents of evil—these it requires sharper acumen than the masses possess, to see at the right time, and in their real character. For example—what invasion was it—they asked—of *their* liberty, for the President to remove the public money from the *Bank*, a wholesale shaving-shop, to other places of deposit?

Besides, Jackson always had the sagacity to disguise his strong measures in popular forms. Whether his acts were always popular or not, his reasoning always was. Whether his proceedings were despotic or not, he defended them upon the principles and in the name of freedom. It was *the Bank*, he charged, that was the tyrant. It was seeking to overturn the government, and to enslave and corrupt the people. *It* was buying up members of Congress, and subsidizing the press. It was producing the panic and pressure, which disordered commerce, and crippled industry, and turned out labor to starve, in order to force upon the people its own financial system, and a renewal of its existence. It had violated its charter. It had closed its doors against investigation. It had been false to its contracts. It had expended vast sums of money in electioneering schemes and practices against the government. It had assumed a tone of haughty insolence towards the President, as disrespectful to the office as to the incumbent. Its president lived in a style befitting a prince of the blood royal. From his palace of Andalusia he came to his marble palace in Philadelphia, to issue his ukases which caused the stocks to rise and fall all over the world. He was the Money King—" the despot with the quill behind his ear," whom John Randolph said he feared more than a tyrant with epaulettes. He could make money plentiful or scarce, property high or low, men rich or poor, as he pleased. He could reward and he could punish; could set up and pull down. His favor was wealth, his enmity ruin. He was a government, over which the people had no control.

Thus, it will be seen, with what exquisite tact the President presented the issue to the people. It was the issue of a powerful money oligarchy, in its last struggles for power denied by the people, warring against the government the people had set up. Jackson stood the impersonation of the popular sovereignty, warring against an usurping moneyed institution—an enormous shaving-shop. St. George and the Dragon was only the ante-type of Jackson and the Monster!

The truth is, that what Jackson lacked of material to make head against the Bank, the Bank more than supplied. Biddle, its president, seems to have been a worse politician than financier. From the first hostile demonstration of the President, to the final explosion of the new institution, into which the assets and management of the National Bank were carried, the whole series of movements was a series of blunders and follies.

If the Bank had been bent upon ruin, it could have taken no surer method of suicide. The opposition of its friends in Congress to an investigation into its affairs; its contributions towards the publication of political papers and pamph lets; its large loans to newspaper editors, and to members of Congress; the immense extension of its line of discounts—these things, however innocent, naturally gave rise to suspicion, and suspicion, in its case, was conviction. The tone it adopted in its report, towards the President, or, rather, towards the paper sent to the cabinet, signed "Andrew Jackson," was in as bad taste as policy. The truth is, the President of the Bank greatly underrated the President of the United States. Jackson was a much abler man than Biddle supposed. The unlearned man of the backwoods knew the American people better than the erudite scholar of the refined metropolis. The tenant of the Hermitage was, by all odds, a wiser politician than the lord of the princely demesnes of Andalusia.

It is true that the crisis was a sharp one. Great distress was felt, great clamor was raised, immense excitement prevailed. The storm burst suddenly, too, and with tropical fury. The President's friends fell off like autumnal leaves in a hurricane. The party leaders grew anxious; many of them were panic-stricken, and some of them deserted; but the pilot at the helm stood like another Palinurus in the storm. The distress was confined mostly to the commercial cities. Jackson's reliance was mainly on the rural districts, and, luckily for him, these contained the great mass of the population, devoted to the calm and independent pursuit of husbandry, and devoted to him. The farmers were, to a great extent, independent of banks and free of debt, and depending for support upon the sale of necessaries, which generally command, under all states of the money market, remunerating prices.

That there was great distress could not be denied. But whose fault was it? The Bank laid the blame on the President; the President laid it on the Bank. Which was to be believed? The *immediate* cause was the conduct of the Bank in withdrawing its circulation; but this was made necessary, it was said, by the withdrawal of the public money. This was denied; and it was charged that the Bank had, by the unnecessary and corrupt extension of its discounts and accommodations, put itself into the necessity of this sharp measure of protection, even if such necessity existed.

But relief was at hand. The deposits were placed in the vaults of the state-banks. The United States Bank was out of the way. The funds of the government, overflowing in all its channels of revenue, became the feeders to numberless Bogus banks all over the country. Bank charters multiplied in the land. A state of almost fabulous prosperity, as it seemed, set in. The revolution went back for the first time. But the calm was worse than the storm—the prosperity worse than the adversity. And here was the great, and, for a time as it turned out, the fatal error of the Democratic party. It had not provided for the exigencies it created. The United States Bank was put down, but where was the substitute? The Bank had been the fiscal agent of the government, in fact the treasury; what was to succeed to its duties? If the public money was not safe in the United States Bank, it could scarcely be considered safe in the various shin-plaster concerns, that had sprung up, like frog-stools, all over the Union; nor could individuals, in such wild and uncertain times, especially without new restrictions and securities, be intrusted with the enormous sums coming into the hands of the government, when every man was a speculator, and every speculation seemed a fortune! It could scarcely have escaped the sagacity of the politicians, who were inveighing, every day, against the evils of the credit and paper systems, that this enormous banking, so suddenly and prodigiously increased, must, at no distant day, lead to a monetary crisis, which, compared with that following the removal of the deposits, would be like a hurricane to a zephyr. But no adequate safeguard was provided. Present peace was purchased at the expense of future overthrow; and it was bequeathed to Mr. Van Buren to reap the whirlwind, from the wind sown by his predecessor.

But, for the present, the sky cleared again. Jackson rallied his hosts. He recovered his lost ground; he regained his captured standards; he cashiered the deserters, and inspired throughout the country a fresher zeal for the party, and an almost superstitious conviction of his own invincibility.

And now we had reached the climax of one of those prodigious hallucinations, which sometimes, like epidemics, sweep over nations, carrying before them all lessons of the past, all experience, reason, sagacity and common sense. The South Sea bubble, the Mississippi scheme in France, the wild years of 1818–19 in our own country, all added together, scarcely paralleled, in their multiplied follies and chicanery the monetary excesses of 1835-6. We need give but a few of the features: Bank paper, by the million of dollars, resting on no foundation better than insolvent promises; an unlimited credit system, inflated to the utmost tension of speculation, without calculation as to means or results; an universal indebtedness, with no medium of payment except paper credits, liable, nay, certain, at the first challenge of their soundness, to prove worthless; an extravagance, in modes of living, forbidden by prudence to wealth, yet indulged in by poverty; enormous importations of goods, bought on credit, and sold, to the sixth remove, on credit; indebtedness by every state and by every corporation, for all it could borrow to make impossible railroads, and to navigate unnavigable rivers; while the whole nett product of the country would scarcely pay the interest on its debt; and this apparently, but a starting point for other enterprises and operations still more magnificent; the whole country turned out to speculation and fortune-hunting; prices up fourfold, and going still higher every day; every channel and department of commerce or speculation foaming with the rushing tides of adventure, and every highway teeming with adventurers, swarming in hordes over the land. It seemed as if a new chapter had opened in history, and that the world had been let out of the school of common sense for a holiday of wild commercial insanity.

At the height of this *mardi-gras*, and in the agony of this wild sport, Gen. Jackson threw down the specie circular. The blow was as sudden as it was effectual. In itself it amounted to no great deal. It required specie for government debts, which any creditor has a right to demand. Gold and silver, to the amount of a few millions, were seemingly no hard requisition on banks that had promised to pay hundreds of millions on demand. But the circular was as effectual as an injunction in chancery not only on the banks, but on every body in trade. It caused examination; it called a halt; men began to take their latitude. It was found they were far out at sea. The confidence of the public was broken. The sole capital of the banks was this confidence, and confidence was now gone. A rush—a suspension—a failure—a crash from Maine to Louisiana, involving ruin, and all the evils which attend the failures of those who seek by mendacity to prevent the results of folly.

In any other country, this prodigious shock would have produced a revolution. Perhaps even here it would have done so, had the ultimate effects of the measure been seen, and had revolution promised any relief. But it remained to be seen how much might yet be saved from the wreck. The suspension of business was as instantaneous as it would be in Boston, if, suddenly, all the railways were taken up, and the telegraphic wires torn down. The shock was so sharp and quick that men had no time for remonstrance or. opposition; and the first moment of cool reflection to an old trader made him feel as ridiculous as an old Calvinistic divine would feel, if, stung by a tarantula and dancing a minuet with the simpering airs of a gallant, he suddenly recovered to a true sense of his situation.

CHAPTER IV.

Jackson's Second Term—Van Buren Elected President—Commercial Distress—Party Excitement—Harrison's Election and Death—Tyler's Administration—Clay's Defeat—Jackson's Death—His Achievements and Character.

THE second term of Gen. Jackson's administration was marked with stirring and startling events. Never, probably, in times of peace, were crowded, into so short a period, so many acts and movements, fraught with all the incidents and excitements of war. Washington City resembled the head-quarters of a commanding general. The whole series of measures affecting the currency—the exciting episode of the French difficulty—the South Carolina business—the distribution of the proceeds of the public lands—the collision with the Senate—Jackson's triumph over it by the passage of the expunging resolutions, these and other measures, coming in quick succession, occupied the public mind, and furnished fuel for continual excitement.

We have spoken of the Compromise and of the agency of Clay in effecting that momentous measure, upon which hung the peace and the integrity of the nation. This agency was most important to his character. It redeemed him from the old charge, in the estimation of those who had been most active and influential in urging it against him. It made him friends in a quarter where, before, he had only enemies. It presented him before the whole nation in an aspect at once of power and of goodness; as a magnanimous man and a public benefactor; and it prepared the way for a co-operation with those, who were to be, afterwards, his most efficient allies. The removal of the deposits furnished an occasion, which was ably improved, for one of those lofty and impassioned appeals to the hearts of his countrymen, which, better than any other of his countrymen, he could make.

Affairs had now changed. The re-action of Gen. Jackson's popularity in particular sections, and, to some extent, over the whole Union, created a corresponding re-action in favor of Clay. A new generation of statesmen and voters was springing up. The young and enthusiastic, such potential allies in a political contest, caught the contagion of the spirit of opposition to usurpation and tyranny, as it was called, which the fervid genius of Clay evoked. The great intellects of the nation, whose eloquence has now become classic, were co-operating in the Senate and the Lower House, and lending the aid of their various and powerful abilities to the cause of opposition. The WHIG PARTY began to be organized. It had the major part of the intellect on its side. It called that intellect, wherever it could do so, into the public service. The public councils of the nation exhibited more of talent than they had ever known before. The great age of eloquence had come. In the Senate alone, a profound and various ability was found, such as, at any other post-revolutionary period, all the departments of the government together could not muster.

In the House, Clay had a brilliant staff, young, fire-eyed enthusiasts, bold, daring, resolute, charging the very heights of power, and eager for the fray with the enemy. The commercial interest, the old manufacturing interest, the State-Rights party, the conservative interest, the old-fogy anti-military party, were now banded together; and, to give greater volume to the stream, that section of the original friends of Jackson, who desired the election of Judge White to the Presidency, instead of Mr. Van Buren, the presidential favorite, united with the opposition. Such a combination would seem to be invincible; but it was not. The opposition divided, and Jacksonism, rallying as Gen. Jackson would have rallied in the field to charge the opening ranks of an enemy, carried the day. Gen. Jackson's career closed "in triumph over all his enemies," and he threw his mantle, as he retired, upon the shoulders of his lieutenant. His sun set grand and lurid, but with the dun, ominous aspect that betokens a coming storm.

But the election of 1836, showed the opposition its underrated strength, and rescued the struggle with the revived hopes of the assailants. In the mean time, the clouds had thickened, and the terrible storm which seemed to be waiting only for the old thunderer to retire, began to blow upon the country like a tropical hurricane. No such period as that awful one of monetary panic and commercial disaster had ever before visited the nation. Scarcely yet recovered from its effects, we remember it with the vivid recollection of a fresh and horrible catastrophe.

Mr. Van Buren was inaugurated just as the embarrassments of the country were beginning to be felt in their first spasms of acute distress. The little Sybarite, looking out from the terrace of the White House, "perfumed like a milliner," saw trees dancing on their heads, and the air filled with missiles, and the waves rising mountain-high, and heard the whistle of the tornado, and felt the ground rocking like an earthquake all around him. It were a curious thing to have seen how the old chief would have met this great crisis. Could he have weathered the storm, the achievement would have been the brightest illustration of his genius. What course he would have taken, we cannot know; but we know what he would *not* have done. He would not have contented himself with holding on by one hand and fending off with the other.

The administration of Van Buren was a long stagger and a fall. Its enemies pushed on their batteries against the citadel; they sat down before it; they cut off his supplies; they dug a trench around him and battered down his walls. The campaign of 1840 opened, and it was obvious to all calm observers that the chances were greatly in favor of the opposition. The Harrisburg Convention met. The country had unequivocally pronounced in favor of Clay, and it was supposed that the only purpose of the Convention was to announce the popular decision. Clay evidently expected the nomination; and his friends congratulated themselves that the long-delayed hour of his triumph had come. Contrary to all expectation, the nomination of the politicians fell upon another—Gen. Harrison—a good, brave, kind-hearted old man, but whose whole brains could have been hid under Clay's bump of comparison.

If Clay felt the disappointment, he did not show it. His voice was the first heard in ratification. The nomination seemed at first to shock the public mind; but it was only the shock of the rail-car as it starts on its rushing course. Clay took the field for his rival. The people rose almost *en masse*. The whole country was divided, as if in civil war, into hostile factions. Banners flouted the sky; the air rang with acclamations; the people met in armies; the pursuits of business were neglected for the strife and strivings of political canvassing; and an excitement careered over the land, which, in any other country, would have drenched it in blood, and upheaved the government from its foundation stones. Tennessee was wrested from the spell of Jacksonism; and, at Nashville, a multitude, which no man might number, composed of the old enemies of Clay, hung upon his accents, and, as he denounced the principles and measures of Jacksonism, rent the air with thunder-shouts of applause, which invaded even the peace of the Hermitage. So near came the old rivals, that they hurled upon each other scorn and crimination. The result we know. Harrison came into office upon a sea-tide of popularity. A month passed. He died and was succeeded. The funeral meats furnished forth the banquet of the enemy. The Whig policy was defeated by the veto of its own President, and Whig spirit and Whig principles were paralyzed. This was the bitterest cup Clay ever drained. Yet he did not despond. He rallied and cheered his broken forces. He bore himself as loftily as ever—nay, more loftily. The party, though shorn of much of its strength, was still powerful. It had still the capacity to win another victory on old issues. It met in convention, and, this time, it made sure of its man. The cowardly policy of indirection and conciliation was discarded. The real leader was put at the head of the army. The Democratic party, with its wonderful recuperative energies, was reanimated and resuscitated, and already in the field panting for an opportunity of avenging its late defeat. The Democratic people had indicated a preference for Van Buren; but the opposition to him, arising out of his anti-Texas opinions, induced the managers to throw the political Jonah overboard, to appease the raging elements. Another was nominated, with a new issue. And all men felt that the great struggle, for life or death, was now to be fought out between the two great parties. The battle was fought with a resolution worthy of the stake. Clay lost it, and, with the old leader, went down the distinctive principles of the party he had built up, sustained and lived for; and the last hope of its permanent ascendency was extinguished for ever.

Shortly after the induction of the new administration, Jackson died. He died at peace with the world, in which he had been so prominent an actor, forgiving all his enemies, the last and greatest of whom was his early rival; an act of Christian grace, tasking his renewed temper, as he declared, to its most difficult exercise. He yielded him submissively to the only foe to whom he had ever submitted, in all his long and stormy career. The grave closed over him, as over meaner victims, and he rested, at a patriarchal age, from his heady conflicts. "After life's fitful fever he sleeps well," by the side of her to whom, through life, in manhood and in age, and for whose memory after her death, through all the tumultuous scenes and stirring exigencies of his eventful career, he had clung with a fond and doting tenderness. Earth to earth, ashes to ashes, is the universal and inevitable doom.

Thus passed from the world one of the most remarkable men, who, in all the generations of mankind, ever made his mark upon his age. It is vain to deny to Jackson a title to greatness. He achieved great things, and won a succession of splendid triumphs, unequalled in the history of any man, save one, of his generation. He achieved them, not by the force of accident, but because of the power within him. It is idle to discuss the ability or the merits of a man, who, in different, and these the highest, departments of human enterprise, succeeds, not in one department or in one measure, but in all departments and in all things throughout a long succession of years and of struggles, against the greatest and most various opposition. Such successes do not come by chance. But if we will not take this general conclusion, let us look to particulars. What did he accomplish? He raised himself, in a profession, of all others, the least suited to his genius, at a time of life, when men of real merit are only preparing themselves for local distinction, to the offices of Attorney-General and of Judge; and when the scene changed from peace to war, he rose at once to the post of General, and, in a few months, won the most brilliant successes and the brightest laurels of the war, and placed himself side by side with the great captains of the world. He took his seat in the Senate of the United States. He was soon the strongest candidate before the people for President, bearing the palm from the veteran politicians and established statesmen of the country. Defeated in the House by the politicians, he turned defeat into victory, and established upon it a sure and lasting ascendency. He was lifted by the strongest tide of personal popularity to the first office of his country, and held power against an opposition more powerful than ever before assailed an administration. But he did much more than this. He impressed his name and character upon the country more deeply than any man, the father of his country only excepted, ever did before or after him. He gave a fresh and awakening influence to the popular mind, threw off the influence of old politicians, and started the government and the people onward in a new and more impulsive career. He opened a new era in American politics, with new measures, new ideas, and new statesmen. He founded a party, more perfect in its organization, and more lasting in its influence, than any before established, giving its own line of statesmen, and its own course of policy to the country ; a party from which was to rise a stronger influence upon the world, and the indefinite increase of the wealth, territory, and population of the Republic He consolidated the strength and energies of the government; made it formidable, feared, and respected by foreign powers ; insomuch that he addressed the head of the second power of Europe, with the imperious tone of a rich creditor pursuing a bilking bankrupt, and forced him to a settlement of a claim, upon an open threat of chastisement. He found a confederacy—he left an empire. He altered the monetary system of the government—struck down the Bank of the United States—raised up and sustained the State Banks, and finally blew them up as so many torpedoes ; and, for a time, nearly abolished the whole credit system of a great trading people. He struck down the doctrines of State Rights, in their sanctions and substance, and in their strongholds, and with them the flower of the disciples of that school, to which he had, in great part, owed his elevation ; and he established national doctrines, which placed the government on the basis vainly contended for by Washington and Marshall. He subdued the Senate. He placed his rejected minister at its head. It rebuked his course. He made it draw black lines around its records. And he raised up another president, if not two, to rule after him; and continued after his retirement, and to the close of his life, the ruling spirit of his own party. This he did without the aid of the politicians ; for he needed no conduit between himself and the people. He operated *directly* upon the public mind. Indeed, the most popular man of his followers held his popularity on the tenure of his will. Desertion of him and his cause was popular ostracism. If he were powerful enough to raise up whom he chose, he was powerful enough to put down whom he chose. His name and his influence were as pervasive as the atmosphere. It fixed the selection and promotion of the cabinet minister even of the President, and also of the lowest official of an obscure municipality.

Calhoun was sitting upon the comfortable perch of the Vice-Presidency, thinking no harm, evidently quite content with the prospect before him. It was seemingly a good time for him. His foible was not supposed to be a criminal indifference, much less an unconquerable aversion, to the high posts of the public service. He was young, just reaching the meridian glory of faculties equal to the discharge of any civic duty to which he could be called. He had already won the highest distinction; and he had won it without calling into exercise half the talent he possessed. Jackson was in the heyday of a popularity such as no man of his country, its father and founder only excepted, had ever held; and he was Jackson's lieutenant; and yet, so unexceptionably had he borne himself, that though identified with the administration, and its early supporter, he had given no offence to the opposition. Indeed, he had run upon its ticket, too, for Vice President. State-Rights doctrines were in the ascendant, and the Executive countenance shone kindly upon them and their supporters. The long-sighted politicians had begun to look upon the Vice President and fawn around him, as the successor! Clay was under the ban. The man of Braintree, like a greater, was on his ocean rock. Crawford was a paralytic. Who and what stood between Calhoun and Dwight's prediction, or rather the fulfilment of it? Serenely, we may imagine him, gazing through the bow-window of the Capitol, up towards the building at the other end of the avenue, and bethinking him that only a few more years, with all the accidents which might shorten that period in his favor, stood between him and the golden guerdon for which so many hearts were fevering. Jackson's angry stamp disturbed the reverie, and, with that stamp, the platform fell beneath him, and he dropped down a thousand feet into the political charnel house below! Where were now the legions of friends with whom his slightest utterance was the definition of a proverb, " the condensed wisdom of a nation?"

> He counted them at break of day,
> But when the sun set, where were they!

The man who offended Jackson was doomed. Like a mighty Nimrod, he threw his lariat from the Capitol, and throttled and brought down to death or submission the most powerful senators, even at the remotest corners of the Republic. Talent, and genius, and learning, and eloquence, and statesmanship cordoned themselves around him in strenuous warfare; but his single arm, like Murat's on the Mount of

Transfiguration, rolled back the brilliant charge and left him still unhurt—not a feather of his plume awry—and in possession of the heights of power.

And, finally, according to T F. Marshall, when he was about quitting the world, he turned Presbyterian, and trampled Satan under foot, the last, and perhaps the greatest of his victories!

It may well be doubted if the records of ancient or of modern times exhibit to us a name, more distinguished for sublime and unfaltering courage, than that of Andrew Jackson. He never seemed to rise to, but ever to stand level with, the loftiest exigencies. There was nothing in the shape of danger or responsibility which he feared to brave—not to meet merely, but to go in quest of—not to endure, but to defy and to master. He was chary of his fame. He loved applause; but when did he pause in the execution of a purpose to count its cost to his reputation? Did he ever falter when the chivalry and flower of his early and later supporters deserted his banner by battalions? If any thing can appal a politician's heart or stay his hand, it is civil war. But, in the case of South Carolina, he contemplated that result and prepared for it, with the coolness and determination of a common-place business matter. He stood forth a peculiar and original man, in the great attribute of conceiving and executing purposes and plans, from the very contemplation of which common-place politicians shrink in dismay.

Yet one thing this great man lacked. He lacked the crowning virtue of magnanimity. Generosity towards a personal or political enemy, and charity for opposing opinion were not numbered among the virtues in his calendar. We are pained to be forced by truth to say that the hero's character, of such robust and stalwart proportions, and vital with such massive and masculine strength, was incomplete. Like some Gothic tower, dimly seen by star-light, it leaves the impression of power akin to the terrific and sublime; but wants the mild and softening light of this absent grace to make it lovely to the contemplation and dear to the heart.

We turn from the Man of Progress to the Man of Conservatism, from the Man of War to the Man of Peace.

CHAPTER V.

Clay in the Senate—His Patriotic Course—Compromise of 1850—Analysis of Clay's Character—His Rank as a Statesman—Compared with Calhoun and Webster—His Death.

THE war with Mexico ended, the questions to which it mediately gave rise transferred the scene of contention to our own country. As this collision was coming on apace, an opportunity came for electing a Whig President; for the New-York politician held one of the arms of the Democracy in the fight. But gunpowder again prevailed. The old claims of the civilian were laid aside for the fresh pretensions of the soldier. The old trick of an inexpedient expediency was revived, and the last chance of electing Clay to the Presidency thrown away.

But, though denied the first office, he was not denied the first position, in the country. That he held by the grace of God, and without the leave of the politicians. Soon was the value of his position to be tested; for the great sectional contest, awaiting only measures of practical legislation in regard to the newly-acquired territory, now broke out in all its fury. The danger of this conflict brought Mr. Clay from his retirement, to the national councils.

He occupied now his true and natural position. He was no longer a candidate for the first office. He was out of the dust and strife of the arena. He was not an object of profitable assault to the politicians. Slander might well afford to intermit its labors of hatred, and prejudice could pause to take a calmer view of his history and character. It is surprising how soon the old calumnies died out; and how soon the great and shining attributes of the illustrious patriot caught and fixed the gaze of his countrymen, of all sections and divisions, however before alienated from him. The truth is, that Clay was hated more from fear than from contempt, or rather, there could be no such thing as contempt or scorn for such a man. His chivalrous and lofty carriage made men respect, even while they hated him. His countrymen were always secretly proud of him, and, in the great crises of the country, felt a confidence in his wisdom and skilful pilotage which they felt in no other. He came now on a national errand. He had sunk the partisan. Modes of administration were a small question, compared to the question of the preservation of the country. The matter in hand *now* was no less an issue than the dismemberment of empire. The grave difficulties, which stood in the way of a settlement of the sectional disturbances inflaming the public mind, had foiled the wisdom of all who had essayed to adjust them. They seemed, indeed, to be impossible of adjustment. Fifteen State legislatures, in the Free

States, had instructed their representatives to insist on the Wilmot Proviso. The Slave States, with equal unanimity, had declared their intention to resist such a measure as an act of dissolution. The public mind had become deeply excited. Sectional parties were becoming more and more inflamed. Crimination and recrimination, insult and obloquy, gross personalities, furious invective, scorn and defiance, were the staple of familiar public and private discourse. The inherent difficulties of the question were even more formidable than these external hindrances to its settlement. The old half-healed, half-covered sore of the slavery question was tortured and lacerated again by the rough fanaticism of the North; and the South, proud and sensitive, as of old, was goaded to the last point of patient endurance. The patriot's heart sank within him at the prospect. It was a dark time for the Republic—the darker because a desire for the adjustment of these fearful questions seemed to depart with hope.

At this juncture, Henry Clay took his seat in the Senate. His very presence there was an event in the political history of the country. The old light was on his lofty brow, and in his eye and in his voice were the fire and the spell which could yet save his country. He seemed, in view of the new work before him, to breathe another youth. With the wisdom of his ripe age, he seemed to have caught from the past the vigor and the prime of his meridian fire. There was patriotism enough in the country to save it; but it was a dormant patriotism. Clay waked it up. Clay was the medium that poured the electric current of the people upon the politicians and the public councils. Never before had he fully shown himself the man God had made him. For fifty years, he had never found a rival for a whole session, as an orator and leader in a deliberative assembly; but men had compared him to himself, and had noted how far he was, in this speech or that, from his high-water mark of excellence. Now he was above himself—above where the flood of his sweeping and surge-like eloquence had ever gone before. As a mere orator, he left the great deeds of his youth and middle age behind. But his oratory was the least remarkable of his claims to attention and gratitude. He was eloquent in every thing—instinct with eloquence, as if possessed by its spirit—in movement—in manner—in writing—in speech—in tone—above all, perhaps, in social intercourse transfusing himself into others; now in the closet, now at the mess table, now in the committee room, in the drive, on the street, every where—in every way—seeking no repose—wanting none—it was the fever and fanaticism of soul that carried him with but one object before him—and yet that fever and fanaticism presided over by a judgment and a tact that never forsook and never misled him.

All know the result. All know how he passed through the long agony of glory and of triumph. He conquered and the Union lived.

Fate awarded him ample justice at the last. He had linked the most brilliant passages of his life to the Union; the last link of the chain, too, he threw around its pillar.

His eloquent life was brought to its peroration, and that peroration was, as in his great speeches, the most beautiful, the grandest, the most eloquent of all its parts.

He could retire now. Why linger "superfluous on the stage?" His sun, trembling on the verge of the horizon, like a tropical sun, gorgeous, yet with a solemn and sacred aspect, magnified even beyond his size at noon, might now go down without a cloud or shadow, lighting up all the sky around with rays of marvellous glory long after he had set!

It is charged upon Clay that he was overbearing and imperious, impatient of contradiction and opposition, defiant of his enemies and exacting towards his friends. He was called a dictator. We wish we could deny this charge. But we cannot. There is too much truth in it. Clay was constitutionally combative and aggressive. He had the go-ahead faculties in a morbid state of activity, both because they were large naturally, and because they were continually exercised. He was fond of victory for its own sake. His temper was high, hot and eager; his impulses quick and strong; his self-confidence supreme; and his courage stubborn and invincible. The early part of his career had been a succession of triumphs, often where success is won, as in ancient warfare, by hand-to-hand conflicts, for immediate results, and against emulous and bitter opposition. The rough school of the frontier, with men struggling for position and leadership,—to impress themselves upon the fluent mass of opinion, and to mould that opinion into policy—that wild and untempered society of young Kentucky, where the strongest will and the boldest bearing were even more essential to success than the most vigorous and the best cultured intellect, made an impression upon his character which subsequent experiences only confirmed. The qualities which give a man what is called common-sense—the knowing, observing, perceptive faculties, gave his mind a practical turn denied to most orators; for Clay's business capacity, in every department of affairs, public or private—his memory, system, order, the facility with which he saw what was to be done, and how it was to be done, and the energy with which he did it, were, taken together, unequalled; and this practical turn made him more solicitous of results than fastidious of means, provided they were effectual. As a captain, there is no prescribing what, under favoring circumstances, would have been either the measure of his abilities or the measure of his success. There was no more—and scarcely, if any, less—of the bull-dog hardihood and resolution of McDonald in him, than in Jackson; but there was more of the out-coming, transfusing enthusiasm, and the show and brilliancy of Murat. We can imagine the effect of the tall figure and homely but expressive features, which identified him to the stranger among a thousand eminent men, in the thick of the fight, at the front of a charging column, or beneath the banner shaking over his head, throwing back in defiant impatience the lock of hair that was wont to fall over his brow, and which, when in the full tide of invective, he had a trick of tossing up, like the lion shaking his mane, as Calhoun described it—we can imagine the effect of such a figure and face, when, loaded like a battery with enthusiasm and energy, his unrivalled voice rang out a charge, or inspirited cowardice into heroism as a standard wavered before the hot pressure of the enemy.

With these high military qualities, he united the military fault of being dictatorial. His temper was usually sweet, his animal spirits high, his disposition kind and generous. This was his sunny side. This was " Cæsar in his tent that day he overcame the Nervii." But Cæsar in the field against the Nervii, was a different man. Clay's resentments sometimes carried him into coarse vituperation—sometimes into injustice; and, it must be confessed that he showed less forbearance towards his party friends or associates, temporary or general, than towards his regular party opponents; for example, than towards Wright, Buchanan and Forsyth. In this way, he injured himself, and he injured the Whig party. He had always the power of carrying a great many persons, indeed, the large majority of his own party with him, in such attacks, and they left a sting which was not removed by the reconciliation that evaporated all bitterness from his own mind; for the assailed felt injured by the assault, and usually had the worst of the engagement. That Clay struggled with this temper, and honestly endeavored to overcome it, and towards the last of his life, in some degree succeeded, must be granted him ; and he seems, in his serene moments, to have felicitated himself on the happy facility of his temper, and the amiable meekness of his nature—as Sir Anthony Absolute had done before him; but when the lists opened, and the bugles sounded, the spirit which they aroused was something short of evangelical. He gave, with much better grace than he took, the railleries, sarcasms and covert allusions licensed by debate; by which the malign spirit is draped, though not disguised, in the robes and gauze of rhetorical and complimentary phrase, and bitter things are said in sweet words. Nothing could be more delightful than the humorous displays of the ridiculous positions of his adversaries, or the sly, ironical cuts, he sometimes gave, in the shape of congratulations over their discomfitures. Some of the most successful parliamentary hits ever made were his, and of this sort. For example, the imaginary scene at the White House after Mr. Tyler's vetoes. But, it must be confessed, that, when the hits came from the other side, he either could not usually see the fun of the thing, or, if he did, he sometimes rudely disturbed it, by a withering sneer or the cut direct.

But this can be truly said: He was incapable of malignity: "He bore resentment as the flint bears fire." He was free to repair with grace, and without stint or reservation, the injustice which he wrought in haste. He was as placable when cool, as he was fierce when hot; and when he became reconciled, his memory retained no trace of the past provocation. His intolerance, too, was mostly of the qualities and conduct alien from his sympathies, because alien from his nature. Bold, straightforward and fearless, he could not well brook an opposition which came from caution, fear or time-serving; and, as is usual with such men, he sometimes put to the account of fear and time-serving, what was only the fruit of prudence.

He took his ground, for the most part, with judgment; always from conscientious conviction; and he was strongly wedded to his favorite projects; hence he was restive under an opposition which, in his view, was opposition at once to himself and to the public interests.

Clay has been charged with ultraism in politics. This imputation has been warmly denied by his friends, who point to his concessions and compromises as proofs of a contrary character. But neither the charge nor the denial represents the whole truth. He was not an extremist in the selection of his ground; he *was* ultra in maintaining it. But his firmness did not run into obstinacy, even when he had taken his position. He abandoned a measure when hopeless, or when its maintenance plainly involved greater evils than its loss. He could conciliate and concede down to a particular point; but beyond that point he could not easily be induced to go. He clung with remarkable pertinacity to the *principle* of a measure; but he was not a stickler for forms; and *modes* were so far indifferent to him, that he willingly agreed, perhaps preferred from policy, to surrender them to the opinions of others. It was the zeal and indomitable perseverance which he put forward in support of a measure, which men mistook for a constitutional proneness to extremes; not marking the difference between an extreme zeal for a thing, and zeal for an extreme thing. He had to struggle between opposite forces. His physical temperament was highly impulsive; his moral temper was conservative; but his mind was eminently practical; and it took the conservative side in his measures, while his physical energies drove them forward with all the vigor and steam-power of Young America.

It seems to be forgotten, too, that Clay was the recognized leader and exponent of a large and powerful party; and what in another man would seem officious dictation, would, in such a leader, be not only proper, but even indispensable. A party to be effective must have organization. To have organization, there must be executive power in the party, even if out of power, answering in some degree to the official power of the party it opposes. Upon Clay was thrown this executive power. There must be yielding and concession, it is true, to keep up party integrity; but this concession certainly had as well come from individual members as from the head, whom, it cannot be doubted, carried with him the confidence and the suffrages of the vast majority. Those of the Whigs who accuse Clay of dictation and ultraism, ought therefore to reflect that the same charge might be retorted upon the minority who opposed him with nearly as much force as it could be made against him who represented the mass of the party.

Great injustice has been done Clay, by instituting comparisons between a single faculty or a few faculties of his intellect, and a single or a few faculties of his illustrious contemporaries; and by a general deduction of his inferiority to them, drawn from this comparison. It might be safely admitted that Clay did not possess the wonderful analysis of Calhoun—that incarnation of logic. It might, also, be conceded, that he had no claim to the Miltonic grandeur of imagination, the classic erudition, the artistic skill in words, and the comprehensive and lucid statement of Webster. Not only Clay's intellect, but his whole organization depends for its just appreciation upon a view of it *as a whole*. It is remarkable for the harmonious proportions, and the large, though equable, developments of all the parts. If, by no one faculty, standing alone, would he have been greatly distinguished, yet in no one faculty was he less than remarkable; while *the whole* made up a complement of distinction and power denied, as we think, to any other man of his time. Reflect, how rare it is to find concentered in one man all the qualities of mind, of body, of temperament, which make a successful manager in war-times, and in those crises of affairs in peace, requiring the highest faculties of the captain. Reflect, how few of his contemporaries could, on any one prominent occasion, have supplied his place. Consider, how few men have the qualities which preserve the confidence of a party for years—how few could have held the undisputed leadership of a furious opposition for nearly a generation. Who else has ever done it? Consider, that with these qualities were blended a business capacity and knowledge of detail, which qualified him for success in every department of practical affairs. Consider, that he showed a genius for diplomacy inferior to that of no man of the age; for his settlement of the sectional questions when they seemed impossible of appraising, called for as high diplomatic ability as the treaties he negotiated. Consider that, as a jurist, notwithstanding the small attention he paid to the practice and study of law, he rose to the first rank at the eminent bar of his own state; and, that, as an advocate, he had no peer in courts, where the most brilliant and eloquent orators of the country pleaded. Consider, too, that he led the policy of the country in every great measure from Madison, indeed, from the last Congress of Jefferson's administration, until he met the man of his destiny in Andrew Jackson; that in Democratic Congresses, he carried almost every one of his leading measures, and was only defeated by the vetoes of the President from fixing upon the country almost the whole line of his policy—a policy so broad as to have embraced nearly the whole scheme of Federal administration. If we look at his measures, we find schemes so large—systems so broad—as to belong only to minds the most capacious; and, besides them, we see faculties of administration so extended as to embrace the fullest details of the bureau or the farm. No man ever had a busier invention in moulding measures, or a more active enterprise in prosecuting his purposes. And, when we add, that, for thirty years, a greater body of intellect looked up to him in reverence or followed him with unhesitating confidence, than any man of his age attracted; that those who knew him longest were those who appreciated him the most highly; that senators and judges applauded him as loudly as the village zealots of his party at the clubs; and that generation after generation or statesmen found him and left him at the post of unquestioned national leadership—at the first post of effective influence on all questions, which, for the time, sank the clamors, and disbanded the organization of party;—we begin to realize the error, which would degrade the intellect of such a man, from the highest class of the gifted sons of genius God has ever given to the earth. In the multiplicity of his accomplishments, in the versatility of his powers, in the grandeur of his schemes, in the strength of his intellect, in the loftiness and range of his ambition, in his sway over the intelligence of his country, and in the monumental measures of his policy, Alexander Hamilton, alone of his countrymen, approaches him.

But the most conclusive proof of his superiority is to be found in the fact, that whenever the country was in imminent danger, and could find extrication only in extraordinary resources and wisdom, the public expectation turned to Henry Clay, as its deliverer; and the discord and prejudice of party and of section hushed their clamors to hear and obey his voice; just as, amidst the terrors of a storm, the instinct of the passengers points to the strong and able man of the ship for safety.

His personal courage was of that daring type, which, in Bonaparte's army, would have raised him from the ranks to a marshal of the empire; and it supported a moral courage of like robustness and enterprise. His emotional nature was powerful and easily excited; and he owed to his strong sensibilities a great portion of that popular *those great executive energies which carried them into execution*

And thou art gone from our midst, gallant Harry Clay! and the world seems drearier than before! Who thinks of thee as of an old man gradually going out of life by wasting and decay; as one, who, in the eclipse or helplessness of physical and mental energies, sinks to his last sleep and rest? No! thou seemest ever young; ever buoyant with a vigorous and impulsive manhood; vital with irrepressible energies, and glowing with Life and Hope and Love; as if all noble feelings and all lofty thoughts were busy in thy heart and brain, claiming from lips and eyes eloquent utterance. We could bear to hear of thy dying thus, though with many a sharp pang of sorrow, and many a thought of sadness mingled with pride and love. But what friend of thine could bear to contemplate thee living—yet receding from life; the noble form bowed down; the lofty crest palsied and lowered; the glorious intellect passing into thick-coming darkness, and bursting only in fitful blaze, if ever, into the life and light of thy old eloquence; the buoyant step now halting on the crutches of senility; words, peevish and garrulous, profaning the tongue that once held senates in transported audience; and rayless and vacant now, the bold and glittering eye, that awed and commanded strong men like a king? Who could have borne to see thee the wreck of thy former self, nothing remaining but the contrast of present nothingness with past grandeur and glory! We were spared that spectacle; for it was mercifully granted to thy prayers to spring out of mortal life at once, with unwasted energies, into the blaze of immortality!

Why pursue further the theme? The grass is just growing green on the sod above him; and the words of eulogy and the deep wail of a nation are almost yet stirring the air. He died bravely as he had lived. He had lived out his term and worked out faithfully his time; and now the Republic mourns, throughout her wide borders, and will honor till its last stone be removed, the greatest orator, and, except Washington, the wisest statesman and most useful citizen this country ever called into her service.

And so the long feud ended, and the leaders' fight is over. The old Knights died in harness and were buried with the honors of war, and chivalrous enemies do homage to their graves.

> The good Knights are dust,
> And their good swords are rust,
> And their souls are with the saints we trust.

THE END.

RECENT PUBLICATIONS

OF

D. APPLETON & COMPANY,

443 and 445 Broadway.

Any of the following Books will be forwarded by mail to any address on receipt of the price.

THE HUMAN ELEMENT IN THE INSPIRATION OF THE SCRIPTURES.

By T. F. CURTIS, D. D. 1 vol., 12mo. Cloth, $2.00.

"The great events recorded in Scripture were witnessed by human eyes, addressed to uninstructed minds, and even the inspired words were uttered by mortal tongues. What allowances shall we make for these mortal impediments to a divine work! The author seeks to solve the problem, and he enters upon his task with a becoming spirit."—*Albany Argus.*

THE PHYSIOLOGY OF MAN;

Designed to represent the existing state of Physiological science, as applied to the Functions of the Human Body. By AUSTIN FLINT, JR., M.D. ALIMENTATION; DIGESTION; ABSORPTION; LYMPH AND CHYLE. 1 vol., 8vo. Cloth. Price, $4.50.

FIRST SERIES.—The BLOOD; the CIRCULATION; RESPIRATION. 1 vol., 8vo. $4.50.

"No previous physiological work with which we are acquainted contains such an exact and minute analysis of the principles of dietetics, or furnishes so many valuable suggestions for the general reader who wishes to combine the pleasures of the table with the preservation of health."—*N. Y. Tribune.*

THE WIT AND WISDOM OF DON QUIXOTE.

1 vol., 12mo. Cloth, $1.25.

"The wisdom of all men lies in the ore, till some cunning mind shapes it into coin, then it becomes current and enriches all. Don Quixote is full of this wisdom condensed into wit."—*Albany Argus.*

THE PRINCIPLES OF BIOLOGY.

By HERBERT SPENCER. 2 vols., 12mo. Price, $5.00. (Vol. II. just published.)

"This volume contains the principles of Morphology as distinguished from Physiology, and is a contribution to the series of the great author, Spencer, who is doing for the science of the day what Bacon did for his age."

D. APPLETON & CO.'S PUBLICATIONS.

THE POLITICAL WRITINGS OF RICHARD COBDEN.

2 vols., 8vo. Cloth, $6.00.

"He was one of those enlightened Englishmen who gallantly took our part against the governing class of their own country, maintaining the justness of our cause, and predicted for it a certain and glorious triumph."—[Extract from Preface by W. C. Bryant.

HAND-BOOK OF PRACTICAL COOKERY, FOR LADIES AND PROFESSIONAL COOKS.

Containing the whole Science and Art of Preparing Human Food. By PIERRE BLOT, Professor of Gastronomy and Founder of the New York Cooking Academy. 1 vol., 12mo. $2.00.

"This volume is the result of actual experience by the Professor, whose lectures in the principal cities were so largely attended."

EZEKIEL AND DANIEL;

With Notes, Critical, Explanatory, and Practical. Designed for both Pastors and People. By Rev. HENRY COWLES, D. D. 1 vol., 12mo, $2.25.

"The first volume of this work met with such a hearty reception that the succeeding one does but recommend itself. All denominations of Christians unite in praise of the author's ability."

BIBLE TEACHINGS IN NATURE.

By Rev. HUGH McMILLAN. 1 vol., 12mo. $2.00

"This admirable book has a prime object to show how the miracles of the Bible are not only emblems of power on the spiritual world, but also exponents of the miracles of nature."

CHRISTIANITY AND ITS CONFLICTS,

ANCIENT AND MODERN. By E. E. MARCY, A. M. 1 vol., 12mo. $2.00.

"It is the latest of the elaborate arguments presented in behalf of the Catholic religion or system, and is perhaps one of the most effective."

PHYSIOLOGY AND PATHOLOGY OF THE MIND.

By HENRY MAUDSLEY, M. D. 1 vol., 8vo. $4.00.

"As the result of the investigations of one whose philosophical deductions are founded on practical experience, Dr. Maudsley's treatise is a valuable work, and deserves the careful attention of all who feel an interest not only in general metaphysical facts, but in those manifestations which mark the boundaries between health and disease in the human mind."

HENRY VIII. AND CATHARINE PARR.

An Historical Novel. By L. MUHLBACH. 1 vol., 12mo. Cloth, $2.00.

"There is a wonderful fascination in the writings of Louisa Mühlbach. Dealing with kings and queens, courts and courtiers of a time long past, she is thoroughly acquainted with their manners and customs, their laws and habits, their weaknesses and crimes; and, following history in its essential features, she weaves a story of court life which has a terrible power to fascinate."

D. APPLETON & CO.'S PUBLICATIONS.

APPLETONS' HAND-BOOKS:

HAND-BOOK OF TRAVEL THROUGHOUT THE UNITED STATES AND CANADAS.
1 vol., 12mo, with Maps. $4.00.

HAND-BOOK OF NORTHERN TRAVEL. $3.00.

HAND-BOOK OF SOUTHERN TRAVEL. $2.00.

"The information is the latest attainable—the result of personal observation."

MARIE ANTOINETTE AND HER SON.

An Historical Novel. By L. MUHLBACH. Translated by Rev. W. L. GAGE. 1 vol., 8vo. Containing eight Illustrations. Paper covers, $1.50; cloth, $2.00.

This novel describes the most thrilling epoch in the history of France. The romantic career of the beautiful and unfortunate Marie Antoinette and the Reign of Terror are depicted with historical accuracy, and in the author's happiest style.

THE MANAGEMENT OF STEEL.

By GEORGE EDE, employed at the Royal Gun Factories Department, Woolwich Arsenal. From the Fourth London Edition. 1 vol., 12mo. Cloth, $1.50.

"In this present attempt, my aim has been to write a work which would be found as useful to the novice or amateur mechanic as to the practical man; and I have endeavored to word the subject in such a homely style, that persons totally unacquainted with the processes will be able to judge for themselves as to the reasonableness of my remarks."—[Ex. from Preface.

THE ROMANCE OF THE AGE;

OR, THE DISCOVERY OF GOLD IN CALIFORNIA. By EDWARD E. DUNBAR. 1 vol., 12mo. Illustrated. $1.25.

"As yet no attempt to give a connected account of the wonderful discovery of gold in California, with the remarkable combination of events attending the occurrence, has been made. In my present effort, I propose simply to rescue some important facts from oblivion, hoping they may prove an instructive, entertaining record at the present time, and of use to the future historian."—[Extract from Introduction.

HALF HINTS:

TABLE D'HÔTE AND DRAWING-ROOM. 1 vol., 12mo. Cloth, $1.25.

CONTENTS: Commonplace—Come—The Universe—Little Ones—Table d'Hôte—Drawing-Room—Gentlemen's Parlor—The Exchange—An Inmate—Not a Sermon—Happiness—Poor Bodies—Poor Souls—And So Forth—Out of the Window.

THE GOOD REPORT:

MORNING AND EVENING LESSONS FOR LENT. By ALICE B. HAVEN, Author of "Patient Waiting no Loss," "No Such Word as Fail," etc., etc., etc. 1 vol., 12mo, beautifully printed, 318 pages. Cloth, $1.50.

"The name on the title-page of this book will be recognized by many as a dear and familiar one, though no longer responded to on earth by her who once bore it. To them the book will come as a welcome message from the pure heart and earnest mind that so often ministered to them in the past—but now rests from her labors for evermore."

D. APPLETON & CO.'S PUBLICATIONS.

SYBIL'S SECOND LOVE.

By JULIA KAVANAGH, Author of "Adele," "Nathalie," &c. 1 vol., 12mo. Cloth. 432 pages. Price, $2.00.

"A clever, interesting, and eminently readable novel. The plot is well worked out. The characters are excellently drawn."—*Globe*.

A JOURNEY IN ASHANGO-LAND

AND FURTHER PENETRATION INTO EQUATORIAL AFRICA. By PAUL B. DU CHAILLU, Author of "Explorations in Equatorial Africa." 1 vol. 8vo, with Map and 30 Illustrations. $5.00.

Guardian.—"Du Chaillu's New Travels is a picturesque and interesting story."

Morning Herald.—"No one will grudge M. Du Chaillu the honor and fame he has acquired."

HOME LIFE: A JOURNAL.

By ELIZABETH M. SEWELL. 1 vol., 12mo. $2.00.

"In the present story her laudable aim is to illustrate a few of the fundamental principles of education, and also the difficulties and disappointments attendant upon the endeavor to carry them out under ordinary circumstances, and amongst ordinary people."—*Phil. Inquirer*.

A NEW SYSTEM OF INFANTRY TACTICS,

DOUBLE AND SINGLE RANK. Adapted to American Topography and Improved Fire-Arms. By Brevet Major-Gen. EMORY UPTON, United States Army. One thick volume, 16mo. Price, $2.00.

Order adopting this Volume, to the exclusion of all others.

HEADQUARTERS OF THE ARMY,
ADJUTANT-GENERAL'S OFFICE,
WASHINGTON, *Aug.* 1, 1867.

GENERAL ORDERS No. 73.—The following order, received from the War Department, is published for the information and guidance of the army:

WAR DEPARTMENT,
WASHINGTON CITY, *Aug.* 1, 1867.

ORDER IN RELATION TO UPTON'S INFANTRY TACTICS.—The new system of Infantry Tactics, prepared by Brevet Major-General Emory Upton, United States Army, recommended for adoption in the place of all others by a Board of Officers, of which General Grant is President, having been approved, is adopted for the instruction of the infantry of the army of the United States, and for the observance of the militia of the United States.

To insure uniformity throughout the army, all infantry exercises and manœuvres not embraced in that system are prohibited, and those therein prescribed will be strictly observed.

EDWIN M. STANTON, Secretary of War.

By command of   GENERAL GRANT.

E. D. TOWNSEND, Assistant Adjutant-General.

THE COMPARATIVE GEOGRAPHY OF PALESTINE AND THE SINAITIC PENINSULA.

By CARL RITTER. Translated by Rev. W. L. GAGE. 4 vols., 8vo. $14.00.

"It would be impossible to mention all the good things in these volumes. Ritter allows no hint in any known quarter to escape him. Classical or Oriental, ancient or modern, there is no language from Sanscrit to Spanish but if necessary he calls into requisition."

LOUISA OF PRUSSIA AND HER TIMES.

An Historical Novel. By L. MUHLBACH. 1 vol., 8vo. Illustrated. Paper covers, $1.50; Cloth, $2.00.

"This interesting historical novel takes the reader to Prussia during the period of the invasion of Germany by Napoleon. It gives us the German side of the war, showing how deeply they felt the humiliation which Napoleon's victories compelled them to endure. The character of the beautiful and beloved Louisa of Prussia, whose memory is cherished by Prussians as that of a saint, is charmingly portrayed."

THE CULTURE DEMANDED BY MODERN LIFE.

A Series of Addresses and Arguments on the Claims of Scientific Education. Edited, with an Introduction on Mental Discipline in Education, By EDWARD L. YOUMANS, M. D. 1 vol., 12mo. Cloth. Price, $2.25.

Most of the Lectures in this volume have not been before published in this country, and the authors of several have kindly revised their productions for this work. It may be added, that several of the discussions are important, not only as presenting the claims and educational value of their subjects, but also as suggesting the best methods of their study. Professor Liebig's late Lecture on the "Development of Ideas in Physical Science" has so direct a bearing upon the position and claims of science, especially in this country, as to deserve a place in the present collection; and an excellent translation of it has been expressly made for this volume.

SOUND.

A Course of Eight Lectures Delivered at the Royal Institution of Great Britain. By JOHN TYNDALL, LL. D., F. R. S. 1 vol., 12mo. Illustrated. Price, $2.50.

"In the following pages I have tried to render the science of Acoustics interesting to all intelligent persons, including those who do not possess any especial scientific culture. The subject is treated experimentally throughout, and I have endeavored so to place each experiment before the reader, that he should realise it as an actual operation. My desire, indeed, has been to give distinct images of the various phenomena of acoustics, and to cause them to be seen mentally in their true relations."—[Extract from Preface.

NAPOLEON AND THE QUEEN OF PRUSSIA.

An Historical Novel. By L. MUHLBACH. Translated by F. JORDAN. 1 vol., 8vo. Paper covers, $1.50; Cloth, $2.00.

"This novel is the second of the series written by this author and published under the general title of 'Napoleon in Germany.' The incidents which she so charmingly tells can nowhere be found in the histories of the time."

COUSIN ALICE:

A Memoir of ALICE B. HAVEN. With Portrait. 392 pages. Beautifully printed. 1 vol., 12mo. Cloth, $1.75.

"A memoir of one of the most gifted, as well as one of the best, American women. It is a sad sweet record of a life of suffering borne with the resignation of a martyr, and ending with a saint-like beatification."—*Boston Gazette.*

THE FOREIGN TOUR OF MESSRS. BROWN, JONES, AND ROBINSON.

1 vol., 4to. Price, $6.

BEING A HISTORY OF WHAT THEY SAW AND DID IN BELGIUM, GERMANY, SWITZERLAND AND ITALY. Illustrated with 80 pages of Comical Plates.

"Probably no volume ever issued from the press possesses the same amount of genuine humor. The illustrations are drawn to the life, and any one who has visited the Continent of Europe will recognize the scenes as real."

IRON MANUFACTURE OF GREAT BRITAIN,

Theoretically and practically considered, including descriptive details of the Ores, Fuels, and Fluxes employed, the preliminary operation of Calcination, the Blast, Refining, the Puddling Furnaces, Engines and Machinery, and the various processes in union, etc., etc. By W. TRURAN. Second Edition. Revised from the Manuscripts of the late Mr. TRURAN by J. ARTHUR PHILLIPS, author of "A Manual of Metallurgy;" and WILLIAM H. DORMAN, C. E. 1 vol., large 8vo. Illustrated with 84 Plates. Price, $10.

"Mr. Truran's work is really the only one deserving the name of a treatise upon and text-book of the iron manufacture of the Kingdom. It gives a most comprehensive and minute exposition of present practice, if the term may be applied to iron manufacture as distinguished from strictly professional subjects. The author does not go out of his way to theorize upon how iron should be or may be made, but he describes how it is made in all the iron districts of the Kingdom."—*Engineer.*

A COMPREHENSIVE DICTIONARY OF THE BIBLE.

Mainly abridged from DR. WM. SMITH'S Dictionary of the Bible. With important Additions and Improvements, and 500 Illustrations. Price of each Number, in a neat paper cover, Thirty Cents.

Dr. Smith's Dictionary of the Bible, published in 1860–'63, and containing, in its three large octavo volumes, nearly 3,200 pages, is a work of acknowledged excellence; but its size, cost, and scholarly character, must prevent any extensive circulation of it among the great mass of those who desire and need a Dictionary of the Bible. The "Comprehensive Dictionary," on which nearly two years of editorial labor have already been expended, owes its origin to a settled conviction, on the part of the Editor and Publishers, of the need of such a modified abridgment of the original work as should make the results of modern scholarship generally accessible.

The Editor, Rev. Samuel W. Barnum, M. A., is well known among the graduates of Yale College as an accurate and thorough scholar. His experience in 1845–'47, as the principal assistant of the late Prof. Goodrich, in the revision of Webster's Dictionary (unabridged and royal octavo editions), made him familiar with the details of lexicography; and his subsequent labors as an official expounder of the Scriptures, gave him a practical acquaintance with the wants of the people in the field of Biblical knowledge.

The Dictionary will be issued in semi-monthly numbers of 48 royal octavo pages each. The whole work will probably be contained in about 22 numbers.

FREDERICK THE GREAT AND HIS FAMILY.

By L. MUHLBACH. 1 vol., 8vo. Illustrated. Paper covers, $1.50 Cloth, $2.00.

"To any person who has read a single one of these pictorial and dramatic romances, the name of the author will assert the vivid interest of the book. They are more than entertaining; they are valuable as careful studies of history, minutely and appreciatively drawn."—*Chicago Republican.*

D. APPLETON & CO.'S PUBLICATIONS.

BERLIN AND SANS-SOUCI;

Or, Frederick the Great and His Friends. By L. MÜHLBACH. 1 vol., 12mo. Cloth, $2.00.

"We have on several occasions, in noticing the works of the great German authoress, Miss Mühlbach, expressed our admiration of them, but are now, after much careful reading of each volume as it has come from the press, almost constrained to pronounce them matchless; unrivalled in the whole domain of historical romance."—*Chicago Journal of Commerce.*

JOSEPH II. AND HIS COURT.

An Historical Novel. Translated from the German by ADELAIDE DE V. CHAUDRON. 1 vol., 8vo. Paper, $1.50; Cloth, $2.00.

"In 'Joseph II.' she transcends her previous efforts; not only is the story wrought out in a masterly manner, but the real characters that figure in it have been carefully studied from the detailed chronicles of the time."—*Philadelphia Inquirer.*

THE NEW FRENCH MANUAL.

A New, Simple, Concise, and Easy Method of Acquiring a Conversational Knowledge of the French Language, Including a Dictionary of over Ten Thousand Words. By M. ALFRED HAVET. 1 vol., 12mo, 332 pages. Half bound, $1.75.

"It is, in the opinion of some of our foremost teachers, emphatically the best system for teaching French."

THE ANNUAL CYCLOPÆDIA.

Commenced in 1861. Six volumes now out. The same price per volume, and uniform with the New American Cyclopædia. One volume published annually. Registering all the important events of each year—valuable as a work of reference. Price and style of binding: In extra cloth, per vol., $5.00; in library leather, $6.00; in half turkey morocco, $6.50; in half russia, extra gilt, $7.50; in full morocco antique, gilt edges, $9.00; in full russia, $9.00.

"It is an enterprise of immense value to the public, and ought to be in every library, publi and private, as an invaluable book of reference."—*Atlas and Argus, Albany, N. Y.*

"We can confidently and conscientiously recommend the 'Annual Cyclopædia' to all who would have an accurate and readable history of contemporary events close at hand, and as a safe work of reference."—*Evening Traveller.*

THE HOUSEHOLD BOOK OF POETRY.

Collected and Edited by CHARLES A. DANA. Eleventh Edition, Revised and Enlarged. 1 vol., royal 8vo, half bound, gilt top, $7; half calf, extra, $9; morocco antique, $10.
Elegant Illustrated edition, royal 8vo.

"Within a similar compass there is no collection of poetry in the language that equals this in variety, in richness of thought and expression, and of poetic imagery."—*Worcester Palladium.*

"It gives us in an elegant and compact form such a body of verse as can be found in no other volume or series of volumes."—*Boston Transcript.*

D. APPLETON & CO.'S PUBLICATIONS.

THE COMBINED SPANISH METHOD.

A New Practical and Theoretical System of Learning the Castilian Language, embracing the most advantageous features of the Best Known Methods. With a Pronouncing Vocabulary, containing all the Words used in the course of the work, and References to the Lessons, in which each one is explained, thus enabling any one to be his own instructor. By ALBERT DE TORNOS. 1 vol., 12mo. 470 pages Price, $2.00.

"The present volume is the result of the experience of twenty years as a teacher of the Spanish tongue. All the good features of the various systems are combined in this work."

THE HISTORY OF THE NAVY DURING THE REBELLION.

By the REV. CHARLES B. BOYNTON, D. D., Professor at th U. S. Naval Academy, and Chaplain of the House of Representatives. Illustrated with numerous Engravings. Price of the work: In extra cloth, per vol., $5.00; library leather, per vol., $6.00; in half turkey morocco, per vol., $7.50. To be complete in two elegant octavo volumes of about five hundred pages each, Embellished and Illustrated with some ten full-page Engravings in chromo tints, and with the same number of full-page Wood-cuts, Portraits on steel of Distinguished Officers, and numerous Vignettes from Sketches made by Commander M. B. WOOLSEY, U. S. Navy, and with numerous Maps and Charts from government surveys and official plans furnished for this work exclusively.

The author has had unusual facilities for collecting original and reliable information, and has produced *the only authentic work* on the subject, forming a volume of sterling value and great merit, and one with which there can be no competition. It will be an invaluable work to *Ship-builders, Captains, and Yatchmen;* to *Officers and Seamen;* and to *Relatives and Friends* of those who have fought our battles on river and sea.

Among the numerous Illustrations are several fine large-page Drawings of the most celebrated vessels of modern time, including the Dunderberg, Miantonomoh, Puritan and other iron-clads, with the ships Hartford, Kearsarge, Wabash, etc., etc.

It will be issued in the very best style, on paper of excellent quality, and printed in clear, elegant type. The beautiful and costly Illustrations will be engraved in the highest style of the art.

WILLIAMS & PACKARD'S ORIGINAL GEMS OF PENMANSHIP.

1 vol., 4to. Price, $5.00.

The work is one of extraordinary merit, and will be prized by all lovers of the art, not alone as a triumph of skill and an embodiment of grace and beauty, but as a most acceptable, because useful, treatise on Practical and Ornamental Penmanship. In fact, we hazard nothing in the assertion that no work hitherto published has covered these requisites with the same fidelity and success, or combines within its pages so many and such varied studies of exquisite beauty and grace.

The authors have spared no pains to present an acceptable volume, and one which will answer all reasonable demands as a text-book for Schools, Academies, and Business Colleges, as well as a guide for the private student and adept.

Especially will the work be valuable, as embracing the very best studies in Off-hand Flourishing and Pen-Drawing, for which Professor Williams has been long famous.

D. APPLETON & CO.'S PUBLICATIONS.

THE
NEW AMERICAN CYCLOPÆDIA.

EDITED BY
GEORGE RIPLEY AND CHARLES A. DANA.

PUBLISHED BY
D. APPLETON & COMPANY, New York.

In 16 Vols. 8vo, Double Columns, 750 Pages each.

Price, Cloth, $ *Sheep,*   *Half Mor.,* $ *Half Russ.,*
per Volume.

EVERY one that reads, every one that mingles in society, is constantly meeting with allusions to subjects on which he needs and desires further information. In conversation, in trade, in professional life, on the farm, in the family, practical questions are continually arising, which no man, well read or not, can always satisfactorily answer. If facilities for reference are at hand, they are consulted, and not only is the curiosity gratified, and the stock of knowledge increased, but perhaps information is gained and ideas are suggested that will directly contribute to the business success of the party concerned.

With a Cyclopædia, embracing every conceivable subject, and having its topics alphabetically arranged, not a moment is lost. The matter in question is found at once, digested, condensed, stripped of all that is irrelevant and unnecessary, and verified by a comparison of the best authorities. Moreover, while only men of fortune can collect a library complete in all the departments of knowledge, a Cyclopædia, worth in itself, for purposes of reference, at least a thousand volumes, is within the reach of all—the clerk, the merchant, the professional man, the farmer, the mechanic. In a country like ours, where the humblest may be called to responsible positions requiring intelligence and general information, the value of such a work can not be over-estimated.

PLAN OF THE CYCLOPÆDIA.

The New American Cyclopædia presents a panoramic view of all human knowledge, as it exists at the present moment. It embraces and popularizes every subject that can be thought of. In its successive volumes is contained an inexhaustible fund of accurate and practical information on Art and Science in all their branches, including Mechanics, Mathematics, Astronomy, Philosophy, Chemistry, and Physiology; on Agriculture, Commerce, and Manufactures; on Law, Medicine, and Theology; on Biography and History, Geography and Ethnology; on Political Economy, the Trades, Inventions, Politics, the Things of Common Life, and General Literature.

The Industrial Arts and those branches of Practical Science which have a direct bearing on our every-day life, such as Domestic Economy, Ventilation, the Heating of Houses, Diet, &c., are treated with the thoroughness which their great importance demands.

The department of Biography is full and complete, embracing the lives of all eminent persons, ancient and modern. In American biography, particularly, great pains have been taken to present the most comprehensive and accurate record that has yet been attempted.

In History, the New American Cyclopædia gives no mere catalogue of barren dates, but a copious and spirited narrative, under their appropriate heads, of the principal events in the annals of the world. So in Geography, it not only serves as a general Gazetteer, but it gives interesting descriptions of the principal localities mentioned, derived from books of travel and other fresh and authentic sources.

As far as is consistent with thoroughness of research and exactness of statement, the popular method has been pursued. The wants of the people in a work of this kind have been carefully kept in view throughout.

It is hardly necessary to add that, throughout the whole, perfect fairness to all sections of country, local institutions, public men, political creeds, and religious denominations, has been a sacred principle and leading aim. Nothing that can be construed into an invidious or offensive allusion has been admitted.

DISTINGUISHING EXCELLENCES.

While we prefer that the work should speak for itself, and that others should herald its excellences, we cannot refrain from calling attention to the following points, in which we take an honest pride in believing that the New American Cyclopædia surpasses all others:—

I. IN ACCURACY AND FRESHNESS OF INFORMATION.—The value of a work of this kind is exactly proportioned to its correctness. It must preclude the necessity of having other books. Its decision must be final. It must be an ultimatum of reference, or it is good for nothing.

II. IN IMPARTIALITY.—Our work has undergone the examination of Argus eyes. It has stood the ordeal. It is pronounced by distinguished men and leading reviews in all parts of the Union, strictly fair and national. Eschewing all expressions of opinion on controverted points of science, philosophy, religion, and politics, it aims at an accurate representation of facts and institutions, of the results of physical research, of the prominent events in the history of the world, of the most significant productions of literature and art, and of the celebrated individuals whose names have become associated with the conspicuous phenomena of their age—doing justice to all men, all creeds, all sections.

III. IN COMPLETENESS.—It treats of every subject, in a terse and condensed style, but fully and exhaustively. It is believed that but few omissions will be found; but whatever topics may, through any oversight, be wanting, are supplied in an Appendix.

IV. IN AMERICAN CHARACTER.—The New Cyclopædia is intended to meet the intellectual wants of the American people. It is not, therefore, modelled after European works of a similar design; but, while it embraces all their excellences, has added to them a peculiar and unmistakable American character. It is the production mainly of American mind.

V. IN PRACTICAL BEARING.—The day of philosophical abstraction and speculation has passed away. This is an age of action. *Cui bono* is the universal touchstone. Feeling this, we have made our Cyclopædia thoroughly practical. No man of action, be his sphere humble or exalted, can afford to do without it.

VI. IN INTEREST OF STYLE.—The cold, formal, and repulsive style usual in works of this kind, has been replaced with a style sparkling and emphatically readable. It has been the aim to interest and please, as well as instruct. Many of our writers are men who hold the foremost rank in general literature, and their articles have been characterized by our best critics as models of elegance, force, and beauty.

VII. IN CONVENIENCE OF FORM.—No ponderous quartos, crowded with fine type that strains the eyes and wearies the brain, are here presented. The volumes are just the right size to handle conveniently; the paper is thick and white, the type large, the binding elegant and durable.

VIII. IN CHEAPNESS.—Our Cyclopædia has been universally pronounced a miracle of cheapness. We determined, at the outset, to enlarge its sphere of usefulness, and make it emphatically a book for the people, by putting it at the lowest possible price.

Such being the character of the New American Cyclopædia, an accurate, fresh, impartial, complete, practical, interesting, convenient, cheap Dictionary of General Knowledge, we ask, who can afford to do without it? Can the merchant, the statesman, the lawyer, the physician, the clergyman, to whom it gives thorough and complete information on every point connected with their several callings? Can the teacher, who is enabled, by the outside information it affords, to make his instructions doubly interesting and profitable? Can the farmer, to whom it offers the latest results of agricultural research and experiment? Can the young man, to whom it affords the means of storing his mind with useful knowledge bearing no any vocation he may have selected? Can the intelligent mechanic, who wishes to understand what he reads in his daily paper? Can the mother of a family, whom it initiates into the mysteries of domestic economy, and teaches a thousand things which more than saves its cost in a single year? In a word, can any intelligent American, who desires to understand the institutions of his country, its past history and present condition, and his own duties as a citizen, deny himself this great American digest of all human knowledge, universally pronounced the best Cyclopædia and the most valuable work ever published?

CONTRIBUTORS TO THE CYCLOPÆDIA.

The best talent in all parts of the country, and many distinguished foreign writers, have been engaged in the New American Cyclopædia. We give below the names of several of the most prominent contributors, from which the public may form some idea of the character of the work.

Hon. GEORGE BANCROFT, LL.D., New York.
Hon. J. R. BARTLETT, late U. S. and Mexican Boundary Commissioner, Providence, R. I.
Rev. HENRY W. BELLOWS, D.D., New York.
Hon. JEREMIAH S. BLACK, U. S. Attorney General, Washington, D. C.
Capt. GEORGE S. BLAKE, U. S. Naval Academy, Annapolis, Md.
Hon. ERASTUS BROOKS, New York.
EDWARD BROWN-SÉQUARD, M.D., London.
JOHN ESTEN COOKE, Esq., Richmond, Va.
Rev. J. W. CUMMINGS, D.D., Pastor of St. Stephen's Church, New York.
Prof. JAMES D. DANA, LL.D., Yale College, New Haven, Conn.
Hon. CHARLES P. DALY, Judge of the Court of Common Pleas, New York.
Hon. CHARLES S. DAVIES, LL.D., Portland, Me.
RALPH WALDO EMERSON, Concord, Mass.
Hon. EDWARD EVERETT, Boston, Mass.
Pres. C. C. FELTON, LL.D., Harvard University, Cambridge, Mass.
D. W. FISKE, Esq., Secretary of the Geographical and Statistical Society, New York.
CHARLES L. FLINT, Esq., Secretary of the Massachusetts Board of Agriculture, Boston, Mass.
JOHN W. FRANCIS, M.D., LL.D.
Prof. CHANDLER R. GILMAN, M.D., College of Physicians and Surgeons, New York.
Prof. HENRY GOADBY, M.D., State Agricultural College of Michigan, Ann Arbor, Mich.
HORACE GREELEY, Esq., New York.
GEORGE W. GREENE, Esq., New York.
R. A. GUILD, Esq., Librarian of Brown University, Providence, R. I.
Prof. CHARLES W. HACKLEY, D.D., Columbia College, New York.
Hon. JAMES HALL, Cincinnati, Ohio.
GERARD HALLOCK, Esq., editor of the "Journal of Commerce," New York.
Prof. A. W. HARKNESS, Brown University, Providence, R. I.
JOHN R. G. HASSARD, Esq., New York.
CHARLES C. HAZEWELL, Esq., Boston, Mass.
M. HEILPRIN, Esq., New York.
RICHARD HILDRETH, Esq., author of "History of the United States," &c., New York.
Rev. THOMAS HILL, President of Antioch College, Ohio.
Hon. GEORGE S. HILLARD, Boston, Mass.

CONTRIBUTORS TO THE CYCLOPÆDIA.

J. S. HITTELL, Esq., San Francisco, Cal.
JAMES T. HODGE, Esq., Cooper Institute, New York.
Prof. L. M. HUBBARD, D.D., University of N. C., Chapel Hill, N. C.
Rev. HENRY N. HUDSON, author of "Lectures on Shakespeare," &c., Litchfield, Conn.
Prof. S. W. JOHNSON, Yale College, New Haven, Conn.
J. C. G. KENNEDY, Esq., Washington, D. C.
Hon. JOHN B. KERR, late U. S. Minister to Central America, Baltimore, Md.
Rev. T. STARR KING, San Francisco, Cal.
CHARLES LANMAN, Esq., Washington, D. C.
CHARLES G. LELAND, Esq., Philadelphia, Pa.
Prof. JAMES R. LOWELL, Harvard University, Cambridge, Mass.
R. SHELTON MACKENZIE, D.C.L., Philadelphia, Pa.
Rev. H. N. McTYEIRE, D.D., editor "Christian Advocate," Nashville, Tenn.
CHARLES NORDHOFF, Esq., author of "Stories of the Island World," &c., New York.
Rev. SAMUEL OSGOOD, D.D., New York.
Prof. THEOPHILUS PARSONS, LL.D., Harvard University, Cambridge, Mass.
Prof. E. R. PEASLER, M.D., New York Medical College, New York.
JOHN L. PEYTON, Esq., Staunton, Va.
WILLIAM C. PRIME, author of "Boat Life and Tent Life," &c., New York.
J. H. RAYMOND, LL.D., Principal of the Polytechnic Institute, Brooklyn, New York.
GEORGE SCHEDEL, Esq., late British Consular Agent for Costa Rica, Staten Island, N. Y.
Prof. ALEXANDER G. SCHEM, Dickinson College, Carlisle, Penn.
Hon. FRANCIS SCHROEDER, JR., late U. S. Minister to Sweden, Paris.
Hon. WILLIAM H. SEWARD, U. S. Senator from New York, Auburn, N. Y.
WILLIAM GILMORE SIMMS, LL.D., Charleston, S. C.
Prof. HENRY B. SMITH, D.D., Union Theological Seminary, New York.
Rev. J. A. SPENCER, D.D., author of "The History of the United States," &c., New York.
Rev. WILLIAM B. SPRAGUE, D.D., Albany, N. Y.
Hon. E. G. SQUIER, author of "The States of Central America," "Nicaragua," &c.
ALEX. W. THAYER, Esq., Berlin, Prussia.
JOHN R. THOMPSON, Esq., editor "Southern Literary Messenger," Richmond, Va.
GEORGE TICKNOR, LL.D., Boston, Mass.
OSMOND TIFFANY, Esq., Springfield, Mass.
R. T. TRALL, M.D., author of "Hydropathic Encyclopædia," New York.
Baron DE TROBRIAND, New York.
W. P. TROWBRIDGE, Esq., U. S. Coast Survey, Washington, D. C.
HENRY T. TUCKERMAN, Esq., New York.
ALEXANDER WALKER, Esq., editor of the "Delta," New Orleans.
CHARLES S. WEYMAN, Esq., New York.
Rev. W. D. WILSON, D.D., Hobart Free College, Geneva, N. Y.
E. L. YOUMANS, Esq., author of "The Hand-Book of Household Science," New York.

www.ingramcontent.com/pod-product-compliance
Lightning Source LLC
Chambersburg PA
CBHW030402230426
43664CB00007BB/703